OUTSOURCING AND INSOURCING IN AN INTERNATIONAL CONTEXT

OUTSOURCING AND INSOURCING IN AN INTERNATIONAL CONTEXT

MARC J. SCHNIEDERJANS

ASHLYN M. SCHNIEDERJANS • DARA G. SCHNIEDERJANS

M.E.Sharpe
Armonk, New York
London, England

Library of Congress Cataloging-in-Publication Data

Schniederjans, Marc J.
  Outsourcing and insourcing in an international context / Marc J. Schniederjans, Ashlyn M.
Schniederjans, Dara G. Schniederjans.
      p. cm.
  Includes bibliographical references and index.
  ISBN 0-7656-1585-1 (hardcover: alk. paper); ISBN 0-7656-1586-X (pbk.: alk paper)
  1. Contracting out--Management. I. Schniederjans, Ashlyn M. II. Schniederjans, Dara G.
III. Title.

HD2365.S36 2005
658.4'058--dc22   2005010488

Brief Contents

Detailed Contents

Part 2. Methodologies for Different Types of Outsourcing-Insourcing Decisions

**Chapter 5. International Outsourcing-Insourcing Metrics-Based
Methodologies • 75**

List of Tables and Figures

Figures

Tables

Preface

Outsourcing, which includes the decision of insourcing, is not just a popular phenomenon, but is viewed as one of the most important management strategies of our time. Indeed, there have been calls in the literature to elevate the process of outsourcing-insourcing to the status of a new management function that can replace entire purchasing, information systems, operations, marketing, finance, and accounting departments. This is particularly important to business operations the world over because of the international nature of outsourcing. Considering that half of the outsourcing-insourcing decisions meet with failure, making the right decision may be the difference between long-term success or failure for a firm. The need to make the right outsourcing-insourcing decision has never been greater than it is now.

As the outsourcing industry grows by double digits every year, students seeking jobs increasingly need to know about this new industry. Even more urgent, practitioners in industry, regardless of position, need to be educated on issues, concepts, philosophies, procedures, methodologies, and practices of outsourcing.

The purpose of this textbook is to provide current concepts and methodologies that can help individuals understand and use outsourcing strategies. The book is designed for an upper-level undergraduate course or a graduate course in business. It can also be useful to professionals in any field of business or engineering that is affected by outsourcing issues. This would include practitioners at the board of director or CEO level down through an organization's structure to front-line supervisors who are interested in and make outsourcing decisions. Other faculty, trainers, and graduate students will also find this textbook useful. The book assumes a reader has had exposure to business terminology that undergraduate students are normally exposed to in business or industrial management degree programs. Throughout this textbook, important terms are italicized and are usually followed by a definition. The location of the definitions can be found in the index at the end of the book.

The contents of this book are organized into two parts. In Part 1, "Introduction to Outsourcing-Insourcing in an International Context," four chapters are presented that help to overview the concepts and strategies defining outsourcing-insourcing in an international context. In Part 2, "Methodologies for Different Types of Outsourcing-Insourcing Decisions," four chapters are focused on methodological techniques for implementing outsourcing-insourcing decisions.

The authors wish to thank all the people who have helped completing this textbook. One of the major sources of outsourcing information on which we relied is *FSO Magazine*. We thank the many contributors to that online publication, whose work in the outsourcing industry is greatly appreciated by all. We also thank the editorial staff at M.E. Sharpe for their professionalism and responsiveness. It was a joy to work with them. Finally, we wish to thank Jill Schniederjans, wife and mother, who spend countless hours editing drafts. She has made a significant contribution to this textbook. While many people have had a hand in the preparation of this book, its accuracy and completeness are the responsibility of the authors. For all the errors this book may contain we apologize in advance.

Marc J. Schniederjans
Ashlyn M. Schniederjans
Dara G. Schniederjans

Part 1

Introduction to Outsourcing-Insourcing in an International Context

1

Introduction to Outsourcing-Insourcing

Learning Objectives   After completing this chapter you should be able to:

- Describe outsourcing and insourcing.
- Describe what is meant by an international context in outsourcing and insourcing.
- Explain the relationship between subcontracting and outsourcing.
- Describe various types of outsourcing-insourcing.
- Explain why businesses use outsourcing-insourcing as a balancing strategy.
- Explain the relationship between core competencies and outsourcing-insourcing.
- Describe theories used to justify outsourcing-insourcing.
- Describe outsourcing trends.
- Describe risks in the outsourcing-insourcing process.
- Explain the importance of considering risk in an outsourcing-insourcing decision.

What Is Outsourcing-Insourcing?

Outsourcing is defined by Chase et al. (2004, 372) as an "act of moving some of a firm's internal activities and decision responsibilities to outside providers." Lankford and Parsa (1999) similarly state "outsourcing is defined as the procurement of products or services from sources that are external to the organization." These and other definitions agree that outsourcing involves allocating or reallocating business activities (both service and/or manufacturing activities) from an internal source to

an external source. Conversely, *insourcing* can be defined as internal sourcing of business activities. So, insourcing can be viewed as an allocation or reallocation of resources internally within the same organization, even if the allocation is in differing geographic locations.

For clarity, we will distinguish between the two basic organizations that make up an outsourcing arrangement as follows: (1) the firm that seeks to outsource their internal business activities will be referred to as the outsourcing *client firm,* and (2) the firm providing the outsourcing services to

Figure 1.1   **Balancing Outsourcing and Insourcing Benefits and Costs**

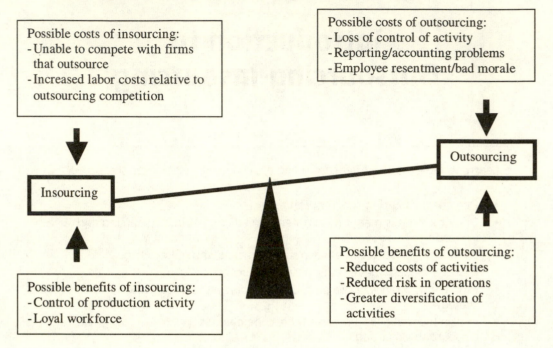

the client firm will be referred to as the *outsource provider*. The services or manufacturing activities, tasks, and jobs to be outsourced can vary substantially with the firm, but generically will be referred to in this book as *business activities*.

Early in their life cycle, most businesses insource their activities. As businesses mature and grow, however, they may find limitations on labor/services, materials, or other economic resources in a particular geographic location. This can force them to subcontract services or procure materials from external sources. Sometimes these are geographically distant sources. Those labor/service or material procurements represent the act of outsourcing if they are acquired from a source external to the organization (i.e., not owned by the outsource provider). As Figure 1.1 depicts, today's modern organization has to balance the potential benefits of outsourcing

with its potential costs in order to determine the proportion of outsourcing to insourcing that will best achieve the organization's objectives. The wrong proportion of outsourcing to insourcing can result in business failures. But planning outsourcing-insourcing based on some calculated ideal proportion also involves risk because the benefits and costs used in the calculation are potential and not certain; they may never materialize and actually have only a probability of materializing.

The idea of *outsourcing-insourcing* (O-I) can become confusing as it applies to large organizations that operate plants in differing locations. For example, if a corporation owns two plants, A and B, and they reallocate production activity from Plant A to Plant B, are they outsourcing? The answer is no, if the corporation considers itself one organization (i.e., they have simply insourced production activity from Plant A to Plant B within the same corporation). In outsourcing, as we are defining it here, the allocation must be "external" to the organization. All other transfers of production activity (e.g., between departments, divisions, or companies within a single corporation) can be viewed as insourcing.

What Is Outsourcing-Insourcing in an International Context?

Another potentially confusing dimension of O-I is the fact that it is often conducted in an international context. An *international context* means activity between nations or between the boundaries of two or more countries. For example, moving production from a plant in Country A to a plant in Country B can be either outsourcing or insourcing. It is outsourcing if the plants in the two countries are owned by different organizations. It is insourcing if the plants in the two countries are owned by the same organizations (i.e., just transferring the same organization's production activity but to a different country). What if a U.S. firm located in the United States allocates production activity to a European firm located in the United States? Is that outsourcing in an international context? It is outsourcing if the U.S. firm does not own the European firm, but it will not be in an international context unless the production activity crosses a border (because the production activity is staying within the U.S.). If the non-U.S.-owned European firm does the work for the U.S. firm in a foreign country, however, it is outsourcing in an international context. Outsourcing in an international context also includes *global outsourcing*. While international outsourcing involves at least one foreign firm, global outsourcing involves many international, external firms.

Another source of confusion in discussions of the international context relates to the term *offshoring* (i.e., the process of moving business activities to a foreign country). A company can offshore some of its business functions by starting its own business in a foreign country. This is an example of offshoring, not outsourcing. Some companies prefer to offshore rather than outsource ("U.S. Companies to Shift Jobs . . ." 2004). If a client company outsources some of its business activities outside the country to a provider firm that the client firm does not own, it is engaging in *offshore outsourcing*. Some client firms actually want their outsourcing partners to possess offshore outsourcing capacity because partners with such capabilities may offer them lower costs and other international context advantages ("Outsourcing Expectations Surpass . . ." 2004).

According to James and Weidenbaum (1993, 42), outsourcing is not a new concept; it is simply another name for the longstanding practice of *subcontracting* production activities. The use of external lawyers, accountants, and consultant provider firms can be viewed as outsourced services. Purchasing manufactured parts and assemblies from external organizations domestically or internationally can also be viewed as outsourcing. Indeed, the classic "buy-or-make" decisions concerning products, processes, and facilities that companies have been making for many decades are examples of the outsourcing-insourcing decision (Russell and Taylor 2003, 126).

This textbook takes the position that O-I in an international context is a logical evolution for business organizations that originates from the concept of subcontracting. That is, it is not a revolution but an evolution of the business organization, as depicted in Figure 1.2. Why has O-I in an international context recently become a major driving force in business the world over? Partly it is due to the rapid development and deployment of technology, particularly advancements in telecommunications and personal computers. The *Internet* and *World Wide Web* permit firms anywhere in the world to

Figure 1.2 **Evolution of Business Organizations and Outsourcing**

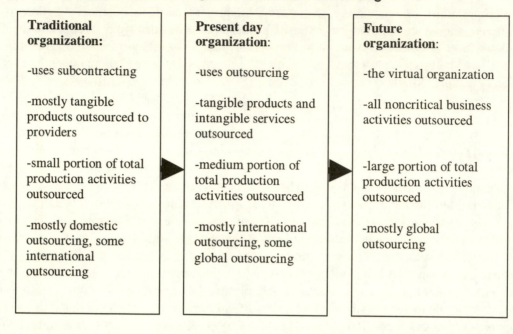

Traditional organization:	**Present day organization:**	**Future organization:**
-uses subcontracting	-uses outsourcing	-the virtual organization
-mostly tangible products outsourced to providers	-tangible products and intangible services outsourced	-all noncritical business activities outsourced
-small portion of total production activities outsourced	-medium portion of total production activities outsourced	-large portion of total production activities outsourced
-mostly domestic outsourcing, some international outsourcing	-mostly international outsourcing, some global outsourcing	-mostly global outsourcing

provide services previously limited geographically, supplying the connectivity necessary to support the growth of O-I in an international context.

Paralleling the growth of O-I is the growth of international business. With the passage of landmark international trade agreements like the 1993 *North American Free Trade Agreement* (NAFTA), and the work of the *World Trade Organization,* the *European Union,* and other international trade zones established throughout the world, governments have been setting the stage for the greatest expansion of international business in history. Combined with the availability of inexpensive computer and communication technology, it has resulted in enormous growth in international business. In the early 1990s, Cateora (1994, 419) reported that "service operations" were the fastest growing sector in international trade, and as we will see later in this chapter, the international outsourcing of services has continued to grow at an increasing rate.

It is not just the parallel growth between O-I and international business that supports this textbook's combination of these two areas of business planning. Any O-I business decision must be considered in an international context if it is to be optimized (because the economic advantages of outsourcing are chiefly available only in an international context). For purposes of this textbook we will refer to *outsourcing-insourcing* (O-I) as a "project" type of management involving a discrete time period (i.e., start and end dates) and requiring a decision to implement the balancing of resource allocation or reallocation.

Types of Outsourcing-Insourcing

A general contractor in the construction industry that subcontracts various construction activities required to build a home is a perfect example of an outsourcer. Every component of the building

Table 1.1

Types of Cooperative Agreements Serving as a Basis for Outsourcing

Types of cooperative agreements between an outsourcing client firm and an outsource provider	Extent of interorganizational dependence
Equity joint venture (e.g., a long-term partnership and sharing of resources to operate a business that will be jointly owned by both organizations)	High
Equity strategic alliance (e.g., a medium-term partnership and sharing of R&D resources to develop a product that will jointly be owned by both client and provider organizations)	
Non-equity alliance (e.g., a temporary partnership and sharing of resources between client and provider organizations)	
Finance, management, marketing, information systems service agreements (e.g., allowing provider firm to perform basic internal business functions in specific areas within the client firm)	Medium
Franchising (e.g., obtaining selected services/products from a provider firm)	
Production and assembly work (e.g., a limited contract in which a provider firm agrees to assemble components for a fixed period of time for the client firm)	
Legal services (e.g., obtaining government permits for a new product with the help of a legal service provider firm)	
Technical training (e.g., training on a new software package from a software provider firm)	Low

process, including the architect's home design, a consultant's site location analysis, a lawyer's work to obtain the building permits, plumbing, electrical work, drywalling, painting, furnace installation, and landscaping, and the sales agent selling the home, can be outsourced.

Any business activity can be outsourced or insourced. All or part of any business function (e.g., accounting, production and operations, administration, research and development, purchasing, finance, marketing, information systems, etc.) which have been historically insourced can be outsourced today. Unlike insourcing, however, outsourcing requires an agreement with an external organization. As Table 1.1 shows, there can be many different types of cooperative agreements

between client firms and outsource provider firms (Contractor and Lorange 1992, 203–215; Hayes et al. 2005, 23–25; Schniederjans 1998, 135–143). Each of these types of outsourcing agreements require different degrees of interorganizational dependence between the client firm and the outsource provider. Indeed, if a contract can be written to define any type of business activity between a client organization and its potential outsource provider, then that business activity can be outsourced.

There continues to be a variety of emerging, differing types of outsourcing activities requiring unique agreements. Some commonly used terms for outsourcing found in the literature are listed in Table 1.2. Different types of outsourcing fall at different places along a continuum of organizational

Table 1.2

Common Types of Outsourcing

Type of outsourcing	Description
Offshore outsourcing	Outsourcing to a provider located in a different country from the client firm. In a variant of this a client firm offshores their operations to another country by starting up their own business in the foreign country. This type of *offshoring operation* is not considered outsourcing, but is a form of insourcing.
Nearshore outsourcing	The same as international outsourcing, but in this case the countries are neighbors (e.g., U.S. firm outsourcing to a firm in Canada, or France outsourcing to Germany)
Transitional outsourcing	Outsourcing an older business system so the firm can concentrate on making a new system work (e.g., letting an outsourcer run an older computer-based ordering system for current customers, while the client firm installs a new system and makes it operational)
Co-sourcing	Outsourcing where the provider's payment is based on achieving a particular goal such as improving the client's business performance
Spin-offs	Outsourced business activities of one company being brought together into a completely new and separate firm (e.g., an outsourced accounting department becoming a separate accounting services firm)
Backsourcing	A kind of insourcing where a client firm, having experienced less than desirable outsourcing, moves the outsourced business activities back to the client firm
Business process outsourcing (BPO)	Outsourcing of an entire process or department within a firm (e.g., outsourcing all information systems services or the finance or accounting departments)
Business transformation outsourcing (BTO)	BTO typically focuses on helping the client firm create a new infrastructure or business model
Value-added outsourcing	Client and provider strengths are combined to market products or services
Netsourcing	Renting computer applications, services, and infrastructure over Web networks
Shared outsourcing	When one outsource provider works for more than one client firm at the same time (e.g., a software outsourcing provider working on the same computer software code for several banks all of which require the same type of software for their customers)
Multisourcing outsourcing	When multiple outsource providers are used simultaneously to ensure, for example, competitive bidding in the outsourcing arrangements

change. On one end of the continuum, there is *business transformation outsourcing* (BTO), where a client firm uses outsourcing only to make changes within its own structure, as when an in-house training session helps educate a client firm's executives on a particular topic ("Transformational Outsourcing . . ." 2003, 4). At the other end of the change continuum is *business process outsourcing* (BPO), one of the fastest growing sectors of the outsourcing market. A report by IDA (a research firm) titled "Worldwide and U.S. Business Process Outsourcing (BPO) 2004–2008 Forecast and Analysis" predicted that the outsourcing market for the nine business process functions currently outsourced (viz., human resources, procurement, finance and accounting, customer care, logistics, engineering/R&D, sales and marketing, facilities operations and management, and training) will increase to almost $700 billion in 2008, representing a compound annual growth rate of 11 percent from 2004 ("Global BPO Market . . ." 2004).

BPO can involve some of the cooperative agreements listed in Table 1.1. For example, many U.S. firms seeking to avoid the political backlash that results from outsourcing jobs to outsource providers in foreign countries are now offshoring by setting up their own development centers (solely owned or as an equity joint venture with a provider) in the same foreign countries they might have outsourced to ("U.S. Firms Set Up . . ." 2004). In this way they can reallocate the business activities to be performed in foreign locations without removing their name from the business or suffering negative reactions from client firm stakeholders.

Why Use Outsourcing?

Beyond the legitimizing historical context of subcontracting, there are many reasons why outsourcing has become an important planning activity in business. There are strategic and economic reasons and important trends, which make outsourcing a critical factor for present and future business success.

Strategic Planning of Core Competencies

One reason why outsourcing is a critical issue is its position in the organization's *decision making structure* (i.e., relationship of strategic, tactical and operational decision making) and the trend toward international outsourcing. Structurally, outsourcing has changed from a *tactical decision* (e.g., medium-term subcontracting of a small portion of a company's unit production) to a *strategic decision* (e.g., long-term subcontracting of a major portion of a firm's production, administration, and inter-

nal departmental services). While acknowledging that outsourcing is not a new concept, Yang and Huang (2000) point out that *strategic outsourcing* is relatively recent. Research literature is only now starting to identify its potential contribution to organizations.

All business organizations develop strategies by setting long-term goals as a general guide for their business operations. (We will discuss strategic planning more fully in Chapter 3.) As Figure 1.3 shows, the strategic planning process begins with an examination or establishment of the organization's basic mission statement, which sets general goals for the organization, such as making profit, providing quality services or products, serving the community, and so on. Once the mission is set, strategic planners next undertake an internal analysis of the organization to identify how much or little each business activity contributes to the achievement of the mission. It is during this *internal organization analysis* that firms identify their strengths—what they do well, or better than their competitors. These strengths are also known as *core competencies* (King et al. 2001). Greaver (1999, 87) defines core competencies as "innovative combinations of knowledge, special skills, proprietary technologies, information, and unique operating methods that provide the product or service customers value and want to buy." Focusing on core competencies has long been recognized in the literature as a critical strategy for the success and long-term survival of any firm (Prahalad and Hamel 1990). Core competencies can be any type of human, systems, or technology resource. The internal organization analysis may identify core competencies internally, based on the informed opinions of the firm's executives, or externally through market research involving the organization's customers. Basically, it involves identifying what the firm does better than anyone else. Common sense dictates those are the business

Figure 1.3 **Strategic Planning and Core Competencies**

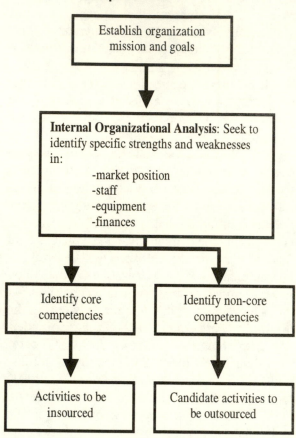

activities the firm should insource and not permit others to perform. Selecting the wrong core competency to outsource or sell can be costly. For example, Trans World Airlines used to have the best reservation system (a technology core competency) in the airline industry. Sadly, they were forced to sell the technology and have never regained the market position they held at the time of that sale.

By contrast, non-core activities, which can be a sizable portion of any organization's total business activities, are good candidates for outsourcing. Again, common sense dictates that if an outsource provider can do a job better than a client organization, then it makes economic sense to engage the outsourcing firm's services and utilize their competitive advantage.

Consider a simple example to see the connection between strategic planning, core competency, non-core competency, and outsourcing. Suppose a firm has set a strategic goal of growth in market share (i.e., the strategic plan). To achieve this goal, the organization will have to produce more products to meet the hoped-for increase in demand. They have identified marketing, in any market they choose, as an organizational strength (i.e., marketing is a core competency). So increasing demand for the organization's products to achieve the growth goal is not a problem. Unfortunately, they have also found an organizational weakness in their production facilities. The organization does not have the production capacity (a non-core competency) to meet the growth goal by producing additional units of product over an extended period of time. By establishing a long-term production agreement with an external outsourcing provider firm, the client firm can acquire the additional production capacity they will need to achieve their strategic growth objective. As this example demonstrates, outsourcing can become a strategy for success. The example also illustrates why outsourcing is a logical component of any organization's strategic planning efforts.

The Economics of Outsourcing

The justification for any business strategy, action or conduct can usually be found in one or more economic theories. Borrowing from classic economics, the *transaction cost theory* is based on the premise that firms seek to economize on transaction costs. Originally formulated by Coase (1937), this theory proposes that investments, including investments in outsourcing, help reduce transaction

Figure 1.4 **Transaction Cost Theory and Outsourcing**

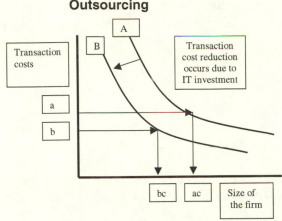

Figure 1.5 **Agency Theory and Outsourcing**

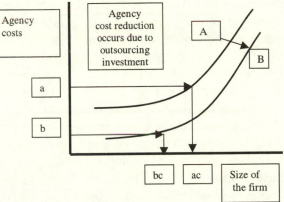

costs, and in turn, reduce the size of the firm, making it more productive (Putterman and Kroszner 1995). As Figure 1.4 shows, a shift in transaction costs from "A" to "B," measured by a reduction in transaction costs from "a" to "b," results in a reduction in the size of the firm (i.e., employees, physical facilities, etc.) from "ac" to "bc." Most of the literature uses this economic theory to justify outsourcing (Aubert et al. 2004; Domberger 1998; Kern and Willcocks 2001; Murray and Kotabe 1999; Pint and Baldwin 1997).

Another economic theory that applies to outsourcing is *agency theory* (Laudon and Laudon, 2004, 83). Agency theory deals with the impact of outsourcing on employees, or "agents," who work for the owners of client businesses. According to this theory, as a firm grows in size and its supply chains and employee interactions increase, the owners need to increase the number of employees who work as agents to support the complexity of the organization. Thus, an investment in outsourcing saves the firm time, improves its control over its business activities by moving non-core activities outside the firm, and requires fewer employees. As Figure 1.5 shows, these agency cost reductions (from "A" to "B") move the agency costs curve

from "a" to "b," causing a reduction in the size of the firm from "ac" to "bc," principally a reduction in employees.

To be fair to the emerging body of knowledge seeking to justify outsourcing, there is one additional, non-economic theory worth mentioning. This social exchange theory is called *interorganizational relationship theory* (Kern and Willcocks 2001, 54–57). According to this theory, relations arise for a number of reasons, each possessing a particular set of behavioral and structural elements. This theory helps to explain the outsourcing relationships that evolve and change over time. It is best used to explain the reasons for interorganizational relationships that are based on exchanges in the differing organizational structures (i.e., between the firms outsourcing to each other) in terms of behavioral aspects. Understanding the relationships allows an economic theory, like transaction cost theory, to better explain the efficiencies observed in the outsourcing process.

Whatever the theoretical foundation of outsourcing used, the motivation for outsourcing *in an international context* is supported in the economic theory of *comparative advantage* (Forslid and Wooton 2003; Hall and Soskice 2001). Applied in the context of trade between countries, this theory focuses on the basic economics of outsourcing internationally. According to this theory, if an external outsourcing provider firm, regardless of its geographic location, can perform work activities more productively than the client firm, the client firm should allow the external outsourcing provider firm to do the work. This allows the client firm to focus on what they do better (i.e., on their core competencies) than their competitors— and better than the provider firm. By focusing solely on their core competencies, according to this theory, both the provider and client firms will enjoy more success in their respective markets. Indeed, many firms have used international outsourcing to achieve a competitive advantage they would not otherwise have been able to attain (Kotabe and Murray 2004). International outsourcing has grown rapidly in the last few years (Lee et al. 2003; Zsidish 2003). Countries that have benefited from international outsourcing, such as India, China, and Russia, have made it a government priority and have set up agencies to support the easy transition of foreign-based client firms into their outsourcing markets. Case studies of many firms of all sizes adopting the outsourcing strategy are now common in the literature (Lee et al. 2003).

Outsourcing Trends

In a survey of fifty-two major corporations (83 percent of them U.S. firms), executives were asked what they felt were the most important reasons for outsourcing. The top reasons include cost savings (77 percent), to gain outside expertise (70 percent), to improve services (61 percent), to focus on core competencies (59 percent), and to gain access to technology (56 percent) (Goldsmith 2003). The study also revealed that in addition to outsourcing business activities (e.g., information system user support, computer help desk services, etc.), whole business departmental functions (e.g., accounting, marketing, finance, operations management, information systems, etc.) were being outsourced. To ascertain future outsourcing trends, the study asked executives who had outsourced business functions about their plans for future outsourcing. While 35 percent said they would continue or expand outsourcing, 40 percent said they would continue outsourcing but revise their outsourcing arrangements, and a significant 25 percent said they would reduce outsourcing or choose to insource their work. Apparently, then, those with experience in outsourcing are not completely satisfied with this strategy for success.

Nevertheless, other surveys appear to reveal significant expansion trends in outsourcing. For example, according to the research and analysis firm, Gartner, Inc., outsourcing will account for 53 percent of the total worldwide *information technology* (IT) service market, and is estimated to make up 56 percent of the market by 2007 ("IT Outsourcing Likely to Grow . . ." 2004). Also, the Forrester research firm found that a total of 315,000 jobs had been shifted offshore from the U.S. in 2003 and predicted that the number will have increased to 830,000 in 2005 ("U.S. to Offshore . . ." 2004).

The loss of these U.S. jobs, and jobs in other countries, has fueled anti-outsourcing rhetoric and action from government officials. For example, in early 2004 the governor of Tennessee signed an anti-outsourcing bill that made the state the first to give businesses an incentive for not outsourcing information systems work to cheaper offshore locations. The law requires state procurement officials to give preference in bids for information system services to contractors employing workers only in the U.S. ("Tennessee Governor Curbs Outsourcing . . ." 2004). A recent study noted that legislators in thirty-six U.S. states have introduced more than a hundred bills to curb or ban offshore outsourcing though most of these bills have not yet become law. Still, this seems to indicate a trend that more such bills may become law ("U.S. Federal Anti-Outsourcing Laws . . ." 2004). Finally, on the federal level, the *Thomas-Voinovich Amendment,* which passed as part of an omnibus appropriations act in January 2004, prohibits some federal contracts from being outsourced overseas if U.S. government employees had previously done the work.

Despite the negative impression created by government actions, the press, and current public opinion, the latest U.S. government data suggests foreigners outsource far more services to the U.S. than American companies send abroad ("U.S. Creates More Jobs. . . ." 2004). The U.S. Commerce Department reported the value of U.S. exports of private services (e.g., legal work, computer programming, telecommunications, banking, etc.) jumped to $131.01 billion in 2003, up over $8 billion from the previous year. The value of U.S. imports of the same private services was $77.38 billion for the year, also up almost $8 billion from 2002. When looking at the broader economic picture and measuring imports against exports, the U.S. posted a $53.64 billion surplus in 2003 in trade in private services compared with the rest of the world.

One additional trend worth mentioning is the perception that outsourcing is not just a stand-alone activity to undertake every so often, but a formal practice that should be part of all organizational planning efforts. Sen (2004) suggests that outsourcing has become a philosophy of managing entire organizations. Sen's *Enterprise Outsourcing Management* (EOM) technique is a way for organizations to undertake and shape outsourcing projects to empower firms to be more competitive. Under EOM the firm is continually monitored in terms of its strategic perspectives and goals, its operational practices, and its resulting business performance. When carefully applied and regularly assessed, outsourcing is viewed as a strategy that can help

Figure 1.6 U.S. Outsourcing Market for Information Services for Select Years

the firm meet its goals and move it toward ideal benchmarks or *industry best practices.*

Further support for the idea that outsourcing is now a business institution comes from the recent development of information systems to aid outsourcing activities ("Infosys to Follow . . ." 2004). The *Modular Global Sourcing* system marketed by Infosys, a major international software developer, splits business processes and information systems into individual modules (i.e., separable computer software modules) that can be purchased to support just the areas of the firm where outsourcing is to be undertaken—those that represent non-core competencies—while avoiding the purchase of other modules that involve business activities the client views as core competencies. What this system permits is an enterprise-wide view to align the goals of sourcing with business strategy, modularizing to achieve greater flexibility, transparency, and shared control. This approach will help to achieve necessary business innovation and is essential for companies that want to derive more value from global sourcing ("Infosys to Follow . . ." 2004).

In summary, the trend toward outsourcing is ever growing. The statistics on the U.S. information technology outsourcing market in Figure 1.6 show just how dramatic the growth trend is (Lackow 2001; "Offshore Outsourcing Boosts . . ." 2004). Yet other observed trends (e.g., government anti-outsourcing legislation, executives' sense that they need to revise existing outsourcing arrangements, *backsourcing*, or the return of business activity with the firm, by experienced outsourcers, etc.) indicate that the current practice of outsourcing needs improvement.

Risk in the Outsourcing-Insourcing Process

Hall (2003) reports that half of all outsourcing agreements fail because firms run risks by not performing appropriate analyses which could show how insourcing some of the outsourced activities could be more productive. As we will see in Chapter 2, some organizations consider outsourcing a means of migrating risk to other firms (e.g., the outsource provider takes on the risks of investing in human resources, technology, etc., while the client firm avoids those risks and simply pays a fee for the services). Yet case study research is showing that the very act of outsourcing brings with it a different set of risks. For example, Natovich (2003) reports that, while some risks are indeed absorbed by the outsource provider, the client assumes a set of risks inherent to the outsourcing arrangement. To identify these risks, we must begin by examining the conceptual outsourcing procedure (See Table 1.3). As shown above in Figure 1.3 and below in Figure 1.7, candidate outsourcing activities are identified from non-core competencies. As Figure 1.7 shows, the conceptual steps in a typical outsourcing process continue from the strategic plan of the organization (Baldwin et al. 2000; Chorafas 2003, 36; Minoli 1995, 207). (We will explain in detail the conceptual steps of the process more fully in Chapter 4.) Each step in this conceptual process listed in Figure 1.7 carries risks that might minimize or eliminate the benefits of the entire outsourcing project.

Figure 1.7   Conceptual Steps in a Typical Outsourcing Process

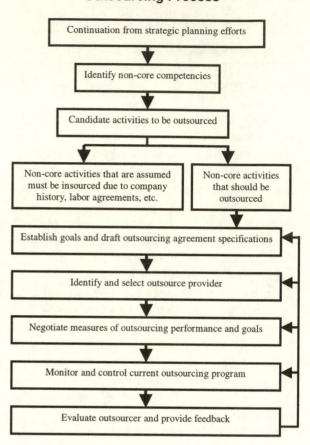

The specific types of risk that a client organization or its managers face depends on a number of factors, including the type of outsourcing undertaken. Greaver (1999, 37–58), Chorafas (2003, 49–70), and Kern and Willcocks (2001, 39–80) break up the risks of outsourcing according to which management phase—design, transition, or follow-up—the risk is associated with. Table 1.4, which briefly describes and provides examples of these phases of outsourcing risk, gives some idea of the range of concerns for managers undertaking outsourcing projects.

Judging from all the risk factors mentioned

Table 1.3

Possible Risks in the Conceptual Outsourcing Process

Outsourcing steps	Examples of possible risks
Identify non-core competencies	Can be incorrectly identified as a core and not a non-core competency
Identify candidate activities to be outsourced	Can be incomplete
Identify non-core activities assumed must be insourced	Can be an incorrect assumption since historic needs change
Identify non-core activities that should be outsourced	Can be an incorrect assumption unless an outsource provider can be found who will complete the job more efficiently
Establish goals and draft outsourcing agreement specifications	Goals can be set so high failure is certain Language in agreement may not be clear enough for understanding and compliance by outsource provider
Identify and select outsource provider	Can incorrectly identify those who should be excluded as candidates Can select the wrong outsource provider
Negotiate goals and measures of outsourcing performance	Misinterpretation of measures and goals, how they are measured, and what they mean Cost of negotiations might be greater than cost advantages of outsourcing
Monitor and control current outsourcing program	Inability to timely monitor or control operations Inability to control finished product quality
Evaluate outsource provider and provide feedback	Inability to evaluate outsource provider accurately Inability to provide timely information to outsource provider A non-responsive outsource provider (i.e., one that ignores feedback)

in the table, outsourcing looks like a very risky proposition, and indeed it is. It becomes even more risky when done in an international context. Meisler (2004) points out that few promoters of international O-I mention the erratic power grids in some foreign countries, or the difficulties with local government officials, inexperienced managers, and unmotivated employees common in international outsourcing. Meisler (2004) goes on to report that international outsourcing fails fifty percent of the time because client organizations have not factored the risks of the international context into their O-I decision. Some firms today are reversing

their international outsourcing decision, bringing outsourced activities back in house (Metz 2004). This is partly due to the perceived failure of outsourcing to achieve the expected gains, such as a 75 percent reduction in the cost of labor reported by Meisler (2004). When client company managers set an outsourcing goal of 75 percent cost reduction and receive only a 30 or 40 percent reduction, they view the outsourcing as a failure, when, in fact, it may be a success. The previously mentioned survey of executives (Goldsmith 2003) identified the top five challenges for companies doing offshore outsourcing as understanding cultural differences and

Table 1.4

Outsourcing Risk Categories and Examples

Risk phase	Description and examples
Design	Setting up the initial outsourcing project within the firm. Examples of risks in this phase include: –Senior management not supporting project –Employees reacting negatively –Unable to align outsourcing efforts with organization goals –Necessary cost and performance information unavailable –Incomplete analysis of outsource provider capabilities –Poorly written agreement or contract
Transition	The process of moving the business activities from the client firm to the outsourcing provider. Examples of risk in this phase include: –Technical problems delay handoff of activities –Outsource provider experiences start up problems –Management of client firm does not willingly participate in handoff of activities to outsource provider –Client firm employees resent and resist transfer of their work
Follow-up	After the handoff of business activities, the client firm must still manage the relationship with the outsourcing provider and the exchange of work between the firms. Examples of risk in this phase include: –Outsource provider fails to meet obligations –Performance measures are not understood or observed –Performance measures are not reported or misreported to client firm –Provider defaults on outsourcing agreement –Outsourcing agreement penalties must be paid by both parties

dealing with political uncertainty (the top reason), evaluating contract performance, the client firm's ignorance of what the outsource provider is doing for them, accountability, and travel expenses to visit and evaluate the outsource provider. These challenges represent a substantial barrier to growth in O-I in an international context, as suggested by the fact that 52 percent of respondents to the same survey are not even considering offshore outsourcing, while only 27 percent are planning on international outsourcing of some kind in the next three years.

Of all the reasons given for O-I failures, the most common is that the O-I decision was made without sufficient analysis, especially quantitative analysis (Meisler 2004). A review of the current outsourcing literature reveals the need for a more quantitative approach to O-I decisions. Though many outsourcing books have been published in the last decade, most treat the O-I decision as purely conceptual, rather than quantitative (Chorafas 2003; Cullen and Willcocks 2003; Gouge 2003). Unlike quantitative methods, conceptual methods of analyzing O-I decisions tend to focus on one variable at a time. This type of analysis runs the risk of missing any potential changes attributable to the dynamic interaction among the many variables in the O-I process. Examples of this type of analytic failure will be presented in Chapter 8, where by combining the total resources of possible outsourcing and insourcing simultaneously, an optimal proportion of allocation can be achieved between both of these variables. This quantitative analysis may be superior to a conceptual approach, which just considers the outsourcing variable.

What can be done to mitigate risk, particularly the risk of O-I in an international context? The outsourcing literature suggests a careful analysis that considers risk, particularly those connected with outsourcing in an international context, since much of the growth in outsourcing will be international. It is to this end this textbook seeks to provide an analytical framework and a collection of methodologies that will permit organizations of any size to incorporate risk analysis into their O-I decision process.

How This Book Is Organized

The remaining chapters in this book all use the same pedagogical method, which is designed to aid the reader's understanding. In addition to the basic content, each chapter includes the following sections: (1) Learning objectives: declarative statements of what a reader can expect to learn from the chapter. These are also useful as a review tool; (2) Introduction: a brief overview of the content of the chapter; (3) Summary: a brief review at the end of the chapter to remind readers of major points; (4) Review terms: a list of key terms to remind readers of their importance; (5) Discussion questions: questions intended to stimulate further thinking about the chapter's contents; (6) Concept questions: questions that can be used as assignments or as a self-test for readers; (7) Problems: problems presented at the end of chapters on methodology for assignment purposes and also to help readers

understand computational aspects of the methodologies, while expanding their understanding of how they can be applied in O-I decision making; (8) References: a listing of works cited in the chapter. Readers can use these reference citations to locate the publication and learn more about topics discussed or mentioned in the chapter.

This textbook is divided into two parts. Part 1, "Introduction to Outsourcing-Insourcing in an International Context," consists of four chapters. Chapter 1, "Introduction to Outsourcing-Insourcing," gives a basic overview of outsourcing-insourcing, what it involves, why it is used, and how it is related to a firm's management planning. Chapter 2, "Advantages and Disadvantages of Outsourcing-Insourcing," provides a justification of O-I. This chapter also identifies the need for businesses to do more risk analysis to ensure successful outcomes. Chapter 3, "Outsourcing-Insourcing Strategy and International Risk Factors," explores the connection between O-I and international business. The chapter introduces the idea of risk in an international context, a central theme in this textbook. Chapter 4, "Planning International Outsourcing-Insourcing" elaborates on the business planning process and its connection with O-I projects. The chapter also outlines strategies to overcome risks and use O-I successfully.

Part 1 having laid out the "what, why, and where" of O-I in an international context, Part 2, "Methodologies for Different Types of Outsourcing-Insourcing Decisions," examines a series of methodologies that will help explain "how" O-I should be undertaken. Chapter 5, "International Outsourcing-Insourcing Metrics-Based Methodologies" introduces a variety of methodologies used to measure O-I risks and business performance. Chapter 6, "Financial Methodologies for the Initial Outsourcing-Insourcing Decision," introduces methodologies used when O-I is initiated within a firm. Chapter 7, "Methodologies for Selecting Outsourcing-Insourcing Partners," introduces methodologies that help a client firm find the best outsource provider. Chapter 8, "Methodologies for Allocating Business Activities Between Outsourcers and Insourcers," introduces methodologies that help a client firm determine the optimum allocation of business activities between insourcing and various outsource providers. The epilogue, "There Are Wrong Ways and Rights Ways to Outsource-Insource in an International Context," reminds the reader of the consequences of not exercising good judgment and using effective methodologies when making O-I decisions.

Summary

This chapter briefly introduced the subject of O-I in an international context. It covered basic ideas, such as the balancing of resources between outsourcing and insourcing, how outsourcing is an evolutionary bridge between the traditional firm and the organization of the future, the parallel growth of international outsourcing and international business, and an overview of the types of O-I. These basic concepts provide the background necessary to begin to appreciate the role of O-I, appreciation that will be expanded in the following chapters. Also, this chapter explained various strategic and economic reasons why outsourcing is an important trend in business today. Finally, the chapter introduced the issue of risk in O-I decision making, an important theme throughout the rest of this textbook. Managers should know both the pros and cons of outsourcing a given business activity so that they can better assess if risks are worth taking. While this chapter mentions some justifications for O-I in general and some risks that might discourage its use, Chapter 2 will focus on the advantages and disadvantages of O-I in an international context.

Review Terms

Agency theory	Internal organization analysis
Backsourcing	International context
Business activities	Interorganizational relationship theory
Business process outsourcing (BPO)	Nearshore outsourcing
Business transformation outsourcing (BTO)	Non-equity alliance
Client firm	Offshore outsourcing
Comparative advantage	Offshoring
Core competencies	Outsource provider
Co-sourcing	Outsourcing
Decision-making structure	Outsourcing-insourcing (O-I)
Enterprise outsourcing management (EOM)	Shared outsourcing
Equity joint venture	Spin-offs
Equity strategic alliance	Strategic decision
Franchising	Strategic outsourcing
Global outsourcing	Subcontracting
Industry best practices	Tactical decision
Information technology (IT)	Transaction cost theory
Insourcing	Transition outsourcing

Discussion Questions

1. How is the international context connected to outsourcing-insourcing?
2. What is the connection between subcontracting and outsourcing?
3. How is the present-day business organization really a way station between traditional and future business organizations?
4. What is the difference between offshoring and offshore outsourcing?
5. How has corporation strategy legitimized outsourcing?
6. Which of the three theories (i.e., transaction cost theory, agency theory, and interorganizational relationship theory) best explains why outsourcing is a reasonable approach to business?
7. How would you summarize outsourcing trends?
8. Why should we consider risk when we are making an outsourcing-insourcing decision?

Concept Questions

1. What is the difference between outsourcing and insourcing? Explain.
2. What benefits and costs might affect an outsourcing-insourcing decision?
3. What types of cooperative agreements might exist between an outsourcing client and outsourcing provider?
4. What is co-sourcing?
5. What is backsourcing?
6. What is a core competency, and how is it related to outsourcing?
7. What kinds of risk does an organization run when undertaking an outsourcing program?
8. What are the conceptual steps in a typical outsourcing process?

References

Aubert, B. A.; Rivard, S.; and Patry, M. "A Transaction Cost Model of IT Outsourcing." *Information and Management* 41, no. 7 (2004): 921–932.

Bahli, B., and Rivard, S. "Validating Measures of Information Technology Outsourcing Risk Factors." *Omega* 33, no. 2 (2005): 175–187.

Baldwin, L. H.; Camm, F.; and Moore, N. Y. *Strategic Sourcing: Measuring and Managing Performance.* Santa Monica, CA: Rand, 2000.

Cateora, R. *International Marketing.* 8th ed. Homewood, IL: Irwin, 1994.

Contractor, F. J., and Lorange, P. "Competition vs. Cooperation: A Benefit/Cost Framework for Choosing Between Fully-Owned Investments and Cooperative Relationships." In *International Strategic Management*, edited by Root, F., and Visudtibhan, K., 112–140. Washington, DC: Taylor and Francis, 1992.

Chase, R. B.; Jacobs, F. R.; and Aquilano, N. J. *Operations Management for Competitive Advantage.* 10th ed. Boston: Irwin/McGraw-Hill, 2004.

Chorafas, D. N. *Outsourcing, Insourcing and IT for Enterprise Management.* Houndmills, Great Britain: Palgrave/MacMillan, 2003.

Coase, R. "The Nature of the Firm." *Economica* 4 (1937): 386–405.

Cullen, S., and Willcocks, L. *Intelligent IT Outsourcing.* London: Butterworth-Heinemann, 2003.

Domberger, S. *The Contracting Organization: A Strategic Guide to Outsourcing.* Oxford: Oxford University Press, 1998.

Forslid, R., and Wooton, I. "Comparative Advantage and the Location of Production." *Review of International Economics* 11, no. 4 (2003): 588–604.

"Global BPO Market to Touch $682.5 Billion, Says IDC." *Outsourcing Intelligence Bulletin: FSO Magazine* 4, no. 6 (May 9–16, 2004), editor@fsoutsourcing.com.

Goldsmith, N. M. *Outsourcing Trends.* New York: The Conference Board, 2003.

Gouge, I. *Shaping the IT Organization.* London: Springer, 2003.

Greaver, M. F. *Strategic Outsourcing.* New York: American Management Association, 1999.

Hall, M. "Outsourcing Deals Fail Half the Time." *Computerworld* 37, no. 44 (2003): 10.

Hall, P., and Soskice, D., eds. *Varieties of Capitalism: The Institutional Foundations of Comparative Advantage.* Oxford: Oxford University Press, 2001.

Hayes, R.; Pisano, G.; Upton, D.; and Wheelwright, S.

Operations, Strategy, and Technology: Pursuing the Competitive Edge. New York: Wiley, 2005.

"Infosys to Follow 'Modular Global Sourcing Strategy': The Future of Outsourcing." *Outsourcing Intelligence Bulletin: FSO Magazine* 4, no. 7 (May 23–30, 2004), editor@fsoutsourcing.com.

"IT Outsourcing Likely to Grow, Says Gartner." *Outsourcing Intelligence Bulletin: FSO Magazine* 4, no. 7 (May 23–30, 2004), editor@fsoutsourcing.com.

James, H. S., and Weidenbaum, M. *When Businesses Cross International Borders.* Westport, CT: Praeger, 1993.

Kern, T., and Willcocks, L. P. *The Relationship Advantage: Information Technologies, Sourcing, and Management.* Oxford: Oxford University Press, 2001.

King, A.; Fowler, S.; and Zeithaml, C. "Managing Organizational Competencies for Competitive Advantage: The Middle-Management Edge." *Academy of Management Executive* 15, no. 2 (2001): 95–107.

Kotabe, M., and Murray, J. Y. "Global Sourcing Strategy and Sustainable Competitive Advantage." *Industrial Marketing Management* 33, no. 1 (2004): 7–15.

Lackow, H. M. *IT Outsourcing Trends.* New York: The Conference Board, 2001.

Lankford, W. M., and Parsa, F. "Outsourcing: A Primer." *Management Decision* 37, (1999): 310–316.

Laudon, K. C., and Laudon, J. P. *Management Information Systems.* 8th ed. Upper Saddle River, NJ: Person/ Prentice Hall, 2004.

Lee, J.-N.; Huynh, M. Q.; and Kwok, R. C.-W. "IT Outsourcing Evolution—Past, Present, and Future." *Communications of the ACM* 46, no. 5 (2003): 84–90.

Meisler, A. "Think Globally, Act Rationally." *Workforce Management* 83, no. 1 (2004): 40–45.

Metz, C. "Tech Support Coming Home?" *PC Magazine,* February 17, 2004, 20.

Minoli, D. *Analyzing Outsourcing.* New York: McGraw-Hill, Inc., 1995.

Murray, J. Y., and Kotabe, M. "Sourcing Strategies of U.S. Service Companies: A Modified Transaction-Cost Analysis." *Strategic Management Journal* 20, no. 9 (1999): 791–809.

Natovich, J. "Vendor Related Risks in IT Development: A Chronology of an Outsourced Project Failure." *Technology Analysis and Strategic Management* 15, no. 4 (2003): 409–420.

"Offshore Outsourcing Boosts IT Service Market in 2003, Says Gartner." *Outsourcing Intelligence Bulletin: FSO Magazine* 9, no. 2 (June 27–July 4, 2004), editor@fsoutsourcing.com.

"Outsourcing Expectations Surpass Just Cost Savings as CFOs Demand More." BOBSGUIDE, http://www.bobsguide.com/guide/news/7137.html (accessed November 5, 2004).

Pint, E. M., and Baldwin, L. H. *Strategic Sourcing: Theory and Evidence from Economics and Business Management.* Santa Monica, CA: Rand, 1997.

Prahalad, C.K., and Hamel, G. "The Core Competence of the Corporation." *Harvard Business Review* 68, no. 3 (1990): 79–92.

Putterman, L., and Kroszner, R. *The Economic Nature of the Firm: A Reader.* Cambridge: Cambridge University Press, 1995.

Russell, R. S., and Taylor, B. W. *Operations Management.* 4th ed. Upper Saddle River, NJ: Prentice-Hall, 2003.

Schniederjans, M. J. *Operations Management in a Global Context.* Westport, CT: Quorum Books, 1998.

Sen, S. "Enterprise Outsourcing Management, the New Mantra." *Outsourcing Intelligence Bulletin: FSO Magazine* 4, no. 2 (March 21–28, 2004), editor@fsoutsourcing.com.

"Tennessee Governor Curbs Outsourcing by Introducing Anti-Outsourcing Bill." *Outsourcing Intelligence Bulletin: FSO Magazine* 4, no. 7 (May 23–30, 2004), editor@fsoutsourcing.com.

"Transformational Outsourcing—It's All in the Contract." *Global Computing Services* (July 25, 2003): 4.

"U.S. Companies to Shift Jobs by Offshoring Rather Than Outsourcing." *Outsourcing Intelligence Bulletin: FSO Magazine* 4, no. 5 (May 2–9, 2004), editor@fsoutsourcing.com.

"U.S. Creates More Jobs in the Country Compared to Outsourcing Overseas." *Outsourcing Intelligence Bulletin: FSO Magazine* 4, no. 2 (April 4–11, 2004), editor@fsoutsourcing.com.

"U.S. Federal Anti-Outsourcing Laws Violate Anti-Protectionist Trade Rule." *Outsourcing Intelligence Bulletin: FSO Magazine* 4, no. 3 (April 18–25, 2004), editor@fsoutsourcing.com.

"U.S. Firms Set Up Offshoring Units in India." *Outsourcing Intelligence Bulletin: FSO Magazine* 4, no. 6 (May 9–16, 2004), editor@fsoutsourcing.com.

"U.S. to Offshore 830,000 Jobs, Predicts Forrester." *Outsourcing Intelligence Bulletin: FSO Magazine* 4, no. 7 (May 23–30, 2004), editor@fsoutsourcing.com.

Yang, C., and Huang, J. B. "A Decision Model for IS Outsourcing." *International Journal of Information Management* 20 (2000): 225–239.

Zsidish, G. A. "Managerial Perspectives on Supply Risk." *Journal of Supply Chain Management* 39, no. 1 (2003): 14–26.

2

Advantages and Disadvantages of Outsourcing-Insourcing

Learning Objectives   After completing this chapter you should be able to:

- Describe how outsourcing is becoming an industry.
- Describe outsourcing advantages and cite examples.
- Describe outsourcing disadvantages and cite examples.
- Describe how insourcing is related to the outsourcing advantages and disadvantages.
- Describe international outsourcing advantages and disadvantages.
- Explain how risk mitigation is used to justify outsourcing.
- Explain value migration in outsourcing.

Introduction

Chapter 1 introduced the *outsourcing-insourcing* (O-I) decision as a balancing of proportions of outsourcing and insourcing to achieve an organization's strategic goals. Managers then determine the proportions they need to understand the advantages and disadvantages outsourcing and insourcing can bring to their organization.

In this chapter we seek to explore a variety of advantages for both outsourcing and insourcing. Since there is only one outcome in the O-I decision, either outsource or insource business activity, an advantage for one can be seen as a comparative disadvantage for the other. Thus, while this chapter focuses on the advantages and disadvantages of outsourcing, it will in effect relate to insourcing at the same time. In addition, this chapter continues its discussion of the role of risk in the O-I decision by examining the connection of risk to various advantages used in justifying outsourcing.

Outsourcing as an Industry

To recognize the advantages and disadvantages of outsourcing, it is important to understand how the industry of outsourcing is structured to meet the needs of client firms. Of the ten functional areas mentioned by Goldsmith (2003), the most commonly outsourced functional area is *information technology* (IT), and the least commonly outsourced is *human resources* (HR). These commonly outsourced functional areas are representative of the broader outsourcing industry and provide an overview of activities now taking place.

Information Technology (IT) Outsourcing Industry

The IT outsourcing industry currently takes on a wide range of projects, from small-scale projects to complete business process solutions, where the entire IT function is provided by an outsourcer. Lackow's (2001) survey of the industry shows a diverse set of IT provider service categories, including user support, voice network management, disaster recovery, software development, data network management, software maintenance, data center operations, IT strategy and planning, support services, application hosting, and business processes. The survey predicted IT outsourcing would continue and grow in importance. A follow-up survey of forty-four companies by Goldsmith (2003) confirmed the prediction by estimating that 79 percent of U.S. firms outsource IT. Other research by Lee et al. (2003) confirms that clients continue benefiting from outsourcing IT, and it is considered a valuable strategy.

Characteristic of the IT outsourcing industry is the ever-dominant strategy of *offshore outsourcing.* The *Meta Group* (a forecasting organization) predicts growth in offshore outsourcing of IT is expected to increase at a yearly rate of 20 percent ("Offshore Outsourcing Market . . ." 2004). Meta goes on to predict that by 2009 the average enterprise will outsource 60 percent of its IT application work offshore.

One common trend in the IT outsourcing industry is *multi-sourcing,* the practice of using multiple outsource providers to mitigate the risk of having to deal with just one provider. Having many outsource providers may give a client firm more flexibility and access to more competitive pricing ("Multi-sourcing . . ." 2003). According to both Lackow

(2001) and Goldsmith (2003), the offshoring and multi-sourcing strategies that presently characterize the IT outsourcing industry are chiefly driven by the wish to minimize costs. With projections that U.S. firms will save almost $21 billion in IT expenses by offshoring from 2003 to 2008, it is difficult to argue against the cost savings reasoning (McDougall 2004). This theme recurs in other IT outsourcing literature ("Offshore Outsourcing Poised . . ." 2004). What is only now beginning to surface is the recognition of the need to make risk assessment part of the decision process ("Offshore Outsourcing Poised . . ." 2004; Bhattacharya et al. 2003; "Negotiating the Contract . . ." 2004; "Discover Weighs the Risk" 2004). Indeed, IT outsourcing clients are now starting to realize that outsourcing risks can result in greater costs and poorer quality than expected ("Challenges to Consider" 2004; "Offshoring Call Centers" 2004; Natovich 2003; Soliman and Chen 2003).

Human Resource (HR) Outsourcing Industry

According to Adler (2003) the HR outsourcing industry has three main segments: HR consultants, HR administrative-service providers, and HR technology enablers. *HR consultants* provide classic consulting expertise on HR business activities such as compensation, employee benefits, and workplace diversity. This industry segment is represented by very large firms such as *Hewitt Associates* and *Mercer Human Resource Consulting*, in addition to smaller, more specialized firms. *HR administrative-service providers* handle large-scale HR business activities such as payroll and benefits processing. Interestingly, many HR administrative-service providers started in one HR area, like payroll, and expanded into other areas, like benefits. Examples of firms in this segment of the HR outsourcing industry include *ADP* and *ProBusiness Services, Inc., HR technology enablers*, according to Adler (2003), are responsible for HR information system implementation, software maintenance, data management, network activities, and continuous IS monitoring services that might traditionally have been performed by IT consultants. Firms in this segment of the industry include *Exult* and *Synhrgy HR Technologies.*

Within each of the three industry segments observed by Adler (2003) some firms are considered specialists (i.e., firms working in only one type of business industry, like HR companies whose clientele is limited to the travel industry) while others are generalists (i.e., firms that work with any kind of client, in any business industry). Also, some providers compete in only one industry segment, while others, like *IBM's PriceWaterhouseCoopers,* are vertically integrated generalists that offer a full range of HR services spanning HR consulting, HR administrative-services, and HR technology.

Currently, the HR outsourcing industry is experiencing an industry trend toward integration and consolidation (Adler 2003; "Filippelli Joins the . . ." 2004). This will mean many of the HR consulting and HR administrative-service providers will be able to give greater breadth of HR solutions and fuller integration within client firms. This will result in a "one-stop" service positioned to perform complete *business process outsourcing* (BPO) service in HR. As with any consolidating industry, which moves from a competitive environment to a more oligopolistic environment, the logical consequences for the industry's clients will be an increased risk of higher fees and standardization of services, which will lead to greater inflexibility. A Web site set up to assist in the education of HR outsourcing complete with case studies is: www.outsourcing.com/micr02/ sponsored by *The Outsourcing Institute.*

HR outsourcing, like all functional areas of business, exists in an international context. For example, a survey of 524 Asian companies ("HR Outsourcing in Asia . . ." 2004) revealed 39 percent of the firms outsourced some of their HR processes, and the Asia-Pacific area growth in the HR industry market more than doubled from 1999 to 2004. Some of the fastest growing HR business activities include HR payroll services, education and training, and benefits administration. Another study of HR outsourcing, by the *Conference Board* and *Accenture* (both noted forecasting firms), showed that 80 percent of 120 companies that have outsourced HR business activities would do so again. None of the companies in the study planned to *backsource,* or bring the outsourced activities back in-house ("Most of the Financial Firms . . ." 2004). The study concludes that HR outsourcing is a firmly embedded part of HR service delivery in both North America and Europe. Significantly, the study also finds that while most firms fully outsource some HR business activities and programs, they often deliver other HR services through a blended, or proportioned, solution that combines both internal and external capabilities and may even use multiple outsource providers. Apparently using both internal and external outsourcing staff has proven a successful strategy. (Chapter 8 discusses how this proportioned strategy can be determined.) Clearly, many HR experts support HR outsourcing (Flannery and Heckathorn 2003; Garcia 2004; Stefanic 2004).

Industry Recognition and Support

As outsourcing has evolved into a multi-billion dollar business, organizations have been formed that support the outsourcing industry. One such organization is *FS Outsourcing Company* (www.fsoutsourcing.com), a leading media, research, and event-planning organization that supports outsourcing in the financial services industry. Founded in 2003, it offers diverse products and

Table 2.1

Outsourcing Advantages: Cost Savings and Gaining Outside Expertise

Reasons for outsourcing	Potential advantage
Cost savings	The cost of business activities outsourced to a provider can be less than the cost of insourcing the same activity.
	When a client firm outsources business activity, they can be left with assets (e.g., technology), which can be converted to cash to deal with short-term cash problems (i.e., saving interest costs on loans). In many cases, the outsource provider purchases the assets, at market value or above, making the outsource provider a short-term source of funds.
	Can turn fixed costs (assets) into variable costs (leasing agreements).
	Can reduce nonproductive assets on balance sheet.
	When external financing is too costly to invest in a capital expansion, a firm can outsource the need for the capital investment.
	Client firm becomes part of the outsourcing provider's network or supply-chain, helping to reduce costs for both parties.
Gain outside expertise	Gain access to a broad base of expertise and skills unavailable by insourcing.
	Outsourcers can be a source of original ideas for improvements in core and non-core competency services and products.

services, including print publishing, online publishing, events and conferences, market research and products, education and training, and global consulting solutions. There are also conferences held throughout the world that focus exclusively on outsourcing, providing outsource information and networking opportunities. The annual *Outsourcing World Summit*, for instance, brings executives, managers and providers together for outsourcing education.

What Are the Advantages of Outsourcing (or Disadvantages of Insourcing)?

Goldsmith's (2003) survey found five main reasons why executives outsource business activity. They are, in order of importance, cost savings, gaining outside expertise, improving service, focusing on core competencies, and gaining outside technol-

ogy. These results are presented in detail in Tables 2.1, 2.2 and 2.3 (Chorafas 2003; Cullen and Willcocks 2003; Greaver 1999; Gouge 2003; Hayes et al. 2005; Lackow 2001; Lee et al. 2003; Minoli 1995; Thibodeau 2003).

Clearly, the number one reason driving outsourcing is the possibility of significant cost savings, particularly on labor. While other kinds of cost savings are mentioned in Table 2.1, the possibility of reducing labor costs, which traditionally represent 60 to 100 percent of total cost of products or services, by as much as 75 percent has drawn much attention to outsourcing. Yet the labor cost reduction obtainable by outsourcing is more often 20 to 25 percent or perhaps 30 to 40 percent, according to Meisler (2004). According to Tyson (2004), a 10 to 30 percent reduction in the price of technology is also a reasonable expectation. Domberger (1998) reported that outsourcing resulted in a 10 to 30 percent cost reduction for

Table 2.2

Outsourcing Advantage: Improve Service

Reason for outsourcing	Potential advantage
Improve service	Improves operations flexibility allowing the client firm to more easily increase production during boom times in customer demand and to quickly decrease production during decline periods by ending outsourcing agreements.
	Can provide the flexibility to transform the organization to be more efficient.
	Reduced costs resulting from outsourcing can increase customer value and satisfaction.
	Improved business performance resulting from outsourcing can include higher quality, since the provider can focus efforts more precisely on that factor; increased output, since the client firm adds the provider's production to their own with little or no investment, resulting in better utilization of client firm's reduced assets.
	The psychological impact of outsourcing some business activities tends to motivate remaining client organization employees to work harder in an effort to retain their jobs.
	Can be used to rapidly introduce new products and services in order to meet shifting customer demand.
	Can be used to introduce new technologies or systems incrementally into the client organization.
	Can help new products achieve a faster time to market.
	Can help a client firm develop and gain access to new distribution channels quickly.

client firms, with 20 percent being the most commonly cited figure. Firms that set too high a cost reduction goal will undoubtedly fail to achieve cost objectives, as MacInnis (2003) has observed in his study of the information systems field.

The range of cost reductions reported above becomes interesting when compared with the estimates needed to make an outsourcing project worth the effort. One article asserts that client firms need at least a 35 percent cost reduction to make outsourcing projects successful ("Clients to Blame . . ." 2003). When comparing the needed 35 percent to an average 20 percent, it appears the likelihood of an outsourcing project being successful is small.

The advantage of gaining outside expertise is reasonable in situations where the client firm takes the time to get to know and help the outsource provider grow in its abilities to provide service to the client. Firms that simply pay contractual retainer fees to a provider without any integration and alli-

ance activities necessary for maintaining a healthy partnership are running significant risks. It is not surprising that gaining access to outside expertise is the second highest rated reason for outsourcing according to Goldsmith (2003).

The third most frequently cited reason for outsourcing according to Goldsmith (2003) is to help the client firm improve services. Many of the advantages listed in Table 2.2 are related to flexibility and promoting organizational change in the client firm. A problem with this rationale for outsourcing is the impossibility of accurately predicting how the change will affect the client firm. How, for example, can we measure the psychological impact on morale, loyalty, trust, and dedication of seeing one's co-workers' jobs disappear because of outsourcing?

Table 2.3 lists the lower-ranked reasons for outsourcing. As we pointed out in Chapter 1, focusing on core competencies is one of the main reasons

Table 2.3

Outsourcing Advantages: Focus on Core Competencies, Gain Outside Technology, and Other Advantages

Reasons for outsourcing	Potential advantage
Focus on core competencies	Allows the client firm to focus efforts on outputs and outcomes, while the provider focuses on inputs and processes.
	Provides the client firm the discipline to identify and learn what their core competencies are, and in doing so, aids strategic planning.
	Frees up assets to reallocate to core competencies.
	Client firms can gain unique market access and business opportunities that the outsource provider brings with them.
	Client firms may find they have outsource capacity that they can sell to other firms.
	Outsource provider brings their core competencies to the client, helping the client maintain state-of-the-art performance.
Gain outside technology	Can outsource to state-of-the-art providers instead of retaining older legacy systems (i.e., pick and choose newer technology anytime it is needed, since the client firm does not have to invest in such technology).
	Can help client firm personnel learn newer technology.
Other	Can offer client firm employees an alternative career path, since the outsource provider may offer better opportunities for advancement.
	Client firms can improve their image by association with an outstanding outsource provider.
	Can mitgate risk by transferring problems with human resources, technology, and systems to the outsource provider.
	Changes the culture of a client firm to be more productive
	Can be used as a strategy for downsizing or reengineering a client firm.
	Separation of outsource client and provider may benefit the client firm in situations where customers will inevitably have complaints (i.e., the client firm can blame the provider for any problems).
	Allows the client firm to conserve capital to invest in core competencies.

justifying outsourcing, yet it is the fourth most commonly cited reason in the Goldsmith (2003) survey of executives, and other researchers have also found that it tends to be downplayed by executives (Antonucci et al. 1998; Beaumont and Costa 2002; Lankford and Parsa 1999; Yang and Huang 2000). One factor leading to its lower ranking is that it is a fairly intangible objective. Unlike many of the measurable cost or service objectives, core competencies have to be identified, which the literature indicates is not always an easy or accurate process (Milgate 2001, 27–44; Sen 2004). Sadly, many firms feel justified in outsourcing any activity at all (Lisle 2003; Rothery and Robertson 1995, 123–124), which can lead to the loss of a core competency or a *near-core competency* (i.e., a competency that may soon become a core competency if developed).

Particularly striking is the fact that *risk mitigation* (i.e., the process of reducing risk) is not included in the top five reasons for outsourcing in Goldsmith's (2003) survey and was included by us in the "other" category of Table 2.3 due to its appearance in other outsourcing literature (Antonucci et al. 1998; Beaumont and Costa 2002). Some books on outsourcing devote a whole chapter to the outsourcing advantage of risk mitigation (see Kern and Willcocks 2001, chapter 2), and others devote detailed "how-to" sections to this subject (see Gouge 2003, 149–156). The literature also has many case studies in which different types of risk are mitigated by transferring activities to outsource providers. For example, an IT outsource provider, *Johnson Controls,* was hired by another firm to operate and maintain their North American data center facilities (Sawyer 2003). Since system failure is commonly caused by overheating of IT equipment, Johnson Controls conducted a temperature-mapping analysis (something the IT client had not done) and determined two areas in the IT facilities ran a risk of overheating. The client suggested the purchase of two additional cooling units, but Johnson Controls determined that existing cooling units, if repositioned, would protect the components from overheating. The result was that the client saved $60,000 on the purchase of the unneeded cooling systems and avoided the risk of computer failure due to overheating, all at a cost of only $15,000 per year (Sawyer 2003).

The fact that risk mitigation does not show on any particular survey as being an advantageous factor in favor of outsourcing does not mean it is not important. In an executive survey executives did not reveal mitigation as important. Their reasoning may be flawed in not considering risk in outsourcing decisions. Perhaps executives do so because of its perceived negative impact. Willcocks and Choi (1995) identified management trends to downplay the risk-reward in outsourcing arrangements. As Aubert et al. (2004) have observed, uncertainty or risk is a major deterrent to outsourcing, and if out-

sourcing is a strategy that executives want to adopt, why give opponents the potential, damaging risk information, which might prevent the adoption of the risk strategy?

Linking an International Context with Outsourcing Advantages

In addition to all the advantages of outsourcing that we have already mentioned, there are several more, listed in Table 2.4, that are unique to outsourcing in an international context. It is interesting to note that the reasons for outsourcing summarized in Tables 2.1 to 2.4 mirror the reasons why firms internationalize operations, as shown in Table 2.5 (Rodrigues 1996, 80–84; Schniederjans 1998, 7–10). It is the commonality of the pro-outsourcing and pro-internationalization reasons, which supports the thesis of this textbook: O-I in an international context is an international business activity and deserves the same kind of detailed and careful analysis that successful international business decision making has mandated for decades.

While Goldsmith (2003) reports that only 21 percent of the firms contacted for his survey have undertaken international outsourcing, an additional 27 percent said they planned on undertaking it in the next three years. This trend was confirmed by more recent research that has looked back at actual economic behavior in 2003 ("Offshore Outsourcing Boosts . . ." 2004).

What Are the Disadvantages of Outsourcing (or Advantages of Insourcing)?

Businesses operate in a risk decision making environment. Every advantage previously mentioned in favor of outsourcing (or against insourcing) has only a probability or risk of actually occurring. None of the advantages of outsourcing

Table 2.4

Advantages of Outsourcing in an International Context

Reasons for outsourcing	Potential advantage
Increased profits	Greater profits because the cost of business activities outsourced to a foreign provider operating under less restrictive laws (e.g., environmental protection laws, labor laws, etc.) can be considerably less than insourced costs of the client firm. Takes advantage of currency exchange rates to benefit the client in contracts with foreign outsource providers.
Improved operations	Takes advantage of outsource provider foreign markets for raw materials and labor otherwise unavailable to client firm.
Improved markets	A first step and learning experience for the client firm in going international. What better way to learn about running a foreign operation, expansion into foreign markets, and taking advantage of all the other benefits a foreign location has to offer than to work closely with outsource providers in that country. Protect home country markets from imports, since it takes advantage of lower cost foreign labor and materials.
Other	Outsource provider can serve as a de facto branch of a client firm, which can thus avoid going international and also the complexity of dealing with currency and language issues, multinational accounting problems, etc.

Table 2.5

Reasons Why Organizations Internationalize

Reasons why organizations internationalize their business operations	Type of advantage
Reduced costs	Tangible
Reduced risks	
Secure supply and materials sources	
Improved customer service	
Attracts new markets	
Learning to improve business activities and systems	
Attracts human resources from a global market	Intangible

are certain. Likewise, the disadvantages listed in Table 2.6 are not certainties, but have been observed and reported in outsourcing literature (Cullen and Willcocks 2003; Domberger 1998; Goldsmith 2003; Gouge 2003; Greaver 1999; Kern and Willcocks 2001; Kotabe and Murray 2004; Minoli 1995). The list in Table 2.6 is hardly complete, but it provides a basic overview of the disadvantages that have caused the majority of business organizations reported on in the literature either to revise their outsourcing agreements or reverse their decision and start insourcing business activities (Goldsmith 2003).

The loss of control by client firm managers is a disadvantage that can permeate and be linked to all other disadvantages. For example, as Allen et al. (2001) observe, when managers lose control of some operations, costs usually increase because there is no way for the manager to assess and control costs. Some outsourcing contracts, for example, allow the provider to purchase items for the client without approval, leaving the client at great risk for material cost escalations. But materials are not as major a cost risk factor as human resources. As Beaumont and Costa (2002) note,

Table 2.6

Disadvantages of Outsourcing

Reasons for not outsourcing	Potential disadvantage
Increased costs	Lag time in service from outsource provider due to distance can add substantially higher delivery costs (e.g., air freight, air mail, etc.) to client's customers.
	Can be costly and difficult to change an outsourcing agreement without costly penalties. Excessive transition costs for provider training.
	The expense of negotiating, maintaining, and enforcing outsourcing agreements may outweigh the benefits.
Loss of control	A dependence by the client on the outsource provider can lead to a variety of problems (e.g., loss of markets, higher costs, etc.).
	Loss of flexibility in controlling business activities, final product, etc. by client managers.
	Lack of contractual flexibility.
Negative impact on employees	Negative impact on client firm employees' morale when they become outsource provider employees.
	Causes organizational restructuring, resulting in dislocation and social costs for employees.
Negative impact on customers	Lag time in service from foreign outsource provider may delay delivery and increase costs to the client firm's customers.
	Can disrupt operations during the transition of the outsourced activity from client to outsource provider.
Difficulties in managing relationship	Can be difficult to quantify the advantages of outsourcing.
	Design changes in products can be more difficult when ordered from a distance.
	Excessive investment of time in building a relationship with the outsource provider.
	Client firm finds itself unable to communicate with the outsource provider.
	Outsource provider may be unable to communicate difficulties and opportunities.
Other risks	Sharing knowledge with an outsource provider who may later share it with a competitor.
	Can be costly and difficult to reverse outsourcing decision in terms of recruiting personnel in the longer term.
	Outsource provider may fail to achieve client objectives.
	All of the outsourcer's risks are also assumed by the client firm (provider's financial limitations, poor service, older technology, etc.).
	Requires an alliance with a undesirable provider (e.g., a provider with a negative reputation).
	Outsourcing business activities may cause the client firm to lose skills that might be needed in the future.
	Outsourcing business activities may cause the client firm to lose its corporate knowledge within the firm over time.
	Weakens innovative capacity in the longer term.
	Failure in outsourcing can mean the eventual failure of client firm.
	Outsourcing can result in security or confidentiality breaches.

employees are usually the focus of a manager's angst, and employee morale goes down when functions are outsourced, particularly when close colleagues' jobs are outsourced. Employees believe they may be next, and indeed they may, costing the client firm productivity, loyalty, and trust, all of which are necessary for a healthy, growing business (Antonucci et al. 1998). Like employee-manager relations in the client firm, the relationship between the client firm and the outsource provider can be strained by outsourcing, particularly by the notion that outsourcing provides the client with operations flexibility. Many firms find that their outsource agreement actually allows them little flexibility to alter business activities, unless the client firm is willing to pay extra for additional flexibility. And changing the outsourcing agreement may disrupt the outsource provider's internal operations, causing dislocations, poor morale, and so on. Changes might even cause the outsource provider to fail in delivering promised business activities at the agreed-upon time or place. The only recourse then may be to cancel the outsourcing agreement. Yet penalties for premature cancellations can be substantial. Perhaps this may explain the 50 percent failure rate of outsourcing reported by Hall (2003).

As for the "other risks" disadvantages of outsourcing (and to a lesser degree, all of the disadvantages), they tend to be longer-term than the advantages of outsourcing. In other words, many of the risks client firms run by outsourcing will not show up on the bottom line of the firm's cost and profit statements until some time into the future. This permits CEOs who prefer short-term planning and other managers interested only in bottom-line improvements to use the outsourcing strategy to make quick gains at the expense of longer-term objectives and company survival.

Linking an International Context with Outsourcing Disadvantages

As a part of the Goldsmith (2003) survey of executives, specific challenges of offshore outsourcing are identified. There are six areas where substantial disadvantages or "challenges" for the future of international outsourcing are observed. Ranking them by percentage of frequency of response, they include cultural differences and political uncertainty, the inability to evaluate outsource provider performance, client management ignoring their outsourcing responsibilities, lax accountability, costs to send client managers to outsource provider locations, and staff turnover. Goldsmith (2003) also reports that 52 percent of firms in the survey have no plans to use international outsourcing in their planning horizons. When contrasted with the 21 percent of firms in the study, which undertook international outsourcing, there clearly are obstacles preventing the majority of firms from embracing international outsourcing. This perception may be fostered by prohibitive government legislation ("Several U.S. States to Curb . . ." 2004). Research on 603 Canadian firms reveal that 88 percent would not be willing to send BPO work offshore ("ITAC to Study Impact . . ." 2004).

Every disadvantage that is listed in Table 2.6 (and many more that are not) is exacerbated in an international context. Distance causes problems in technology-based communication and adds cost to travel when client firm employees are needed at distant locations. Language differences make it difficult to communicate ideas in a timely fashion. Foreign laws and regulations slow business transactions and add costs. Social customs make it difficult to manage without offending someone. Even time zones can disrupt the smooth flow of commerce between plants and markets in different countries. These international factors diminish the advantages of outsourcing and heighten the dis-

Figure 2.1   **Da Rold Transfer-of-Risk Model in Outsourcing**

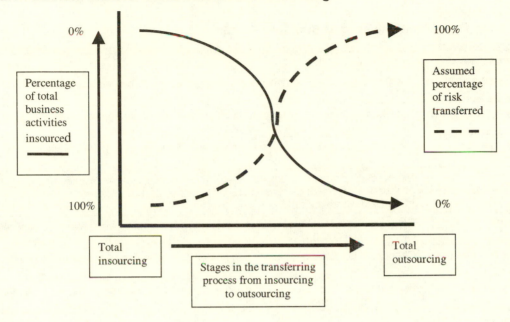

advantages. This should not be surprising because conducting business in an international context adds risk to any operation.

Risk and Outsourcing Advantages and Disadvantages

One theory of risk mitigation is that as client firms increasingly outsource business functions, risks associated with running a business are increasingly passed on to the outsource provider (Antonucci et al. 1998; Beaumont and Costa 2002). It follows that the more outsourcing, the less the risk for a client firm. This relationship is depicted in the outsourcing risk-transfer graph in Figure 2.1, which is based on a model proposed by C. Da Rold. The model assumes that the outsource provider will accept ever-increasing risks as their role in the client organization's business expands (Gouge 2003, 150–152). Additionally, it assumes

that as more client firm operations are given over to an outsource provider, the client firm receives greater advantages and fewer disadvantages (i.e., the client has passed those risks increasingly on to the provider). Underlying this risk model is a further assumption that outsource providers are trustworthy and as interested in helping their client as they are in being in business. Sadly, client firms' notions about providers' trustworthiness are often disappointed. Yet every outsourcing agreement is based on trust. Not surprisingly, the most commonly raised issue in outsourcing arrangements, in addition to hidden costs, is the credibility (or trustworthiness) of the provider's claims (Kerns and Willcocks 2001, 39).

One factor that may fuel distrust is the concept of *value migration* (Domberger 1998, 106–109). Value migration involves business activity being transferred from the client to the outsource provider without compensation to the client. For example,

Table 2.7

Outsourcing Risks That Will Lead to Business Failure

Type of risk issue	Description
Customer complaint issues	Client firm customers' complaints are elevated by move to outsource provider (Smith 2004).
Security issues	Sending individual and corporate accounting records to foreign countries may open the firm to substantial security and confidentiality risk (Wolosky 2004).
Employee issues	Outsource providers may fail to listen to their own employees ("Employees Ignored . . ." 2002).
Client-Provider relationship issues	Not building relationships, taking a passive role managing the outsourcing project, and poor understanding of outsourcing benefits and costs, advantages and disadvantages ("Clients to Blame . . ." 2003).
Cost issues	Cutting the costs on the outsource provider results in the provider reducing service to the client (Digman 2003).
Government issues	Changes in laws and regulations can reduce cost advantages of outsourcing ("Accounting Rule Wipes . . ." 2003).
Structural issues	Experiments in different types of outsourcing (e.g., multisourcing) may fail in the longer term ("Multi-Sourcing Just . . ." 2003).

when a client firm bids out contracts to outsource providers, often only insourcing direct and indirect costs (e.g., labor, materials, overheads, etc.) are considered in establishing a contract fee. Yet there are implicit costs or opportunity costs, which are not always considered. Examples of these implicit costs include excessive client management transfer time to help the outsource provider learn new jobs, or a loss of goodwill on the part of the client firm employees who must instruct outsource provider employees in how to complete these jobs. These loses represent a value that migrates to the outsource provider and is a hidden cost in an outsourcing agreement. As the value continues to migrate to the outsource provider, this organization may eventually take over the business entirely. An example of this occurred in the 1980s, when General Electric (GE) outsourced microwave oven production to a small Korean firm, Samsung (Jarillo 1993). Samsung was able to produce microwave ovens less expensively and with higher quality than GE's U.S. plants. Gradu-

ally, within a few years GE stopped all U.S. microwave oven production and shifted it to Samsung in Korea. Shortly afterward, GE ended all domestic microwave appliance production, leaving Samsung to become the world's largest manufacturer of microwave ovens (Jarillo 1993).

The lack of trust, justified by the possibility of value migration and general uncertainties connected with outsourcing, has been substantiated by research and is included among the major reasons why firms choose not to outsource (Aubert et al. 2004). Research by Natovich (2003) also finds lack of trust at the heart of many failed outsourcing decisions. It suggests that placing all risks on the outsource provider is impractical. Instead, the client and outsource provider should take a partnership approach, sharing risks and rewards of the outsourcing project. There are risks taken every day by client firms in their outsourcing arrangements that bring into question possible advantages outsourcing promises. Those in Table 2.7 have led to outsourcing failures and caused perceived advantages to become disadvantages. In every example, client managers fail to recognize possible risks.

In summary, risk is not mitigated by outsourcing as the Da Rold model in Figure 2.1 contends, but actually appears to be increased by outsourcing. This is exactly what Natovich (2003) observed in the area of IT outsourcing. Indeed, one of the lessons learned from the merger of the Hudson and Nash automobile companies in the 1950s is that when you put two firms with problems together, you end up with twice the problems. These merged firms quickly went out of business, and that is exactly what can happen when a client firm with a problem picks an outsource provider without careful analysis of the risks that provider brings to the project. While it is difficult for a potential client firm to obtain information on outsource providers in other countries, it is an essential prerequisite activity if the client firm is to avoid or at least minimize the types of risks mentioned in this chapter.

Summary

This chapter presented various advantages and disadvantages of outsourcing as a way of understanding where outsourcing might be advantageous (or when looking at the disadvantages, where insourcing might be advantageous). Also, the linkages between the advantages and disadvantages in an international context were described. This chapter additionally presented a discussion on the risky nature of outsourcing.

In both Chapters 1 and 2 the connection of core competencies and O-I are presented as a driving force to seek the advantages outsourcing can offer a client firm. These chapters also described the issue and importance of risk consideration in the O-I decision process. In Chapter 3 we provide a more detailed discussion of the types of risks present, which must be considered in any O-I analysis undertaken in an international context.

Review Terms

Backsource
Business process outsourcing (BPO)
General Electric (GE)
Human resources (HR)
HR administrative-service providers
HR consultants
HR technology enablers
Information technology (IT)
Multisourcing
Near-core competency
Offshore outsourcing
Outsourcing-insourcing (O-I)
Risk mitigation
Value migration

Discussion Questions

1. What similarities are there between the IT outsourcing industry and the HR outsourcing industry?
2. Why is an advantage of outsourcing a disadvantage of insourcing?
3. How are reasons for outsourcing really advantages?
4. How can the advantages of outsourcing help an organization focus on core competencies?
5. How can international outsourcing be linked to outsourcing advantages?
6. How are the disadvantages of outsourcing related to risks run by client firms?

Concept Questions

1. What potential cost saving advantages might firms experience using outsourcing?
2. What potential service improvement ad-

vantages might firms experience using outsourcing?

3. What are some of the potential advantages of outsourcing in an international context?

4. What are some reasons for not outsourcing?

5. What is value migration, and how can it harm a firm?

6. Describe the Da Rold transfer-of-risk model. Is it always valid?

References

"Accounting Rule Wipes Billions from Outsourcers' Profits." *Global Computing Services* (October 17, 2003): 2–3.

Adler, P. S. "Making the HR Outsourcing Decision." *MIT Sloan Management Review* 45 (Fall, 2003): 53–60.

Allen, B. A.; Juillet, L.; Paquet, G.; and Roy, J. "E-Governance and Government On-Line in Canada: Partnerships, People and Prospects." *Government Information Quarterly* 18 (2001): 93–104.

Antonucci, Y. L.; Lordi, F. C.; and Tucker, J. J. III. "The Pros and Cons of IT Outsourcing." *Journal of Accountancy* 185 (1998): 26–31.

Aubert, B. A.; Rivard, S.; and Patry, M. A. "Transaction Cost Model of IT Outsourcing." *Information and Management* 41, no. 7 (2004): 921–932.

Beaumont, N., and Costa, C. "Information Technology Outsourcing in Australia." *Information Resources Management Journal* 15 (2002): 14–31.

Bhattacharya, S.; Behara, R. S.; and Gundersen, D. E. "Business Risk Perspectives on Information Systems Outsourcing." *International Journal of Accounting Information Systems* 4, no. 1 (2003): 75–94.

"Challenges to Consider." *Outsourcing Intelligence Bulletin: FSO Magazine* 11, no. 1 (Sept. 19–26, 2004), editor@fsoutsourcing.com.

Chorafas, D. N. *Outsourcing, Insourcing and IT for Enterprise Management.* Houndmills, Great Britain: Palgrave/MacMillan, 2003.

"Clients to Blame for Outsourcing Failure." *Global Computing Services.* (June 27, 2003): 4. www.computerwire.com.

Cullen, S., and Willcocks, L. *Intelligent IT Outsourcing.* London: Butterworth-Heinemann, 2003.

Digman, L. "Outsmarting Outsourcers." *Baseline* (July 2003): 20–21.

"Discover Weights the Risk." *Outsourcing Intelligence Bulletin: FSO Magazine* 11, no. 1 (Sept. 19–26, 2004), editor@fsoutsourcing.com.

Domberger, S. *The Contracting Organization: A Strategic Guide to Outsourcing.* Oxford: Oxford University Press, 1998.

"Employees Ignored in Outsourcing Deals, Says Report." *Computergram Weekly* (Nov. 5, 2002): 5.

"Filippelli Joins the Team." *Corporate Finance* 227 (2004):11.

Flannery, T. P., and Heckathorn, L. "How to Build Your Business Case for Outsourcing." *Benefits Quarterly* 19, no. 3 (2003): 7–12.

Garcia, J. "The Case for Outsourcing Claims." *Best's Review* (July 2004): 84–85.

Goldsmith, N. M. *Outsourcing Trends.* New York: The Conference Board, 2003.

Gouge, I. *Shaping the IT Organization.* London: Springer, 2003.

Greaver, M. F. *Strategic Outsourcing.* New York: American Management Association, 1999.

Hall, M. "Outsourcing Deals Fail Half the Time." *Computerworld* 37, no. 44 (2003): 10.

Hayes, R.; Pisano, G.; Upton, D.; and Wheelwright, S. *Operations, Strategy, and Technology: Pursuing the Competitive Edge.* New York: Wiley, 2005.

"HR Outsourcing in Asia-Pacific to Reach $2.56 Billion." *Outsourcing Intelligence Bulletin: FSO Magazine* 5, no. 1 (May 30–June 6, 2004), editor@fsoutsourcing.com.

"ITAC to Study Impact on Outsourcing in Canada." *Outsourcing Intelligence Bulletin: FSO Magazine* 5, no. 2 (July 11–18, 2004), editor@fsoutsourcing.com.

Jarillo, J. C. *Strategic Networks: Creating the Borderless Organisation.* Oxford: Butterworth-Heinemann, 1993.

Kern, T., and Willcocks, L. P. *The Relationship Advantage: Information Technologies, Sourcing, and Management.* Oxford: Oxford University Press, 2001.

Kotabe, M., and Murray, J. Y. "Global Sourcing Strategy and Sustainable Competitive Advantage." *Industrial Marketing Management* 33, no. 1 (2004): 7–15.

Lackow, H. M. *IT Outsourcing Trends.* New York: The Conference Board, 2001.

Lankford, W. M., and Parsa, F. "Outsourcing: A Primer." *Management Decision* 37 (1999): 310–316.

Lee, J-N.; Huynh, M. Q.; and Kwok, R. C-W. "IT Outsourcing Evolution—Past, Present, and Future." *Communications of the ACM* 46, no. 5 (2003): 84–90.

Lisle, C. "Outsource a Core Competency? Why Private Equity Groups are Outsourcing Business Strategy Due Diligence." *Journal of Private Equity* 7, no. 1 (2003): 72–76.

MacInnis, P. "Warped Expectations Lead to Outsourcing Failures." *Computing Canada* 29, no. 7 (2003): 1–2.

McDougall, P. "The Offshore Equation: Is Offshoring Worth the Heat? The Financials Are Compelling, and the Benefits May Well Ripple Throughout the Economy." *InformationWeek* (Sept. 6, 2004). www.informationweek.com/story/showArticle. jhtml ?articleID=46800044&tid=16008.

Meisler, A. "Think Globally, Act Rationally." *Workforce Management* 83, no. 1 (2004): 40–45.

Milgate, M. *Alliances, Outsourcing, and the Lean Organization.* Westport, CT: Quorum Books, 2001.

Minoli, D. *Analyzing Outsourcing.* New York: McGraw-Hill, 1995.

"Most of the Financial Firms Continue to Outsource HR Functions." *Outsourcing Intelligence Bulletin: FSO Magazine* 4, no. 3 (April 18–25, 2004), editor@fsoutsourcing.com.

"Multisourcing Just a Red Herring?" *Global Computing Services* (July 4, 2003): 3–4.

Natovich, J. "Vendor Related Risks in IT Development: A Chronology of an Outsourced Project Failure." *Technology Analysis and Strategic Management* 15, no. 4 (2003): 409–420.

"Negotiating the Contract: Best Practices in Mitigating the Risks of Changing Business Needs, Evolving Technology, Rising Costs and More." *Outsourcing Intelligence Bulletin: FSO Magazine* 5, no. 2 (June 13–20, 2004), editor@fsoutsourcing.com.

"Offshore Outsourcing Boosts IT Service Market in 2003, Says Gartner." *Outsourcing Intelligence Bulletin: FSO Magazine* 9, no. 2 (June 27–July 4, 2004), editor@fsoutsourcing.com.

"Offshore Outsourcing Market to Grow 20% Annually through 2008." *Outsourcing Intelligence Bulletin: FSO Magazine* 14, no. 1 (November 5, 2004), editor@fsoutsourcing.com.

"Offshore Outsourcing Poised for Double-Digit Growth." *Outsourcing Intelligence Bulletin: FSO Magazine* 14, no. 1 (November 5, 2004), editor@fsoutsourcing.com.

"Offshoring Call Centers." *Outsourcing Intelligence Bulletin: FSO Magazine* 11, no. 1 (Sept. 19–26, 2004), editor@fsoutsourcing.com.

Rodrigues, C. *International Management.* Minneapolis/St. Paul: West Publishing Company, 1996.

Rothery, B., and Robertson, I. *The Truth about Outsourcing.* Aldershot, England: Gower Publishing, 1995.

Sawyer, J. W. "The Optimization Triangle Proves an Rx for Success." *Energy User News* 28, no. 11 (2003): 24–26.

Schniederjans, M. J. *Operations Management in a Global Context.* Westport, CT: Quorum Books, 1998.

Sen, S. "Enterprise Outsourcing Management, the New Mantra." *Outsourcing Intelligence Bulletin: FSO Magazine* 4, no. 2 (March 21–28, 2004), editor @fsoutsourcing.com.

"Several U.S. States to Curb Outsourcing of Jobs Overseas." *Outsourcing Intelligence Bulletin: FSO Magazine* 5, no. 2 (July 11–18, 2004), editor@fsoutsourcing.com.

Smith, D. "Outsourcing: Will Utilities Plug In?" *Electric Perspectives* 29, no. 2 (2004): 22–32.

Soliman, K. S., and Chen, L-D. "APS: Do They Work?" *Information Systems Management* 20, no. 4 (Fall 2003): 50–58.

Stefanic, A. "The Business Case for Outsourcing." *Employee Benefit Plan Review* (February 2004): 11–13.

Thibodeau, P. "Offshore's Rise Is Relentless." *Computerworld* 37, no. 26 (2003): 1–2.

Tyson, L. D. "Outsourcing: Who's Safe Anymore?" *Business Week*, February 23, 2004, 26.

Willcocks, L., and Choi, C. J. "Cooperative Partnerships and Total IT Outsourcing: From Contractual Obligation to Strategic Alliance." *European Management Journal* 13, no. 1 (1995): 67–78.

Wolosky, H. W. "Transparent Outsourcing." *Practical Accountant* 37, no. 3 (2004): 4.

Yang, C., and Huang, J. B. "A Decision Model for IS Outsourcing." *International Journal of Information Management* 20 (2000): 225–239.

3

Outsourcing-Insourcing Strategy and International Risk Factors

---

Learning Objectives   After completing this chapter, you should be able to:

- Explain the relationship between organization planning and international business.
- Explain the relationship between organization strategic planning and outsourcing-insourcing.
- Describe the relationship between outsourcing-insourcing and international business.
- Identify and discuss the risks of international outsourcing-insourcing.
- Identify the complications involved in outsourcing-insourcing risk factors.

Introduction

In the last chapter we examined the advantages and disadvantages of outsourcing. Many of the disadvantages are directly attributable to a failure to treat international outsourcing-insourcing (O-I) as an international business activity with all the risk factors inherent in international business.

In this chapter we seek to establish the connection between O-I and international business and to show that the methodologies commonly used in international business can and should be applied to international O-I analysis. In addition, this chapter introduces a variety of risks connected with international business that should be considered in all O-I decision making. The treatment of these risk factors in this chapter is a conceptual introduction, which will be methodologically extended in the following chapters.

The Relationship of International Business with Outsourcing-Insourcing

Organization Planning and International Business

Organization planning consists of three basic stages, as presented in Figure 3.1: strategic, tactical, and operational. *Strategic planning* tends to be long-term (i.e., five or more years) and seeks to plot a general course for the achievement of organizational goals. *Tactical planning* tends to be medium-term (i.e., one to five years) and seeks to break down strategic plans into smaller steps for implementation. *Operational planning* tends to be short-term (i.e., one day to a year) and seeks to implement, or operationalize, tactical plans.

When an organization decides to expand into markets beyond the boundaries of the country in

Figure 3.1 **Organization Planning Stages**

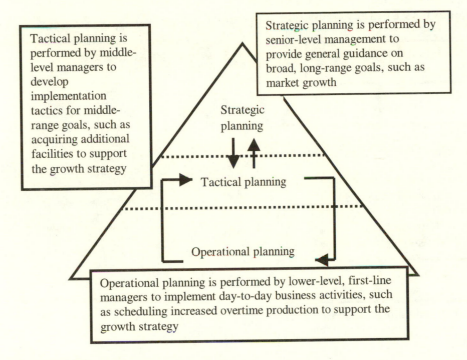

which it operates, it has become involved in *international business*—that is, business activities and transactions that involve imports or exports across two or more national borders (Fatehi 1996, 13–17). Such a decision is made at the strategic stage of organizational planning and requires the selection of a strategy or strategies to guide the organization in its transformation from a domestic to an international business. The steps involved in strategic planning are presented in Figure 3.2.

The first step in strategic planning is to set down or consider the organization's mission statement and goals. This leads to the *external environmental analysis,* which seeks to identify opportunities and risks of going international. The opportunities and risks connected with international business are traditionally thought to involve economics, politics, culture, and demographics, as described in

Table 3.1. Opportunities might include broadening markets to foreign countries, taking advantage of a less costly labor market, or unique access to new technologies. This step also involves identification of "risks." These risks include consideration of the previously mentioned four categories of factors and their related criteria, which might inversely impact an organization's international business plans. From there, an *internal organization analysis* is conducted to identify areas of strength and weakness relative to international competition. Having the necessary funding (or not) might be an example of a strength (or weakness). Finally, assuming the external environmental analysis supports the decision to go international (i.e., opportunities outweigh risks), a decision can be made to select the strategy or strategies that will help the organization take advantage of opportuni-

Figure 3.2 **Steps in the Strategic Planning Stage Leading to the International Business Strategy Decision**

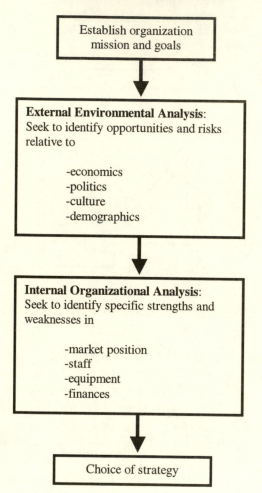

Establish organization mission and goals

External Environmental Analysis:
Seek to identify opportunities and risks relative to

    -economics
    -politics
    -culture
    -demographics

Internal Organizational Analysis:
Seek to identify specific strengths and weaknesses in

    -market position
    -staff
    -equipment
    -finances

Choice of strategy

Table 3.1

International Business Factors to Be Considered in the External Environmental Analysis

Category	Examples
Economics	Labor—number and quality of skilled, semiskilled, unskilled workers
	Capital—amount and stability of currency
	Infrastructure—physical and informational
	Technology—levels and availability
Politics	Government structure—complex or simple
	Ideology—capitalism, communism, or socialism
	Government stability
	Tax structure
	Legal system
Culture	Language
	Religion—its role in society
	Gender roles—inclusive or not
	Social norms
Demographics	Urbanization—its distribution and availability
	Population—age, health status, growth characteristics, diversity

ties available in international business and achieve international goals.

Relationship of Organizational Strategic Planning and Outsourcing-Insourcing

As we observed in Chapter 1, O-I can be international (across borders) or domestic (within borders), yet still may be international if the firms involved are international, multi-national, or global in their approaches to business. While the lines of demarcation between international and domestic O-I can be blurred by international ownership, the focus throughout this textbook is on international O-I.

To adopt an O-I strategy in an international context is to adopt an international business strategy that can have major implications for the entire organization. The O-I strategy decision is part of an organization's overall planning. The decision to pursue O-I is an upper-level decision usually made by an organization's board of directors, president, and vice presidents (DiRomualdo and Gurbaxani 1998). This is not to say middle-level managers do not initiate suggestions for using O-I, but rather control of the final decision usually rests at the highest levels of the organization.

As Figure 3.3 shows, the steps involved in the O-I decision are remarkably similar to those involved in international business strategic planning. Both processes begin with the organization's mission statement and goals. From there an internal organization analysis is conducted to identify areas of strength and weakness (i.e., core competencies or non-core competencies) relative to the competition. As discussed in Chapter 1, once the non-core competencies are identified, they become candidates for O-I in an international context. This leads to the external environmental analysis, which seeks to identify opportunities and risks involved in using O-I. As we discussed in the passage in Chapter 2 on advantages of O-I, opportunities might include saving money on operations, improving product quality, or strengthening competitive position of a client firm by using outsource firm facilities. This step also seeks to identify "risks." The risks may include the inability of outsource providers to help a client firm improve in desired non-core competencies, and the possibility of undermining the client firm's core competencies. If the external environmental analysis supports O-I, the organization will select an O-I strategy or strategies that will help it take advantage of opportunities and achieve organizational goals.

It is important to note that in *classic* strategic management, the normal progression of planning starts with the organization's mission and goals and progresses first to external environmental analysis and secondly to internal organization analysis (Digman 1990; Hill and Jones 1992). This

Figure 3.3 **Steps in the Strategic Planning Stage Leading to the O-I Strategy Decision**

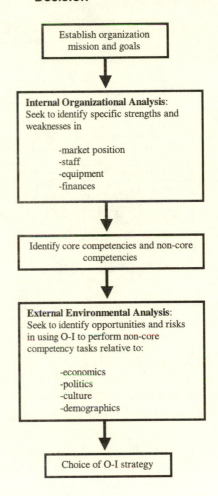

progression, as presented in Figure 3.2, is reversed in Figure 3.3 because the decision to outsource is first based on identifying internal weaknesses and secondly on solving specific internal weaknesses by finding external outsourcing partners, usually in an international context. This divergence from the typical strategic planning process is unique to the outsourcing decision.

Table 3.2

Examples of the Relationship Between International Business and O-I Issues

Category	International business issue	Related O-I issue
Economics	Is the country's currency stable?	What is the likelihood that the outsource provider firm can afford to pay staff if the currency is unstable?
Politics	Is the country politically stable?	What is the probability that laws pertaining to the outsourcing agreement will have to be changed because of a change in government?
Culture	Is there a difference in language between the two countries that might inhibit successful business operations?	Will the outsource provider firm always be able to understand communications?
Demographics	Is there sufficient growth in the population of this country to meet market growth needs?	Can the outsource provider firm find the employees they need to fulfill the O-I agreement if the population has no growth?

Relationship of Outsourcing-Insourcing with International Business

A wide range of factors can be brought into the external environmental analysis that determines whether international O-I is justified. These factors usually fall into the four general categories listed in Figure 3.3: economics, politics, culture, and demographics. As can be seen from Table 3.2, these four categories are also a primary focus in international business (Cavusgil et al. 2002, 40; Fatehi 1996, 44–69; Rodrigues 1996, 42–69). So the decision to enter international business or pursue O-I in an international context is usually based on the same set of criteria, though international business decisions tend to be broader in nature. It is, therefore, not uncommon to experience similar issues in these two areas of strategic planning, as illustrated by the examples in Table 3.2.

The field of international business has long considered the categories listed in Table 3.2 as primary input factors in making international business decisions (Austin 1990; Caslione and Thomas

2002; Cavusgil et al. 2002; James and Weidenbaum 1993). They are viewed as essential factors for any analysis that would lead a corporation to become international. The fact that international O-I is a form of international business, and is closely related to the same steps in strategic planning, makes consideration of the same factors essential for the O-I strategy decision as well.

Outsourcing-Insourcing Strategy and International Risk Factors

It is the external environmental analysis step of strategic planning to which failure of many O-I strategies can be attributed. While there are many reasons why O-I strategies fail, most involve a basic misunderstanding of O-I and its relationship to the strategic planning process, and particularly of the risks involved in all international business operations. For example, Zineldin and Bredenlow (2003) observe that about 50 percent of outsourcing projects fail because an organization treats outsourcing as a short-term solution to a problem. On the contrary, international outsourcing is a long-term strategy with long-term risks that must be considered, not a short-term tactic with short-term risks. According to Natovich (2003) risks in information system outsourcing directly cause O-I failure. These risks include development of adversarial relationships and loss of trust between the provider and client due to misunderstandings about contracts, which in turn lead to lessened commitment by the provider firm's management and finally to difficulties in contractual engagement. Meisler (2004), who like Zeneldin and Bredenlow, asserts that international O-I has a 50 percent failure rate, reports that many in the outsourcing industry believe firms fail to do proper prior planning or consider total risks when engaging in business internationally.

Clearly, a better job of planning O-I projects is called for if the rate of failure is to be reduced. What should a potential client firm do to improve chances for success in international outsourcing? The answer to this question is the focus of this textbook. Fundamentally, one must treat international O-I as an international business project. It should therefore be analyzed with the same rigor and completeness as any international business decision, though reports in the literature suggest this is currently not the norm (Meisler 2004; Hall 2003). Before beginning such an analysis, it is important to first understand the risk factors typically connected to international O-I.

Risk Factors in an International Context

Chapter 1 discussed the assertion in Gouge (2003, 149–154) that outsourcing transfers risk from a client firm to an outsource provider. Indeed, as business functions are transferred to an outsource provider, it is possible to transfer many internal risks (e.g., planning staffing needs, obsolescence of equipment, etc.) along with them. Unfortunately, client firms that contract outsource providers in other countries also

Figure 3.4   Risk Factors in International O-I

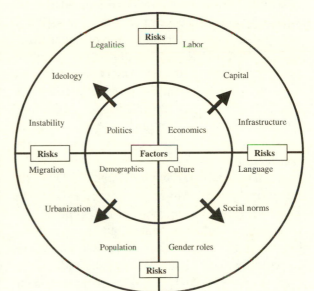

invite substantial new risks that are connected with international business. As Figure 3.4 shows, the same four categories of risk factors used in international business analysis can with some modification be used for analysis of international O-I arrangements.

Each category includes several risks run by firms that outsource in an international context. All these risks need to be evaluated in order to select a successful O-I strategy. The following questions will aid in that evaluation:

Labor (economics factor): Does the outsource provider have the necessary skilled or unskilled labor to do the job they are contracted to perform? If not, does the country in which the outsource provider is located have the necessary labor pool? Without the right mixture of labor skills, an outsource provider will not be able to complete the work and runs the risk of contract non-compliance.

Capital (economics factor): Does the outsourcing firm have the necessary capital to finance operations in fulfillment of a contract? Does the country in which the outsource provider is located have the necessary capital markets (i.e., both domestic and foreign) to support the outsource provider firm's needs? Without adequate funding to the outsource provider firm from internal assets, as well as the banking system within the provider's country, a provider may not be able to finance operations. Even the transference of funds into and out of the outsource provider's country may pose risks for the client firm.

Infrastructure (economics factor): Does the outsource provider have the necessary physical systems (e.g., transportation equipment) and technological/informational systems (e.g., computers) to support contracted business activities? Does the country in which the outsource provider firm's operations are located possess the necessary physical systems (e.g., roads, electrical power systems) and technological/informational systems (e.g., Internet providers, telephone system) to support contracted business activities? Without an adequate infrastructure for transporting physical products or delivering information, outsource providers and their subcontractors risk not being able to deliver business products.

Instability (politics factor): Is the government in the country where the outsource provider operates unstable or likely to change during the period of the outsourcing agreement? Without a stable government, outsourcing firms may not be able to provide security to employees or uphold contracts. Depending on the agreement, the client firm might also risk the confiscation by the outsource provider's government of technology or financial assets that have been loaned to the provider.

Ideology (politics factor): Does the country in which the outsource provider operates have a clear governmental ideology? For our purposes, *ideology* is defined as a government's views, beliefs,

and assumptions concerning its role in controlling the private sector. This would include the type of political system (e.g., capitalism, socialism, etc.) and its role in the economy. Some countries, such as South Korea, have a strong ideology that makes very clear the roles of government and business in relation to each other. As a result, businesses operating in these countries (both outsource providers and client firms) face less uncertainty, and therefore, less risk. Operating in countries with less ideological clarity involves greater risk, since roles of business and government are unclear and can be interpreted in many ways.

Legalities (politics factor): Are the legal systems in the country in which the outsource firm operates understandable or overly complex? Are the legal systems well structured, with formal procedures for adjudication, or are they informal, with preferential treatment, bias, and bribery possible? Without an understandable and well-structured legal system, the outsource firm and the client firm may not be able to defend themselves if legal action is taken against them.

Language (culture factor): Is the spoken and written language of the country in which the outsource provider is located fully understandable to the client firm's employees and customers? If it is not, the client firm runs risks in all communications, including the risk of misinterpreting verbal communications and contractual agreements.

Social norms (culture factor): Might business activities asked of the outsource provider violate social norms in the country in which it is located? *Culture* is a set of shared values, behaviors, and attitudes of a group of people. Culture includes gender roles, religious influence, language, political values, societal divisions, and ideas about trust. If the business activities that an outsource provider has contracted to perform violate any social norms of the country, there are substantial risks to property and risks of legal tort actions to both the outsource provider and the client firm.

Gender roles (culture factor): Might communications necessary for the success of the O-I agreement between different-gendered employees in both the outsource provider and the client firm be culturally upsetting to one or more of the parties involved? The role of women in businesses worldwide has been changing, and so have attitudes toward their contributions. Nevertheless, role expectations can differ substantially in different nations, and firms run gender role risks if they ignore these differences.

Migration (demographics factor): Does the country in which the outsource provider operates have high or low population migration? *Migration* is defined as the movement of people into, out of, or around a country. If a country has a high migration rate, it may be difficult to employ the necessary skilled or unskilled workers needed to run the outsource provider's operation. Also, high migration might add to political instability risks.

Urbanization (demographics factor): Does the country in which the outsource provider operates have highly urbanized or concentrated population centers? Highly concentrated populations in dense metropolitan areas permit easy access to labor markets and more efficiency in reaching customers for marketing purposes. The more evenly dispersed the population, the harder it is to reach labor or customers. Other factors, such as the concentration of transportation and information systems, often follow populations, making urbanization a desirable demographic.

Population (demographics factor): What is the population growth rate, age, and health status of the country in which the outsource provider operates? Growth in population, lower average age levels, and good health are all associated with high employee productivity. A declining or older

population may make finding adequate employees more difficult and costly for the outsource provider. Equally important is the general health of a population. How much cost might be tacked on to an outsourcing agreement with a firm located in an African nation where 25 percent of the population is infected with the AIDS virus?

Adding to the difficulties of dealing with international O-I risk factors is the fact that they can interact, sometimes causing a chain of negative events. As the example in Figure 3.5 shows, an unstable government (a politics risk factor) can create an economics risk factor, a cultural risk factor, a demographics risk factor, and finally another politics risk factor. This kind of interaction, or *interactive chain-effect*, adds to the complexity of an outsourcing arrangement. The number of additional interactions possible here can be far more than provided in this simple example.

Case Studies on the Complication of Risk Factors

Here are three outsourcing case studies reported in the literature that will help you develop some sensitivity to the kinds of complications that can arise in outsourcing arrangements. These case studies are all related to the cultural risk factor of language—specifically, the failure to understand language.

Dell Computer Corporation Case

Dell Computer Corporation is considered one of the best personal computer manufacturers in the United States. Their business model, marketing strategies, and management have succeeded even in the most difficult economic times. When they saw other competitors (e.g., Gateway and Hewlett Packard) moving some operations offshore, they quickly decided to maintain profitable operations by adopting an international

Figure 3.5   **Example of O-I Risk Factors Creating an Interactive Chain-effect**

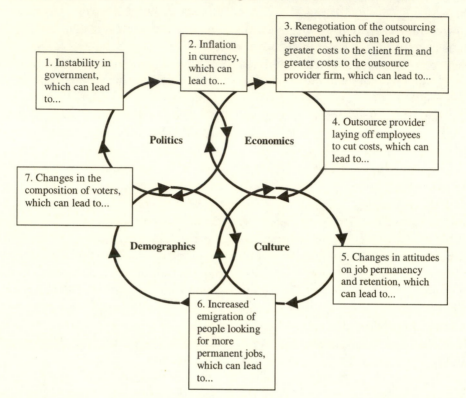

outsourcing strategy as well. Dell believed they could cut labor costs by moving some of their technical support (i.e., "help desk" services) for corporation customers to Bangalore, India (Metz 2004). Corporation customers who had problems with their Dell computers could call a help desk service number where a Dell service technician in India could provide basic technical information that would allow the customer to resolve the problems. As is always the case with Dell management, they planned an outsourcing contract fair to all parties. Unfortunately, corporation customer complaints quickly started surfacing concerning the difficulty of understanding Indian service technicians. Despite the best efforts of the provider firm in India, the accent of the Indian technicians was frequently too difficult for customers to understand, a problem reported in the media (MSNBC 2004). When Dell's customers started to complain, Dell management responded, shifting help desk service phone calls previously routed to Bangalore to locations in Idaho, Tennessee, and Texas (Metz 2004).

Cultural differences in language, even accent, are a risk factor, one that caused this outsourcing arrangement to produce less-than-desirable results. Even in contractual arrangements in which parties in one country say they speak the language of another country "proficiently," it is advisable to ascertain what is meant by "proficiently" in the outsource provider's country. Understanding cultural risk factors is fundamental to any international business activity and critically important in outsourcing arrangements where both parties are highly dependent on each other.

Cable & Wireless PLC Case

Cable & Wireless (C&W), a United Kingdom organization, hired the IBM Corporation, a United States organization, to provide information technology (IT) outsourcing services. Both firms are best at what they do. Everything was arranged by contract using a *global framework agreement* (GFA), an international boilerplate that allows for the standardization of many aspects of an outsourcing agreement. One feature of the contract was to ensure that the services IBM provided met certain benchmarks. To ensure fairness in measuring IBM's services against the agreed-upon benchmarks, Compass America, Inc., a firm specializing in measuring services against benchmarks, was hired by C&W to monitor services IBM provided over the entire fourteen months of the outsourcing contract. At least some of these benchmarks were related to the cost of services IBM charged C&W. The results of the benchmarking process revealed that C&W had consistently been overcharged by IBM (i.e., they had been charged more than an agreed-upon benchmark for cost of services). IBM believed the GFA did not obligate them to repay overcharges. Moreover, IBM stated that under the terms of the GFA they and IBM of Japan were entitled to additional work. They planned to make claims on payment charges due to them from C&W. The matter eventually ended up in litigation ("Clients to Blame . . ." 2003).

Benchmarking is a common and well-respected approach to monitoring performance of O-I agreements (Fancescnini et al. 2003). Despite both companies' being international

in scope, using the same language, and having fairly similar legal systems, the risk factor was their divergent understandings of the language of the GFA—specifically, what the GFA empowered each organization to do in regard to performance of the contract. If, despite the commonalities these organizations shared, they still managed to disagree on the interpretation of an outsourcing agreement, just think of the risks taken when organizations do not speak the same language, have different legal systems, or have no local representatives to work out issues in international outsourcing agreements.

Islington Council Government Service Agreement Case

Islington Council is a United Kingdom appointed government body that awards contracts to private firms for providing government services. Governments tend to insource services in order to create employment opportunities in the home country and to ensure that taxes are spent within the country. But Islington Council believed they might be able to provide better administrative, management, IT systems, and support of housing benefits to clients by outsourcing these functions to ITNet, an international but United Kingdom-based provider firm. In this situation both parties are basically from the same country, same language, and legal system. The outsourcing contract was negotiated on a multiyear basis and involved millions of pounds and penalties to the outsource provider for noncompliance. Despite the clear language and agreed-upon expectations, the outsourcing agreement had to be renegotiated because the Council believed ITNet did not provide proper service to Islington residents (the clients in this case). Eventually, Islington Council decided that ITNet could not provide the level of service agreed on in the outsourcing agreement, and the Council rescinded the parts of the contract that outsourced administrative and management activities, leaving ITNet to handle only the IT systems and support. The Islington Council ended up paying more than two million pounds to end its outsourcing agreement. ITNet had to pay three hundred thousand pounds in contract penalties (Simon 2003).

The interpretation of contractual language and the expectations that such language instills in outsourcing partners were not successfully communicated in this arrangement. Both parties paid a penalty. Even with two parties that use the same language, differing interpretations of a contract can cause outsourcing to fail.

These three case studies illustrate some of the complications and penalties outsource providers and client firms suffer when entering into outsourcing agreements without consideration of all relevant risk factors. While the case studies focus on the single risk factor of language, it is prudent to consider all categories of international risk in any O-I agreement. As we have seen, however, many businesses neglect to do this kind of analysis. This textbook is dedicated to correcting the oversight and to helping equip decision makers with a logical and comprehensive approach to dealing with risk in choosing an international O-I strategy.

Summary

This chapter sought to establish a relationship between the steps in international business strategic planning and similar steps in the O-I strategic planning process. In particular, the chapter pointed out that the factors considered in external environmental analysis of international business and O-I external environmental analysis are basically the same. It also argued that the same care and the same level of analysis that have been applied for decades to international business decisions should also be applied to O-I as an organizational strategy decision. Finally this chapter presented a conceptual introduction to a series of O-I risk factors that play a part in the international O-I analysis to be discussed in the rest of this textbook.

Using the organizational planning model introduced in this chapter, the next chapter will detail the individual O-I planning steps necessary to implement outsourcing. This planning process will provide a general framework whereby any function or business activity can be successfully outsourced.

Review Terms

Culture
External environmental analysis
Global Framework Agreement (GFA)
Ideology
Information technology (IT)
Interactive chain-effect
Internal organization analysis
International business
Migration
Operational planning
Organization planning
Strategic planning
Tactical planning

Discussion Questions

1. Why is it important to see a connection between strategic planning and O-I planning?
2. What is viewed as the basic failure in the current approach to making the international O-I decision?

3. Why is labor considered a risk factor in international O-I?
4. Why is capital considered a risk factor in international O-I?
5. Why are social norms considered a risk factor in international O-I?
6. Why is language considered a risk factor in international O-I?
7. Why is population migration considered a risk factor in international O-I?
8. Why is government instability considered a risk factor in international O-I?
9. How can O-I risk factors interact to create an interactive chain-effect detrimental to an outsourcing agreement?
10. What kinds of mistakes can a firm make in structuring an international O-I agreement that might lead to the agreement's failure?

Concept Questions

1. What are the three stages of organizational planning? Explain each and give an example.
2. What is the connection between the external environmental analysis done in international business planning and the external environmental analysis done in O-I decision making?
3. What are the basic steps that should be taken in the strategic planning stage by a firm considering a move toward international business?
4. What are the four categories of opportunities and risks that should be considered during the external environmental analysis in international business planning? Give examples of each.
5. What are the basic steps that should be taken in the strategic planning stage by a

firm considering an O-I strategy?
6. What are the four categories of opportunities and risks that should be considered during the external environmental analysis by a firm considering international O-I? Give examples of each.
7. What percent of O-I projects succeed?
8. Name twelve international O-I risk factors. Explain each.
9. Why are interactive chain-effects undesirable in O-I projects?
10. What is the major issue leading to O-I agreement failure in each of the case studies?

References

Austin, J. *Managing in Developing Countries*. New York: Free Press, 1990.

Caslione, J.A., and Thomas, A.R. *Global Manifest Destiny: Growing Your Business in a Borderless Economy*. Chicago: Dearborn Trading Publishing, 2002.

Cavusgil, S.T.; Ghauri, P.N.; and Agarwal, M.R. *Doing Business in Emerging Markets*. Thousand Oaks, CA: Sage Publications, 2002.

"Clients to Blame for Outsourcing Failure." *Global Computing Services* (June 27, 2003): 4. www.computerwire.com.

Digman, L. A. *Strategic Management*. 2nd ed. Homewood, IL: BPI/Irwin, 1992.

DiRomualdo, A., and Gurbaxani, V. "Strategic Intent for IT Outsourcing." *Sloan Management Review* 39, no. 4 (1998): 67–80.

Fanceschini, F.; Galetto, M.; Pignatelli, A.; and Varetto, M. "Outsourcing; Guidelines for a Structured Approach." *Benchmarking: An International Journal* 10, no. 3 (2003): 246–261.

Fatehi, K. *International Management*. Upper Saddle River, NJ: Prentice-Hall, 1996.

Gouge, I. *Shaping the IT Organization*. London: Springer, 2003.

Hall, M. "Outsourcing Deals Fail Half the Time . . ." *Computerworld* 37, no. 44 (2003): 10.

Hill, C. W., and Jones, G. R. *Strategic Management*. 2nd ed., Boston, MA: Houghton Mifflin, 1990.

James, H.S., and Weidenbaum, M. *When Businesses Cross*

International Borders. Westport, CT: Preager, 1993.

Meisler, A. "Think Globally, Act Rationally." *Workforce Management* 83, no. 1 (2004): 40–45.

Metz, C. "Tech Support Coming Home?" *PC Magazine* 23, no. 3 (February 17, 2004): 20.

MSNBC. *Nightly News,* February 19, 2004.

Natovich, J. "Vendor Related Risks in IT Development: A Chronology of an Outsourced Project Failure." *Technology Analysis and Strategic Management* 15, no. 4 (2003): 409–420.

Rodrigues, C. *International Management.* Minneapolis/St. Paul: West Publishing, 1996.

Simons, M. "Council's £2m to End Contract." *Computer Weekly* (February 27, 2003): 2.

Zineldin, M., and Bredenlow, T. "Strategic Alliance: Synergies and Challenges: A Case of Strategic Outsourcing Relationship or SOUR." *International Journal of Physical Distribution and Logistics Management* 23, no. 5 (2003): 449–464.

4

Planning International Outsourcing-Insourcing

Learning Objectives   After completing this chapter you should be able to:

- Describe the entire planning process for international outsourcing-insourcing.
- Describe the strategic steps involved in planning international outsourcing-insourcing.
- Describe the tactical steps involved in planning international outsourcing-insourcing.
- Describe the operational steps involved in planning international outsourcing-insourcing.
- Explain how international risk factors can be taken into account in the planning of international outsourcing-insourcing.

Introduction

All management planning can be categorized into three types: strategic planning, tactical planning, or operational planning. These planning categories are sequential, that is strategic precedes tactical planning, and tactical planning precedes operational planning. All organizations have to perform all three types of planning (Bryson 2004; Lasher 2004).

While strategic planning was introduced in Chapters 1 and 3, this chapter focuses on all three types of planning activities and their sequence in an *outsourcing-insourcing* (O-I) project. Specifically, this chapter targets just those planning activities related to the subject of O-I. This permits a more detailed discussion of O-I planning activities that can lead to a successful O-I project.

Planning by its nature is more flexible in scope than most subjects in management. While there is some general ordering of planning tasks, the exact order and content of each step can vary by organization (Arbaugh 2003). The treatment in this chapter is one way of looking at the O-I planning process within organizational planning. It should be recognized there may be other ways of viewing the planning process. Also, it is the contention of this textbook that outsourcing be considered in an international context, or at least international outsourcing should be seen as prudent in today's global business environment and essential to any successful O-I undertaking. The final selection of an outsource provider does not have to be international, only the analysis that leads to a final O-I decision must be internationally inclusive.

To make the discussion less esoteric and more

Figure 4.1   **Strategic, Tactical, and Operational Planning Steps in International O-I**

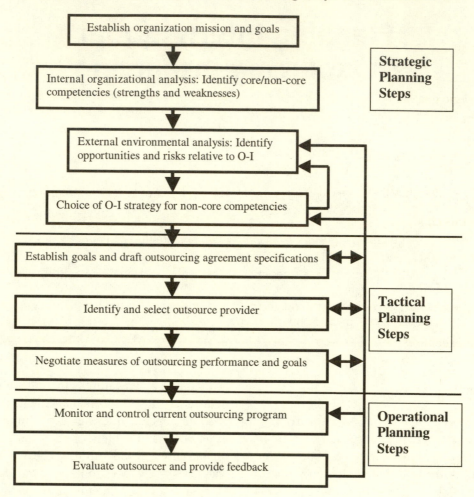

applied, a hypothetical organization will be used to illustrate the types of steps in the international O-I planning process. Explaining where in the organization necessary decisions are made and who makes plans is important to understanding the decision process itself. Assume there is an electronics firm (i.e., the client) located in the U.S. that manufacturers and sells its own products in U.S. markets. The client firm is planning to outsource all of its production function, while continuing to insource other remaining business functions (i.e.,

marketing, accounting, finance, etc.). The client firm will undertake all steps in the international O-I planning process presented in Figure 4.1.

Strategic Planning Steps in Outsourcing-Insourcing

The strategic planning steps for any client firm considering an O-I strategy starts with the firm's mission statement (Quinn and Hilmer 1994; Quinn 1999). The mission statement defines very long-term goals (if not the organization's lifetime goals). Using these as general guides, boards of directors, presidents, and vice presidents usually draft related strategic goals for the organization. For instance, the client firm's mission statement might require the firm to seek generally profitable operations. A related strategic goal might be to achieve an average of 30 percent profit for the next five years. The mission statement might also require the client firm to seek growth. A related strategic goal might be to achieve a market growth in sales of 20 percent per year for the next five years. These two strategic goals for the client firm will be used as examples throughout this chapter.

Internal Organizational Analysis

With a general direction for these two strategic goals originating either directly from the mission statement or the interpretation by its board of directors and executives, the next step in strategic planning is to look internally for strengths and weaknesses as they relate to the tentative goals. Since profitability is directly related to costs of goods sold, lowering the costs of production is one strategy for achieving greater profitability. The client firm would have to identify current costs per product (or product line) and explore strategic internal alternatives for lowering costs sufficiently to achieve the targeted, general goal of an average of 30 percent in profits for the next five years. This might include a strategy for possible reduction in overhead costs by policy changes and in cutbacks in hiring or turnover of personnel who will not be replaced. It might also include a reexamination of company policies on inventory levels (i.e., by lowering required minimum inventory levels, a firm can reduce inventory investment costs, taxes, insurance, etc.).

The goal of growth in sales can only be accomplished by providing more product to the market. This requires an increase in production capacity to meet greater customer demand. Seeking growth in production capacity might be a supportive production strategy for achieving the goal of increasing growth in sales. Clearly, the client firm would focus a great deal of planning toward marketing to obtain the increase in sales, but at this level of planning, all of the functional areas (i.e., production, finance, marketing, accounting, etc.) will seek to develop strategies to support the general strategic goals of the organization. Other firms might wait to complete functional planning at the tactical level. Where the O-I strategy is to be considered at the strategic level for such detailed purposes as product cost reduction, there is a need for at least aggregated information, like aggregate production capacity to be shared with the planners. These planners would then be in a better position to explore internal alternatives, such as insourcing through an expansion of existing production facilities or simply building new production facilities to meet the production growth goals. It is an important step to consider alternatives, such as insourcing capabilities, before considering any outside alternatives.

Looking at possible strategic alternatives, the board of directors or executives might conclude they have insufficient cost reduction alternatives to achieve the profitability goal and insufficient production capacity alternatives to produce the necessary extra product to meet the sales growth goal. (Chapter 5 will discuss some of the methodologies that can be used to make these types of decisions.) These could be viewed as organizational weaknesses to be strengthened by adopting strategies to correct or overcome them. It could also be concluded that the production department does not offer any unique value to the organization and is a hindrance toward achieving general organizational goals (i.e., the production department would be considered a *non-core competency*). This internal organizational analysis might also identify that the marketing department in the client firm is unique and contributes a competitive advantage that other firms cannot meet (i.e., a *core competency*).

External Environmental Analysis

If a client firm's weaknesses cannot be strengthened internally, the next step in strategic planning is to find external solution opportunities and identify risks associated with those opportunities. A firm's executives during this step should explore all possible external alternatives, such as a leasing arrangement for temporary production facilities to increase the production capacity to meet a growth goal. The leasing option might also lower capital costs to help profitability in production or introduce new technology to reduce product cost per unit. The opportunities explored are then compared and those that best meet the organizations strategic needs are selected.

It is at this step in the planning process that outsourcing should be included as a possible solution to overcome weaknesses found in the internal organizational analysis. (Chapter 6 discusses many of the financial methodologies used in this initial O-I decision process.) Because outsourcing may make long-term and possibly permanent changes in the client organization with external organization providers, the use of outsourcing can become a strategic, long-term strategy. The advantages of outsourcing listed in Chapter 2 demonstrate it is an ideal strategy to improve profitability, reducing product costs, and augment production capacity. This clearly fulfills the needs of the hypothetical client firm. Of course, outsourcing can also be viewed as a leasing agreement, since it often involves a fixed monthly payment for provider services for a fixed period of time. Unlike most leasing agreements, the contracted outsource services tend to be complete services, including both tangible

Figure 4.2   Overview of Outsource Provider Selection Steps

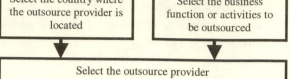

assets and intangible human resource services. Due to the belief that there are substantial benefits of international outsourcing over virtually all possible local O-I alternatives, it is currently one of the most popular strategies to deal with non-core competencies ("Offshored Services . . ." 2004).

Today, any firm seeking a realistic outcome to an outsourcing project has to consider O-I in the international context ("German Firms . . ." 2004). While there are O-I exceptions (some are addressed in other chapters) many of the greatest opportunities provided by outsourcing almost always occur when it is conducted across international boundaries. To maximize the strategic outsourcing advantage, strategic planning efforts must include consideration of all international O-I opportunities and associated risks. Herein lies a fundamental problem that many strategic planning efforts fail to recognize: in an international context, international risk factors must be a part of the analysis. Many organizations (Sen 2004; "Negotiating the Contract . . ." 2004), even governments ("Economic Impact of Outsourcing Risks . . ." 2004) presently overlook risk factors in international O-I.

How the client organization may want to bring international risk factors into the O-I strategy at the strategic phase of planning may depend on other strategic goals being considered. When considering O-I in an international context the steps used to select the provider consist of those in Figure 4.2. Whether the country selection step or busi-

Table 4.1

An Example of Rating International Risk Factors by Country

Risk factors in international O-I	Possible countries			
	England	Mexico	...	Canada
Economic: Labor	1	0	...	0
Economic: Capital	0	2	...	0
Economic: Infrastructure	0	2	...	0
Culture: Language	0	0	...	0
Culture: Social norms	2	0	...	3
Culture: Gender roles	2	0	...	2
Demographics: Migration	0	1	...	0
Demographics: Population	0	0	...	0
Demographics: Urbanization	0	0	...	0
Politics: Ideology	2	0	...	2
Politics: Instability	0	1	...	2
Politics: Legalities	3	0	...	3
Total risk rating score	**10**	**6**	**...**	**12**

Risk rating scale: 0=no risk, 1=minor risk, 2=average risk, 3=high risk

ness activities step is initiated first, or relegated to a later tactical planning, can be important. In the case of the client firm example, the functional area of production has been identified and non-core competency selected for outsourcing.

Suppose the client firm has an even longer-range goal of entering an international market in a foreign country. Using an international outsource provider in a suitable foreign country might be a valuable first step for gaining knowledge about that foreign market. Suppose further the client firm's board of directors believes its products will do best in an English- or Spanish-speaking country. In such a situation the board of directors might want to narrow the country selection decision to English- or Spanish-speaking countries. Just the decision to limit the countries substantially reduces the search considerably. It should be mentioned that countries, like China, India ("India's Proficiency In English . . ." 2004), and Russia, have millions of English-speaking personnel, which outsource providers use in service offerings. For the purposes of this chapter's example, the client firm wants to have an English- or Spanish-speaking consumer market.

To further narrow the selection of countries, the board of directors might want to consider subjectively rating the international risk factors introduced in Chapter 3 for each country where the desired production outsourcing work might be performed. (This type of rating/scoring method will be discussed in detail in Chapter 5.) Once a rating for each risk factor is determined by board members or experts/technical staff, the risk factor ratings can be added up to provide an overall score for each country. An example of this type of simple rating/scoring methodology is presented in Table 4.1. Based on these ratings, Mexico would be the least risky of the locations being considered for an outsourcing partner.

As with many quantitative methods, assessing risk factors is not easy and may require considerable thought and research, along with an in-depth understanding of the client firm's strategic needs. Experts from within and outside the organization, including lawyers with international law backgrounds, international economics experts, and cultural experts from universities, are often employed to aid in making these assessments (Cavusgil et al. 2002, 83).

During the analysis in which a country is selected, board members may find the risks of international O-I are too great and decide not to follow the international O-I strategy. Indeed, the board may also identify new risks that require a revision (note the reversing arrow flow on Figure 4.1) in their external environmental analysis. This, of course, would mean that they would have to find a new strategy to achieve sales and capacity goals. This new strategy may involve outsourcing, just not in an international context.

The analysis should also consider the home country of a client firm in an international comparative analysis like that depicted in Table 4.1. Including the home country in the analysis can help document the conclusion that the home country should either be ruled out or ruled in, based on risks that a domestic outsource provider poses for a client firm compared to risks posed by international providers. Adding the home country to the analysis also will help justify a final strategy selection to those stakeholders who might question it. Indeed, *nearshoring* (i.e., choosing an outsource provider located in the home country or in another country) can be a good strategy for businesses and governments seeking both control and cost advantages (Meisler 2004). For example, Meisler (2004) reports that U.S. client firms are interested in outsourcing to Canadian outsource providers because Canada's cultural similarity and geographical nearness to the U.S. allows the client to exert more control than would be possible in most other countries. This represents a compromise in which some cost savings are sacrificed for greater control because Canada's smaller wage differential does not afford as much labor cost reduction as outsourcing to many other countries.

Choice of O-I Strategy for Non-Core Competencies

The selection, described in Figure 4.2, of the functional area or particular business activities to be outsourced may be relegated to the tactical stage of planning. This is particularly appropriate when the strategic plan calls for changing the organization in some way, but not necessarily giving up any business activities in the long-run. Outsourcing in such a situation can be used as a medium-term, tactical means of organizational change rather than to effect a permanent alteration of the organization. However, in *business process outsourcing* (BPO) (i.e., the outsourcing of whole functional departments, as in the outsourcing of the entire production department in this chapter's client firm example), the importance of the decision and the long-term nature of such a major resource allocation may require a strategic-level decision from the board of directors.

Assume at this point that the hypothetical client firm, having reviewed all possible alternatives, has decided, based on the simple scoring method shown in Table 4.1, that the best opportunity for achieving sales and capacity growth is to outsource the non-core competency production function to a Mexican outsource provider to be chosen later. Having settled on this international outsourcing strategy, the firm now has to draft tactical plans to aid in the implementation of the strategy.

Tactical Planning Steps in Outsourcing-Insourcing

In most organizations, tactical planning is usually performed by middle-level managers, including vice presidents, general managers, district managers, product managers, or department heads. Tactical planning breaks down longer-term strategic goals into medium-term tactical goals that can be accomplished in approximately one to five years. In the tactical stage, an "outsourcing strategic plan" would most likely be converted into an *outsourcing project*, with specific time frames for outsourcing tasks to be accomplished at the tactical level of planning. As noted by Banerjee et al. (2004), project planning is one of the most effective organizational substructures for dealing with international O-I outsourcing. The project would include all activities necessary to accomplish the tactical steps outlined in Figure 4.1.

When a decision is made at the strategic level, it is only a matter of time before it becomes common knowledge within the client firm. An ethical firm will share the outsourcing decision with all employees, including those who may be losing jobs as a result of the outsourcing. Since most people assume the worst about a drastic change strategy like outsourcing, such a decision can harm current employee performance and morale not just in the affected areas but throughout the organization. Case studies have consistently shown that a failure by management to communicate outsourcing decisions to employees can lead to an eventual project failure ("Employees Ignored in Outsourcing Deals . . ." 2002).

Greaver (1999, 37–57) and Gouge (2003, 162–166) suggest that a formal outsourcing project team be established to manage the outsourcing project. The team should be led by a *project champion* to keep the project design, implementation, and follow-up management activities on schedule. The senior management members who might be chosen for the project champion role include *chief information officer* (CIO), *chief executive officer* (CEO) and *chief financial officer* (CFO). On the other hand, many firms that outsource believe outsourcing should not be considered a project (i.e., something with a fixed time limit), but rather a permanent relationship with no time horizons (Weston 2002). Though outsourcing agreements last on average only thirty-nine months, typical projects are eight years or more, according to a business survey by Goldsmith (2003).

It should be noted that cultural differences can sometimes lead to unsuccessful outsourcing projects. In the U.S., for example, a firm is more apt to choose several outsource providers instead of a single firm because of the U.S. cultural orientation toward competitive markets. That is, U.S. firms tend to believe that having more than one outsource provider helps reduce costs by encouraging competition between the providers. Unfortunately, the practice of outsourcing does not bear this belief out ("Multi-Sourcing . . ." 2003). Case studies show outsourcing is more likely to succeed when a firm has a single outsource partner with whom to build a relationship.

Establish Goals and Draft Outsourcing Agreement Specifications

In the tactical stage of planning, medium-term goals are established on the basis of the strategic objectives. In the client firm example, the strategic goals of achieving an average of 30 percent profit for the next five years and achieving a market growth in sales of 20 percent per year for the next five years can be broken down into yearly targets. Then existing client firm capabilities are assessed on an aggregate, yearly basis to determine what is left for the outsource provider to handle. Since the client firm's entire production department is being outsourced, the cost computations are considerably lessened (i.e., product cost does not have to be averaged or proportioned between insourcing and outsourcing—this topic will be discussed in Chapter 8). The client firm will seek an outsource provider to give them a total unit production cost that will help achieve desired profit levels. For example, perhaps a 50 percent reduction in labor and materials is necessary to achieve the client firm's 30 percent average profit goal, and a 20 percent increase in unit production is necessary to support the sales growth goal. Having calculated these figures for cost and production, the client firm is in a position to start drafting an outsourcing agreement.

The agreement should include a number of features. Some typical features are listed in Table 4.2 (Cullen and Willcocks 2003, 67–111; Greaver 1999, 17–32; Milgate 2001, 60; Rothery and Robertson 1995, 221–228).

Many firms have experienced outsourcing failure due to poorly written agreements. Most agreements are viewed as major roadblocks to outsourcing success (Goldsmith 2003). It is advisable to consult an experienced legal advisor during the contract-drafting step ("Negotiating the Contract . . ." 2004). Involving a legal advisor early can help ensure that the outsourcing team considers all applicable options and issues. A legal advisor may also help avoid some of the many risks common to outsourcing arrangements (Earl 1996). Finally, the advisor may aid the team in better organizing data collection to be fed directly into the eventual agreement.

It may turn out during the drafting step of planning, the strategic choice of outsourcing internationally, or in the case of the client firm, going to Mexico, a revision will have to take place. This is why the arrow in Figure 4.1 for this step permits information to be redirected back to the strategic planners if revision is necessary. Assume at this point there is no need to revise the Mexican outsourcing strategic decision for the client firm in this example.

Identify and Select Outsource Provider

Once a basic draft of the proposed outsourcing work is prepared, the next step is to find an outsource provider to do the work. There are many ways client firms can go about looking for an outsource provider. Traditionally, a list of potential providers can be prepared from industry associa-

tion directories and outsourcing directories. Referrals for the candidates on this list can be obtained from experts or other experienced managers, and the results can be compared using a systematic, check-sheet selection process (Rothery and Robertson 1995).

While there are many worldwide sources of information, including those provided by individual governments, outsourcing has attracted companies that specialize in outsourcing research and information. One example of this type of organization is *FS Outsourcing Company* (www.fsoutsourcing.com) mentioned in Chapter 1.

Another approach to identifying potential outsource providers is to establish a set of provider qualifications and use them to identify candidates (Anderson 2003; "Clients to Blame . . ." 2003). The client firm should select qualification criteria that support the firm's particular needs. For example, a client firm with limited capital might want an outsource provider with sufficient capital to finance their own operations. Other qualifications might include service delivery, product quality, problem-solving abilities, engineering capacity, technology, security, trustworthiness, flexibility, and value. Pint and Bladwin (1997) suggest evaluating the provider in terms of current capabilities to meet client needs, costs and risks, knowledge, skills, breadth and depth of experience (including past performance), financial strength, and commitment to technological innovation, quality improvement, and customer satisfaction. Using these as criteria, client firms can then send a *request for information* (RFI) to outsource providers. The RFI asks providers for information about prices/rates and other qualification criteria with which they are most interested. Basically the request asks the provider to state information about the criteria the client firm is most interested in using for selection purposes.

Still another approach to identifying potential

Table 4.2

Common Features in Outsourcing Agreements

Features	Description
Define scope of outsourcing project	The work to be outsourced is within the scope of the provider, but work to be performed by the client firm is out-of-scope. Organizations have operational boundaries and corporate borders that need to be defended against a provider's natural tendency to intrude on them.
Define objectives and goals	Explain, as specifically as possible, the exact set of objectives and related goals to be achieved. Quantification of production in units or service hours provided per specific objective must be well defined. These objectives should include all critical success factors that the client firm believes is necessary to achieve organizational goals. Such success factor criteria as quality, delivery, timeliness, compliance, flexibility, responsiveness, and cost reduction should be established as a guide to encourage the provider to better understand the needs of the client and more successfully work with them as a partner.
Define contribution of resources	Explain what resources will be supplied by both the client and provider firms to make the outsourcing agreement work. Be as specific as possible in terms of human resources, technology, and system resource requirements as they relate to the defined unit/hour service objectives. Also include the details of transitioning resources that are to be transferred to an outsource provider.
Define duties	Explain where the areas of individual and joint management responsibilities are to be located in all phases of the project over the life of the agreement. This will include all issues of governance including roles, responsibilities, meetings, reviews, evaluations, communications, and any management procedures that must be followed. This would also include the transition planning efforts, including training and retaining of staff and transfer of any staff from client to provider.
Establish timeline on goals and objectives	Specific dates for goal and objective accomplishment along with the means of measuring and evaluating, and reporting requirements. This would cover the entire outsourcing project planning horizon.
Establish flexibility procedures	It is critically important to include opportunities for both the client and the provider to initiate some forms of change in the outsourcing agreement. In some cases these changes might come with penalties for non-compliance or rewards when deadlines or goals are exceeded. It is also common to include bonus systems for the provider to help motivate client-desired outcomes in the longer term.
Risk management	It is important to identify possible risks the client firm may face as a result of the agreement. Some assessment of how these risks will be managed (and by whom) and how they should be minimized is necessary. Risks may be determined for each of the risk phases (note Table 1.4 in chapter 1) of design, transition, and follow-up. Critical success factors, such as shifts in costs, information security, and developing a dependence by the client firm on the provider are just a few of the tactical issues that should be addressed here.
Procedure for terminating agreement	Define the circumstances in which either the client or provider may terminate the outsourcing agreement. This may be at a natural, planned end-time for the outsourcing agreement or because of specific circumstances that justify either party's ending the agreement without penalty or risk of legal action.

providers is to prepare a *request for proposal* (RFP). A request for proposal is a document stating the client firm's outsourcing requirements, including the outsourcing project's scope, location of business activity, reasons for outsourcing, time horizons, and general pricing information (Greaver

1999, 184–188). Once the RFP has been prepared, it can be used as an advertisement in outsourcing media or in foreign countries of interest to the client firm. The RFP can also provide a beginning point for negotiations of a final agreement or contract between the client firm and the outsource provider. Thus, the RFP should be clearly written, provide sufficient information so that the provider can understand what is being requested, and contact information to the client organization's outsourcing project team members.

Because the selection of an outsource provider is so critical to the success of the outsourcing project, Chapter 7 is entirely devoted to methodologies used in selecting providers. As with the previous step, a client firm may find during its efforts to find an outsource provider that the initial strategic decision to limiting the search to providers located in a particular country is too restrictive or fails to produce good candidates. In such a situation, the tactical outsourcing team members have to communicate this fact back to strategic planners and request a revised outsourcing strategy. This is again why the arrow for this step in Figure 4.1 permits information to be redirected back to the strategic planners.

Assume at this point there has been an insufficient response to finding a Mexican outsource provider, and that the board of directors authorizes the selection of any international provider as long as the principal spoken language of the provider's country is English or Spanish. In effect, the country decision has now been assigned to the tactical outsourcing team.

Since the focus of the selection process is now on the outsource provider, the country selection becomes a secondary decision, not to be excluded or have the international risks minimized. One way to make this decision is again to use a risk rating/scoring method. In this situation, provider selection criteria can be placed in four categories relevant to the tactical decision, as listed in Table 4.3. The first of these four provider selection categories is *obligatory selection criteria* (i.e., a provider must meet these criteria in order to be considered eligible at all). Table 4.3, which applies to the client firm example, lists as obligatory the two strategic goals and the language requirements. As Table 4.3 shows, once a provider fails to meet any obligatory requirement, further consideration of the provider is unnecessary, saving time and effort. Also, it is important to rate the risks connected with each obligatory requirement so that a provider's potential for noncompliance is factored into the decision process.

The second and third categories of outsource provider selection criteria include the typical *quantitative and qualitative provider selection criteria* items found in the literature used to judge the ability to satisfy (at least to some risk-rated level) the additional "niceties" that a client firm might appreciate. Examples of each are provided in Table 4.3. It should be noted the outsourcing literature warns that just loading-up selection criteria might not only limit the selection process, but could add considerably to the expense of the outsourcing agreement for compliance reasons (Lackow 2001; Sislian and Satir 2000). It is advisable the outsourcing team clearly justify each of the criteria in terms of strategic and tactical objectives. It is also important that the risk ratings be precisely determined, requiring in some cases considerable management assessment time, expert opinion (particularly for the qualitative ratings) and other technical judgments (Minoli 1995, 206–214).

A fourth category of outsource provider selection criteria focuses on the tactical need to eventually implement tactical plans. The *implementation provider selection criteria* listed in Table 4.3 focus on the three phases of implementation risk mentioned in Chapter 1. Experienced outsource providers may have an implementation reputation that can be viewed as either risky or not. As observed

Table 4.3

An Example of Rating Tactical Provider Selection Criteria Risk Factors by Country

Country	Spain	Spain	Canada	Canada	Canada	England	...
Provider number	1	2	1	2	3	1	...
Provider selection criterion							
Obligatory							
Must be English- or Spanish-speaking country	Yes	Yes	Yes	Yes	Yes	Yes	...
–Risk	0	0	0	0	0	0	...
Necessary production capacity to meet future demand goal	Yes	Yes	No	Yes	Yes	Yes	...
–Risk	0	2	–	1	1	2	...
Can reduce costs enough to meet goal	No	Yes	–	No	Yes	Yes	...
–Risk	–	2	–	–	1	1	...
Quantitative							
Financially able to support operations	–	2	–	–	1	0	...
High production quality standards	–	2	–	–	1	0	...
Has adequate personnel for job	–	0	–	–	1	1	...
Qualitative							
Trustworthy	–	0	–	–	0	0	...
Adaptive to changes	–	1	–	–	1	2	...
Outsourcing experience	–	0	–	–	0	1	...
Problem-solving ability	–	1	–	–	0	0	...
Proven customer satisfaction	–	2	–	–	0	0	...
Proven management capabilities	–	1	–	–	1	1	...
Implementation							
Design	–	1	–	–	0	0	...
Transition	–	2	–	–	1	1	...
Follow-up	–	1	–	–	1	1	...
Total risk rating score	–	17	–	–	9	10	...

Risk rating scale: 0=no risk, 1=minor risk, 2=average risk, 3=high risk

Figure 4.3   **Three-Dimensional Rating/Scoring Table for Outsource Provider Selection**

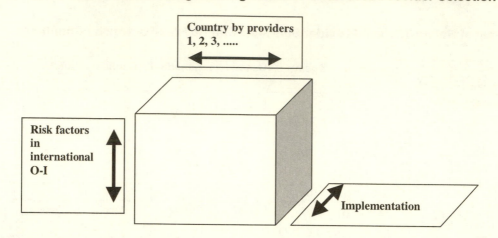

by Dell Computers, some outsource providers can change pricing, making an outsourcing strategy risky business (Metz 2004), or they can experience turnover rates of 50 percent, making operations highly risky (Meisler 2004).

Assuming the risk ratings are accurate, the sum of the ratings in Table 4.3 can now be used as a general guide to a final set of possible candidates. Instead of selecting the one, lowest risk-rated provider, the outsourcing team might select the best two or more candidates whose risk ratings are the lowest. By adopting this less exact solution, the risk that the ratings may not be accurate is reduced, and the solution permits inclusion of international analysis of risk. If the candidates all come from the same country, then the country selection issue might be viewed as being settled. More likely is the situation where the better candidates with the lowest risk will come from two or more countries. In such a situation, prior international risk factors can be brought into consideration in much the same way as they are used in Table 4.1. Indeed, there is an added opportunity to bring important tactical implementation provider selection criteria into consideration in an international context. That is,

consideration of design, transition, and follow-up can be considered in light of various international risk factors in Table 4.1. This would make the rating/scoring table three-dimensional as presented in Figure 4.3. The importance of considering implementation risk in the international context, and with respect to the outsource providers, can be a critical consideration in the success of the project. It has been noted in the literature that locating in a particular foreign country can lead to failure for many reasons, including cultural differences (Meisler 2004; Natovich 2003).

The use of the three-dimensional table in Figure 4.3 would still involve adding up ratings to establish an overall score to guide in the final outsource provider decision. Assume for the client firm example that there are two outsource providers selected from the analysis in Table 4.3 (i.e., Canada 3 and England 1) based on their low risk scores. These two providers can then be compared using the three-dimensional table, presented in Table 4.4, in a two-dimensional format.

Most countries as similar as Canada and England are going to have fairly similar international risk ratings on most of the broad categories in Table

Table 4.4

International Risk Factor Evaluation for Country Selection in Client Firm Example

Risk factors in international O-I	Canada			England		
	Design	Transition	Follow-up	Design	Transition	Follow-up
Economic: Labor	0	1	0	0	1	1
Economic: Capital	0	0	0	0	0	0
Economic: Infrastructure	0	0	0	0	0	0
Culture: Language	0	0	1	0	0	0
Culture: Social norms	0	0	0	1	1	1
Culture: Gender roles	0	1	1	0	1	1
Demographics: Migration	0	0	0	0	0	0
Demographics: Population	0	0	0	0	0	0
Demographics: Urbanization	0	0	0	0	0	0
Politics: Ideology	0	0	0	0	0	0
Politics: Instability	0	1	1	0	0	0
Politics: Legalities	1	1	1	2	2	1
Total risk-rating score	1	4	4	3	5	4
Grand total score			9			12

4.4. Minor differences in cultures (like the use of French language from the Quebec region in Canada or the English legal system differences) might cause subtle differences that will permit a risk rating helpful in differentiating the two countries. For purposes of our client firm example, assume the analysis in Table 4.4 can be summed to show the Canada 3 outsource provider is a less risky choice in an international context than the English provider. Combining this analysis with that prior in Table 4.3, the Canadian 3 outsource provider is the best overall choice for the client firm.

Negotiate Measures of Outsourcing Performance and Goals

The client firm is now in a position to begin negotiation of the actual outsource agreement with the selected Canadian outsource provider. The resulting agreement or contract must clearly list the specific tasks the outsource provider is expected to deliver, and how these goals will be measured in some form of performance achievement. There

are many schools of thought on how negotiations should take place. From a survey of business executives the best advice is to use legal firms with experience in outsourcing or outsourcing consultants (Goldsmith 2003).

Researchers suggest a number of guiding principles when negotiating an agreement (Greaver 1999, 225–250; Milgate 2001, 56–69; Natovich 2003; "Negotiating the Contract . . ." 2004; Sen 2004). While there can be an almost unlimited number of suggestions on items to include in the negotiation process of an outsourcing agreement, some of the more commonly reported items that should be included are listed in Table 4.5.

Let us assume that lawyers and company executives for the hypothetical client firm and the Canadian outsource provider in the example negotiate an outsourcing agreement that appears to meet the client firm's strategic and tactical needs. Such a document then has to be approved by the boards of directors of both firms. Assume for this example that both firms' boards have approved it. As the guidelines in Table 4.5 suggest, the document

Table 4.5

Guiding Principles for Content in Negotiating Outsource Agreements

Negotiating principle	Description
Clearly state strategic intent	The outsourcing agreement should make the client's strategic goals clear to both parties so that the outsource provider can work to build upon the initial relationship and grow in the direction necessary for continued success.
Clearly state goals, objectives, and expectations	In as much detail as possible, the agreement should define the client firm's expectations regarding time, place, who, what, where, and when for all goals and objectives. If possible, expectations should be quantified. It is difficult to quantify criteria like "improved quality," but if quality can be measured by a reduction in customer complaints to the client firm, then such quantification should be included in the agreement.
Establish clear time horizons	In agreements where the outsourcing project is for a fixed period of time, the agreement should clearly state its beginning and end times. Where the agreement has no end time, the agreement should establish fixed periods of review, during which parties can reevaluate the agreement and make changes without penalty.
Define scope of services from the provider	In as much detail as possible, the agreement should define what the providers are expected to do, and what they should not do. This can be quantified in terms of hours of service coverage or units of production. It is important in some agreements that the provider does not go beyond the expected scope of services, which might be perceived as a threat to the client firm's core activities.
Define role of client firm in aiding the provider	The agreement should clearly state the financial, systems, human resource, and technology support to be provided by the client. This should include time horizons and amounts or levels of contributions expected of the client firm. It usually will include a listing of technologies that will be transferred to the provider.
Define transition roles	The agreement should define each party's responsibilities during the transition of the work from the client firm to the provider.
Define management and control activities	The agreement should define who will manage and control the outsourcing process from beginning to end. Control may begin with the outsourcing project team leader in the client firm, but it will end with the provider. Because design, implementation, and follow-up are all crucial to the overall success of the project, each phase should have specifically assigned managers who will oversee and control the process.
Define lines of communication	The agreement should describe in detail the reporting requirements between the client firm and the provider, so that everyone concerned knows whom to report via which lines of communication.
Make the agreement a win-win situation	The outsourcing agreement should not contain hidden surprises or favor one party over the other. Both should see advantages to maintaining the agreements in the short-term and long-term.
Set up provisions to reward benefits and penalties for non-compliance	The agreement should include a reward system that motivates the provider to meet and possibly exceed the client firm's expectations. Likewise, when a provider fails to meet expectations, the costs to the client firm should be paid (in part or in full) by the provider. Rewards and penalties must be stated clearly.
Establish metrics to assess provider performance	The agreement should include a clear statement on the measurement metrics used to define compliance and provider success. The agreement should specify how these measurements are taken, by whom, when, and where, and to whom they will be reported.

(continued)

Establish pricing terms	The agreement should clearly state what the provider can charge the client firm for the basic service agreement but also define provisions for overtime pay or extra service charges and payments to *third-party providers*, where the provider purchases items for the client firm from other subcontractors or outsource providers.
Establish agreement termination provisions	The terms under which either party can terminate the agreement should be clearly defined. The agreement should include definitions of what constitutes noncompliance for both parties and fair time frames for making adjustments to correct problems. They should be tied to the performance metrics and mutually agreed upon by both parties.
Provisions for unexpected contributions	During any partnership, a new idea, technology, process, or product can be developed, including new processes that highly benefit the client firm, where the provider is justifiably due additional compensation for the contribution. A clear statement as to how ownership is to be shared should be included in the agreement.
Establish a provision for unexpected problems	In any relationship, unexpected problems (e.g., markets disappearing, financial problems, labor disputes, wars, etc.) can arise and prevent the agreement from being fulfilled. The agreement should include a system to address these situations in such a way that they do not result in lawsuits or termination of the agreement. Perhaps a panel of outside executives or experts can be used to judge the situation and make fair recommendations to both parties to avoid legal problems.

would detail time horizons and specific timelines for the outsourcing project. The next step (note Figure 4.1) is to implement the tactical agreement for this outsourcing project. This creates the need for operational planning activities.

Operational Planning Steps in Outsourcing-Insourcing

As observed by Insinga (2000), serious pitfalls are often encountered as a strategy is pushed downward into operational planning. At the operational-level of planning the strategic intent tends to be lost in day-to-day, problem-to-problem business environment operations managers face. Outsourcing decisions made at the operational level can easily lead to dependencies on the provider, creating unforeseen strategic vulnerabilities. Most of the possible pitfalls observed at the operational level of planning occur because the outsourcing agreement did not cover them or deal with them as fully as necessary. In a business survey by Lackow (2001), some of the problems with outsourcing agreements included: lack of performance/service level, lack of flexibility, increased costs, lack of agreement on

governance by client firm, length of agreement being too long, and staff turnover for both client and provider firms. These problems apparently have made a difference in recent years. It is interesting to note that while none of the companies in the Lackow (2001) study planned on backsourcing, a follow-up study on outsourcing by Goldsmith (2003), just two years later, revealed that 25 percent of the companies surveyed planned on bringing business functions back to their firms.

Monitor and Control Current Outsourcing Program

The day-to-day efforts of implementing an outsourcing agreement are usually performed by middle-level and lower-level managers in both the client and the outsourcing provider firm. Like the phases of implementation risk mentioned in Chapter 1 (i.e., design, transition, follow-up), there are always risk factors facing mangers in implementing an outsourcing project. While the design of the agreement should be outlined in the outsourcing agreement, there will always be some changes necessary to accommodate the reality of the operational setting. This is particularly true in an international context. Operations personnel from differing countries, even countries as similar as the U.S. and Canada, can be faced with conflicting biases, preferences, priorities, and hidden agendas. Initial agreements, made by upper-level managers, may not work for middle-level or lower-level managers.

To help overcome this initial design issue and move on to the transition phase of implementation, members of the tactical outsourcing project team should hold meetings with the implementation operations managers at all levels of the organization during the design period. The purpose of these meetings is to keep all managers informed of ongoing plans and help bring them into the decision-making process as much as possible by encouraging them to identify and deal with conflicts that might surface during the design or transition periods. Letting people know what is going on in the planning process and how it can affect their jobs is the best way to head off fear, suspicion, anger, and even disruptive behavior. A study of international outsourcing by Elmuti and Kathawala (2000) found that the number one source of problems in outsourcing projects is employee fear of job loss and of change. In the client firm example, international issues, such as cultural differences in work attitudes and other U.S./Canadian differences in social norms, might surface and reveal the need for education and desensitizing.

The way the client firm announces the beginning of the transition process and helps prepare employees for the change is critical to the outsourcing project's success. Meeting with stakeholders, including managers and employees as well as unions, is an important first step in preparing the organization for changes that outsourcing will bring. Reiterating the strategic and tactical reasons for outsourcing, as well as pro-

viding severance packages for those who will be leaving the client firm, can defuse much potential resistance and resentment. It is also important to minimize the fears of all employees not affected by the outsourcing project by making it clear that their positions are secure.

The transition phase of implementation may be outlined in the outsourcing agreement, but the detailed human resource or staff assignments for both client and provider will still need to be made at this planning step. The transition planning at the operational level is by necessity very detailed. It must cover human resources, facilities, equipment, software, third-party agreements, and all functions, processes, and business activities related to the outsourcing agreement. In addition, it must assign the general management responsibilities and functions of day-to-day planning, coordinating, staffing, organizing, and leadership.

There are two dimensions in the transition phase: the "who" and at "what time" are critical in transition planning. Precise questions, such as who reports to whom in either firm on transition issues, must be defined. Also, which employees in the client firm will have their jobs moved to the provider firm and in what time frame, are also important issues. This is a good time to identify employees who will be losing their jobs and determine what benefits and new job opportunities the client or provider firm can offer. It should be noted in many situations, the provider firm hires the ex-client firm employee as a part-time or full-time employee to help with the transition. In an international context this is more difficult, since many citizens of one country will not move to another country. In this situation severance packages are important.

Also during the transition process, measures for monitoring goal achievement must be installed. These measures should be viewed as a quality assurance system, which ensures the client firm that the provider is doing the job they were hired to do. A good monitoring system works for both parties. At the same time the client firm uses the system to monitor goal achievement, the provider should be able to determine if they qualify for extra benefits for doing an exceptional job. (Chapter 5 will discuss some of these measures of performance that can be installed to monitor provider service.) What is important is both the client and provider agree to measures to be taken, who collects information, where and to whom it is reported, and at what times both parties review the measures. International cultural issues, like trust, become important in examining the risk each party bears in accepting the measures (Alijifri et al. 2003; Handby 1996).

A final, important component of any successful outsourcing transition implementation is the installation of a means by which flexibility is structured into the transition process. It is important to establish possible, alternative plans and contingencies for inevitable conflicts during the transition and/or those expected during the subsequent planning horizon of the entire outsourcing agreement. Some of these contingency plans may be based on both the client and provider firms' experiences with outsourcing plans and what was learned during the design and transition process.

The follow-up phase of planning depends on the type of outsourcing agreement undertaken. For the *fixed term agreement* (i.e., where there is a fixed end-time period for the project), there can be a re-transition process undertaken where the provider helps the client firm readjust to insourcing business activities the provider previously handled. For a *continual renewal agreement* (i.e., the outsourcing provider expects to be doing the project indefinitely) the transition process still has to have an end point where the provider is declared the sole operator of the function or activities, which they provide to the client firm. This is necessary because

management responsibilities are shared during the transition process, but at its end, the provider must assume total responsibility.

In the case of the client firm example the strategic and tactical plan is to have a permanent transition of the production department to the Canadian outsource provider. In return the Canadian provider has agreed to hire all U.S. employees willing to eventually move to Canada after the transition period has ended and all of the production department functions are taken over. Other individuals not willing to make the transference to the provider have been given other employment with the client firm or a severance package.

It is important for both the client and provider firms to recognize governmental requirements in making substantial changes in their operations. For example, it is understood by the client firm that because this situation involves the closing of a production plant in the U.S. with more than a hundred employees, the client firm is required to notify employees sixty days in advance of the eventual plant closing. This *Plant Closing Law* was passed by the U.S. Congress in 1988 and is called the *Worker Adjustment and Retaining Notification Act* (WARN) (Bohlman and Dundas 2002, 705). This legal point is introduced to show some laws within a country of origin must be observed to avoid penalties. Likewise, both the client firm and the Canadian provider are fortunate in this example that international agreements, such as the *North American Free Trade Agreement* (NAFTA), are in place to permit the transference of finished products from Canada to the U.S. market without trade barriers and tariffs adding to the cost (Bohlman and Dundas 2002, 400–401). Awareness of such international laws (and the opportunity to use them to a firm's advantage) is another reason why lawyers with outsourcing experience are often brought into the planning process to help identify opportunities and avoid risks.

Evaluate Outsourcer and Provide Feedback

If the monitoring measurements are in place, data are collected and compared to the agreed levels of business performance, and goals meet expectations, then monitoring can be a routine process. This should be viewed as a continuous effort of the follow-up phase of planning to provide a timely system of checks on the provider to insure compliance with the outsource agreement and the expectations of the client firm. Periodic meetings between the outsourcing managers in the client firm responsible for monitoring the project and the provider firm management are an appropriate way of sharing information on the progress of the outsourcing project and providing feedback for corrective control and further improvements.

The evaluations of the outsource provider might also take the form of periodic audits performed by client firm staff or outside auditing firms. The advantage of outside firms is that they represent a third-party opinion with necessary skills to monitor business performance reports underlying accounting records. Auditors also can perform special types of analyses. Effective communication skills are needed in view of the fact that reports could find their way, as depicted in Figure 4.1, to the client firm's board of directors. Third-party auditors could also be used as arbiters in clashes between the client firm and the provider.

Greaver (1999, 272–273) suggests an *oversight council* be appointed to review annual operating plans, provide a forum for discussion of major issues, review performance results, make recommendations for corrective adjustments on the results, and to act as an arbiter if problems arise. Acting much like a board of directors for the ongoing outsourcing project, this group would consist of managers from both client and provider firms in addition to outside experts, such as lawyers or auditors. It could also consist of the same client staffers and managers who led the tactical outsourcing project. They could be empowered to perform a number of management tasks, including evaluation of recommendations on goal changes, flexibility issues, alterations in procedures, and even the outsourcing agreement itself. The group might also provide information back-up through the entire strategic, tactical, and operational planning steps to change, end, or enlarge the original O-I project.

To bring the client firm example to a planning conclusion, assume that a full year of post-transition effort has been completed. During the year, the Canadian outsource provider became agitated by U.S. auditors spending more time in the Canadian production facilities than expected, wasting in their view the manager's time. The Canadian provider requested the U.S. auditors be replaced. Concurrently, the success of the U.S. client firm exceeded their expectations in growth and profitability. The matter was turned over to an oversight council developed to handle such disputes. The U.S. auditors were replaced with a Canadian auditor, which the Canadian firm could not challenge, and the client firm was allowed to re-negotiate the agreement to increase their unit production demands from the provider at a fair price to both parties with no penalties for the change. Such negotiation efforts are common, expected, and should be planned for in an O-I agreement, which on one hand provides flexibility and on the other hand acts to set goals and objectives that must be accomplished.

An International Context Risk Rejoinder

While consideration for international O-I is related to the client firm example in this chapter, the international risk factor categories introduced in Chapter 3 (i.e., economics, politics, culture, and demographics) should always permeate the entire international O-I planning process when considering outsourcing internationally. It is true international risk factors should and usually do impact strategic, tactical and operational planning. While examples of how these risks can be considered in each of the three types of planning are presented in this chapter, it is impossible to cover all the various types of scenarios that can occur. The U.S. client firm example ended in the selection of an international provider in Canada, which from an economic, political, and demographic basis was a good match. In doing so, many international risk factors described in Chapter 3 may not or need not be considered or analyzed in the decision process. Yet, any international O-I selection of a provider can result in unexpected international risks. Being aware of possible risk factors is an important skill for the success of international O-I outsourcing and not doing so is the one consistent reason given for outsourcing failure regardless of the country (Adeleye et al. 2004; Sen 2004"; Your Shout" 2004).

As a way of developing sensitivity to potential unexpected international risks, consider one cultural risk component related to the client firm example: trust. The written outsourcing agreement, which is a contract, forms the basis for trust, but cannot, nor should it be used exclusively as a means of defining a relationship between two parties. As noted by MacInnis (2003) concerning Canadian outsourcing arrangements, "trust" is the key to outsourcing success. When going international, a firm has to deal with "foreigners," and sadly, foreigners can be easily blamed for everything that goes wrong when trust is not present in a partnership. The research study by Natovich (2003) explains how risk taking in an international outsourcing venture develops into an adversarial relationship between a client firm and a provider. This in turn creates a loss of trust between the client and provider, which in turn causes the provider's management to de-escalate commitment to the outsourcing project. Eventually, this leads to breaking the outsourcing agreement completely. Natovich (2003) and others have suggested in order to build trust, both parties must accept risks as partners (i.e., share the risks, rather than have the majority of the risks be given to or migrate to just one partner). As Marshall (1999) and Bracey (2003) point out, building trust is a long-term effort but begins with a relationship based on honesty and shared interests (and that includes shared risks). While the Jupiter Research Corporation (2001) and other firms have developed online training materials to provide very specific guidance on trust-building activities in an international context, there is a need to consider all the ramifications that might substantially impede the progress of an international O-I project. As listed in Table 4.6 the cultural issue of trust can bring into question a great many O-I project risk factors for a client firm to be wary of. Indeed, the list in Table 4.6 could be endless. The consequences listed in Table 4.6 are the prices the client firm might pay for distrusting the provider. The best way to avoid a mistrust issue and all other risk factors is to take them into consideration during the international O-I planning process.

Case Study on Avoiding Risk in International Outsourcing

While some state governments ("Tennessee Governor Curbs Outsourcing . . ." 2004) in the U.S. have been quick to ban or limit international outsourcing of state government activities, other state governments have sought to take advantage of low cost opportunities that international outsourcing can offer. Such ad-

Table 4.6

Selected Questions Reflecting Distrust in the Client Firm Example

Questions that might be raised by a distrustful client firm of the Canadian outsource provider	Possible consequences for the client firm
Will the provider violate Canadian laws?	Increased expense for Canadian legal advice.
Will the provider violate U.S. laws?	Increased expense for U.S. legal advice.
Are the auditing reports from a Canadian auditor accurate?	Increased expense for auditing the auditors.
Will the provider cheat on product quality?	Increased expense for inspections and staff to monitor quality.
Will the provider meet the delivery deadlines?	Increased production quotas to maintain greater inventory levels. This in turn increases the cost of capital in the investment in finished inventory, increases the cost for more inventory staff, accounting, taxes, etc.
Will the Canadian firm try to steal the client firm's business in the future?	The Canadian firm signs a binding contract to prevent this from happening, resulting in added legal expenses for document preparation and possibly future litigation.

vantages are not without risk. For example the state of New Mexico's Labor Department hired TCS-America, an Indian outsourcing firm which is affiliated with Tata Consultancy Services of India (O'Hanlon 2004; Hicks 2004). According to the report by O'Hanlon (2004), TCS-America was hired to redo New Mexico's unemployment compensation computer system. Hicks (2004) reporting on the same story revealed that while TCS-America completed work for other U.S. state governments, including Pennsylvania and New York, it had never worked on a unemployment compensation system. Also, New Mexico agreed to allow them to do all computer software work in India, apparently with insufficient monitoring of the progress completed by New Mexico officials responsible for the outsourcing project. The new system should have been completed in six months, which put the due date at December 2001. Unfortunately, things did not work out well. The initial system was delivered in December 2002,

and as of September 2004 it was still not working. Also, the outsourcing project went way over the budget of $3.6 million up to $13 million. The warrantee for the system ended in 2003, leaving New Mexico with a situation of either suing TCS-America to complete the project (it was estimated at 80 percent complete, but New Mexico officials were not sure, since the work was still being done in India) or hiring someone else to fix it. TCS-America's position is that they complied with the outsourcing agreement and were willing to continue fixing the system if they could receive additional compensation to justify additional work. Where this case will end is still uncertain as of the writing of this study.

In July of 2004, the state of Nebraska signed an outsourcing agreement with TCS-America to develop a similar unemployment compensation computer system (O'Hanlon 2004). The difference in this international outsourcing agreement from the one New Mexico implemented shows the difference planning can make in avoiding international outsourcing risks. Before developing an outsourcing agreement, Nebraska officials interviewed New Mexico government employees who had worked with TCS-America to learn from their experience as to what to expect and what to include in the outsourcing agreement. From those interviews, Nebraska officials developed an agreement that sought to overcome prior problems. For example, Nebraska's agreement required all work be performed in Nebraska, hiring at least 25 percent of employees performing the work locally. This helps the Nebraska government officials mitigate some of the political risks of being perceived as outsourcing American or Nebraskan jobs to foreigners. In this case, outsourcing actually creates jobs in Nebraska, whereas other American outsourcing firms might have done the work out of state. Nebraska's agreement allows a more realistic development period of two years for the project. This avoids completion time risks that might be disruptive to other government systems dependent on the new system. The agreement also permits flexibility by anticipating additional costs above the $7.9 million stated in the contract. This way there can be no surprises on costs that might cause outsiders to perceive or claim the agreement is a failure. Again, this helps avoid a political risk. While TCS-America will bring twenty-one employees from India to Nebraska to do some of the work, sixteen employees will be hired locally for the project. Although somewhat uncertain, TCS-America claims that of the twenty-one employees from India, some might include American citizens presently working in India. This aspect of the agreement could also be used to point out the political disadvantages to being critical of international outsourcing. In addition, the local and state employees are to be trained by the Indian personnel during the development of the project to ensure that once work is completed by TCS-America, Nebraskan workers would be able to run the system without additional costs. This helps avoid risks of dependency on the outsourcer. Because Nebraska state employees will be intimately associated with all aspects of the project, they will be in an ideal situation to help avoid risks during system development and afterward.

While these precautions do not ensure Nebraska will receive the finished system exactly as they expect, their efforts to incorporate within the outsourcing agreement the flexibility, control, and benefits to the state will help reduce risks. As this chapter has pointed out, the planning steps leading to any international O-I agreement require a careful analysis considering risks in both achieving the advantages of outsourcing and avoiding disadvantages.

Summary

This chapter has discussed the strategic, tactical, and operational planning steps undertaken in an international O-I planning process. The various steps and sub-steps were illustrated with a hypothetical example of a U.S. firm that decides to outsource internationally. The chapter provided guidelines and suggestions on the selection of an outsource provider, negotiations, and outsourcing agreement content.

This chapter ends Part 1, which focused on the introductory and conceptual aspects of O-I in an international context. The next four chapters, which make up Part 2, "Methodologies for Different Types of Outsourcing-Insourcing Decisions," will focus on the "how-to," presenting a variety of methodologies for implementing and completing the international O-I process.

Review Terms

Business process outsourcing (BPO)
Chief executive officer (CEO)
Chief financial officer (CFO)
Chief information officer (CIO)
Continual renewal agreement
Core competency
External environmental analysis
Fixed-term agreement
Implementation provider selection criteria
Internal organizational analysis
Mission statement
Nearshoring
Non-core competency

North American Free Trade Agreement (NAFTA)
Obligatory selection criteria
Outsourcing-Insourcing (O-I)
Oversight council
Plant closing law
Project champion
Qualitative provider selection criteria
Quantitative provider selection criteria
Request for information (RFI)
Request for proposal (RFP).
Third-Party provider
Worker Adjustment and Retaining
   Notification Act (WARN)

Discussion Questions

1. Why is planning considered a flexible management activity?
2. What is the purpose of an internal organization analysis?
3. How does the internal organization analysis complement the external environmental analysis?
4. Why is it important to consider international risk factors in the country selection step of planning O-I?
5. Why is the decision on the country of the outsource provider sometimes allocated to the tactical project team?
6. What is the best way to select an outsource provider?
7. Why is it important to monitor an outsource provider once the agreement is in effect?
8. Should a client firm be concerned about violating the law with an outsourcing agreement or should they let the outsource provider deal with those concerns? Justify your answer.

Concept Questions

1. What are the strategic, tactical, and operational planning steps?
2. How does the strategic planning step in international O-I begin?
3. What types of employees conduct the strategic planning of international O-I?
4. Who typically is a "project champion," and why are project champions needed in an O-I project?
5. What are some common features of outsourcing agreements?
6. What criteria can be used in selecting an outsource provider?
7. What are some guidelines for negotiating an outsourcing agreement?
8. How can a cultural issue like trust affect an outsourcing agreement?

References

Adeleye, B.; Annansingh, C.; Nunes, F.; and Baptista, M. "Risk Management Practices in IS Outsourcing: An

Investigation into Commercial Banks in Nigeria." *International Journal of Information Management* 24, no. 2 (April 2004): 167–181.

Alijifri, H. A.; Pons, A.; and Collins, D. "Global E-Commerce: A Framework for Understanding and Overcoming the Trust Barrier." *Information Management and Computer Security* 14, no. 3 (2003): 130–138.

Anderson, A. "Methodology Removes Guess Work." *Communications News* 40, no. 8 (August 2003): 38–39.

Arbaugh, J. B. "Outsourcing Intensity, Strategy, and Growth in Entrepreneurial Firms." *Journal of Enterprising Culture* 11, no. 2 (2003): 89–110.

Banerjee, S.; Agarwal, M.; and Rao, H. R. "The Logistics of Going Offshore." *Outsourcing Intelligence Bulletin: FSO Magazine* 9, no. 2 (June 27–July 4, 2004), editor@fsoutsourcing.com.

Bohlman, H. M., and Dundas, M. J. *The Legal, Ethical and International Environment of Business.* 5th ed. Cincinnati: West, 2002.

Bracey, H. *Building Trust: How to Get It! How to Keep It!* New York: HB Artworks, Inc., 2003.

Bryson, J. M. *Strategic Planning for Public and Nonprofit Organizations: A Guide to Strengthening and Sustaining Organizational Achievement.* 3rd ed. New York: Jossey-Bass, 2004.

Cavusgil, S. T.; Ghauri, P. N.; and Agarwal, M. R. *Doing Business in Emerging Markets.* Thousand Oaks, CA: Sage Publications, 2002.

"Clients to Blame for Outsourcing Failure." *Global Computing Services* (June 27, 2003): 4, www.computerwire.com.

Cullen, S., and Willcocks, L. *Intelligent IT Outsourcing.* London: Butterworth-Heinemann, 2003.

Earl, M. J. "The Risks of Outsourcing IT." *Sloan Management Review* 37, no. 3 (1996): 26–32.

"Economic Impact of Outsourcing Risks: The U.S. Is Overlooking Critical Infrastructure Risk Again." *Outsourcing Intelligence Bulletin: FSO Magazine* 4, no. 7 (May 23–30, 2004), editor@fsoutsourcing.com.

Elmuti, D., and Kathawala, Y. "The Effects of Global Outsourcing Strategies on Participants' Attitudes and Organizational Effectiveness." *International Journal of Manpower* 21, nos. 1/2 (2000): 112–129.

"Employees Ignored in Outsourcing Deals, Says Report." *Computergram Weekly* (November 5, 2002): 5.

"German Firms Look to Outsource Services Overseas." *Outsourcing Intelligence Bulletin: FSO Magazine* 11, no. 1 (August 8–20, 2004), editor@fsoutsourcing.com.

Goldsmith, N. M. *Outsourcing Trends.* New York: The Conference Board, 2003.

Gouge, I. *Shaping the IT Organization.* London: Springer, 2003.

Greaver, M. F. *Strategic Outsourcing.* New York: American Management Association, 1999.

Handby, J. "Outsourcing: Perfecting Partnerships." *Management Consultancy* 11 (1996): 11–20.

Hicks, N. "Connealy Says Company Did Not Finish Job." *Lincoln* (NE) *Journal Star*, September 18, 2004.

"India's Proficiency in English to Ward Off Threat from China as Preferred Outsourcing Destination." *Outsourcing Intelligence Bulletin: FSO Magazine* 11, no. 2 (August 8–15, 2004), editor@fsoutsourcing.com.

Insinga, R. C. "Linking Outsourcing to Business Strategy." *Academy of Management Executive* 14, no. 4 (November 2000): 58–71.

Jupiter Research Corporation. *Building Trust Platforms in the International Arena.* New York: marketresearch.com, 2001.

Lackow, H. M. *IT Outsourcing Trends.* New York: The Conference Board, 2001.

Lasher, W. *Process to Profits: Strategic Planning for the Growing Business.* Mason, OH: South-Western, 2004.

MacInnis, P. "Warped Expectations Lead to Outsourcing Failures." *Computing Canada* 29, no. 7 (2003): 1–2.

Marshall, E. M. *Building Trust at the Speed of Change: The Power of the Relationship-Based Corporation.* New York: American Management Association, 1999.

Meisler, A. "Think Globally, Act Rationally." *Workforce Management* 83, no. 1 (2004): 40–45.

Metz, C. "Tech Support Coming Home?" *PC Magazine* 23, no. 3 (February 17, 2004): 20.

Milgate, M. *Alliances, Outsourcing, and the Lean Organization.* Westport, CT: Quorum Books, 2001.

Minoli, D. *Analyzing Outsourcing.* New York: McGraw-Hill, 1995.

"Multi-Sourcing Just a Red Herring?" *Global Computing Services* (July 4, 2003): 3–4.

Natovich, J. "Vendor Related Risks in IT Development: A Chronology of an Outsourced Project Failure." *Technology Analysis and Strategic Management* 15, no. 4 (2003): 409–420.

"Negotiating the Contract: Best Practices in Mitigating the Risks of Changing Business Needs, Evolving Technology, Rising Costs and More." *Outsourcing Intelligence Bulletin: FSO Magazine* 5, no. 2 (June 13–20, 2004), editor@fsoutsourcing.com.

"Offshored Services by Financial Firms Increase 38% in the Last One Year." *Outsourcing Intelligence Bulletin: FSO Magazine* 11, no. 1 (August 8–20, 2004), editor@fsoutsourcing.com.

O'Hanlon, K. "Chambers: Will State Now Reconsider India Contract?" *Lincoln* (NE) *Journal Star*, September 21, 2004.

Pint, E. M., and Baldwin, L. H. *Strategic Sourcing: Theory and Evidence from Economics and Business Management.* Santa Monica: Rand, 1997.

Quinn, J. B. "Strategic Outsourcing: Leveraging Knowledge Capabilities." *Sloan Management Review* 40, no. 4 (1999): 9–21.

Quinn, J. B., and Hilmer, Frederick G. "Strategic Outsourcing." *Sloan Management Review* 35, no. 4 (1994): 43–55.

Rothery, B., and Robertson, I. *The Truth about Outsourcing.* Oxford, England: Gower Publishing Limited, 1995.

Sen, S. "Enterprise Outsourcing Management, the New Mantra." *Outsourcing Intelligence Bulletin: FSO Magazine* 4, no. 2 (March 21–28, 2004), editor@fsoutsourcing.com.

Sislian, E., and Satir, A. "Strategic Sourcing: A Framework and a Case Study." *Journal of Supply Chain Management* 36, no. 3 (2000): 4–11.

"Tennessee Governor Curbs Outsourcing by Introducing Anti-Outsourcing Bill." *Outsourcing Intelligence Bulletin: FSO Magazine* 4, no. 7 (May 23–30, 2004), editor@fsoutsourcing.com.

Weston, R. "Methodology: Ask the Users." *Information-Week* 915 (November 18, 2002): 40.

"Your Shout." *Computer Weekly*, February 27, 2004, 28.

Part 2

Methodologies for Different Types of Outsourcing-Insourcing Decisions

5

International Outsourcing-Insourcing Metrics-Based Methodologies

Learning Objectives   After completing this chapter you should be able to:

- Describe how executive polling can help outsource decision making.
- Describe how rating/scoring metrics can be used as evaluation outsourcing criteria.
- Use multi-criteria scoring methods for outsourcing decisions.
- Describe how the Delphi method can be used to improve decision model parameter accuracy.
- Describe how external benchmarking can aid in outsource decision making.
- Use gap analysis in international outsourcing-insourcing planning.
- Name sources of information that can be used to assess international outsourcing risks.
- Describe how economic, politics, culture, and demographic international risk factors can be measured.

Introduction

In the last chapter we culminated the *outsourcing-insourcing* (O-I) planning process content of this textbook with a step-wise procedure presented again in Figure 5.1. Starting with this chapter, and throughout the rest of this textbook, a series of methodologies will be presented that are applicable to one or more of the steps in the O-I planning process. In this chapter, we focus on *O-I metrics* or measures that can be used in the evaluation of important decision-making parameters in O-I. The metrics presented in this chapter are applicable to the shaded boxed steps in the O-I planning process in Figure 5.1. Where and how these metrics are

used will be discussed as they relate to application of specific methodologies.

Executive and Board of Director Polling

There is no more valuable source of information than can be obtained by polling the executives in a client firm on any subject or decision-making situation. Who better to know where the problems an organization experiences exist than the internal staffers who interact with each other and see results of fellow employees' business performance day-to-day. Of course, groups of executives (e.g., marketing groups, operations groups, finance

Figure 5.1 **Application of This Chapter's O-I Metric-Based Methodologies in International O-I Planning**

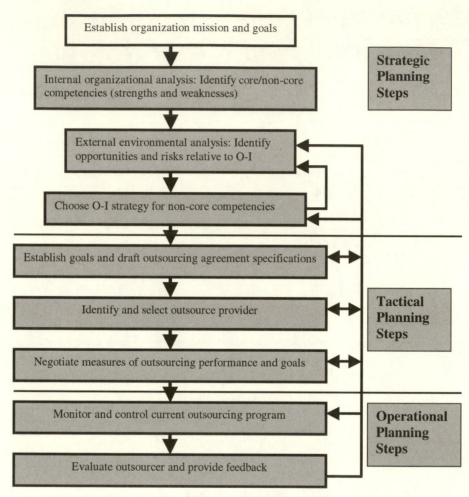

groups, etc.) can have collective biases or orientations, which can make their opinions less useful in the O-I decision process (e.g., marketing groups might favor marketing solutions more than other functional area solutions). It would be a rare occurrence for a functional area, like accounting or information systems, to request to be outsourced. This is why O-I has to start at the strategic level of planning and is usually conducted by boards of directors, who are not usually tied directly to any internal function or area and thus, can be more objective in decision making.

Executive polling of opinions and of board members can be performed orally in routine or special meetings where individuals are free to express themselves (Reid and Sanders 2005, 257). This oral approach is useful in situations where quick opinion information is necessary for a fast decision. A more analytical but time consuming means of polling is to use employee surveys. Questionnaires can be pre-

Table 5.1

Examples of O-I Survey Polling Questions

Organization member	Examples of questions
Director	1. From your experience on the board, which functional area in the organization tends to have the most problems?
	2. How would you rate our firm's reputation for quality when compared to the industry leader's reputation?
Upper-level management	1. Do you know of any O-I providers who are thought to deliver outstanding service?
	2. How would you rate O-I providers in generating useful service information on which to judge goal performance?
Middle-level management	1. How would you rate the usefulness of the information supplied by the O-I provider in helping you to meet your area's goals?
	2. Have you observed any problems in dealing with the O-I provider that should be examined in light of our agreement?
Operational-level management	1. Has the O-I provider made an effort to work with the client staff?
	2. Have there been any problems during the transition period of the O-I agreement that should be re-examined by higher management?

pared to ask differing types of managers and board members a variety of questions, which can lend support to an O-I decision. Such an approach can be performed top-down (i.e., the board of directors down through different management levels of the organization) or bottom-up. The top-down approach is useful when directors have specific ideas about O-I and want to direct the flow of subsequent questions around specific ideas. An example might be where a board is debating between using an offshore outsourcing approach or a nearshore approach for its O-I strategy. By directing the polling questions to executives on operations and implementation issues, the board may be able to find useful internal support for one approach over another. The bottom-up approach can be useful in an exploratory mode when the organization is flexible on possible strategies and seeks to identify a larger range of possibilities, which managers may feel offer unique advantages for the firm.

The types of survey questions that can be used in polling efforts can range considerably. Table 5.1 lists examples of questions that can be used to guide a client firm's board of directors in making an O-I decision as well as implementation questions for other management levels. As can be seen, these questions require an opinion, sometimes expressed with words and other times with a rating scale, which can provide for a quantitative analysis of the responses.

Areas of application of polling in international O-I include determining criteria that should be considered in selecting strategies and tactics in implementing O-I, selecting O-I providers, and evaluating O-I agreements. While polling is particularly useful in finding decision-making criteria, there is an equally important need to compare criteria. This requires establishing measurable criteria.

Rating/Scoring Metrics and Multi-Criteria Scoring Methods

When an outsource provider is being selected, more than a single criterion for services must be consid-

Table 5.2

MCSM Table for Unweighted Outsource Provider Selection Problem

Selection criteria	Outsource provider A	Outsource provider B	Outsource provider C
1. Flexibility	5	1	9
2. Trustworthiness	5	5	2
3. Price	4	3	6
4. Delivery	5	6	6
Total Score	**19**	**15**	**23**

ered. Trustworthiness, care for quality service, and flexibility are some of the multi-criteria that should go into the decision. Likewise, when a board of directors is considering which of several functional areas they might want to outsource, they must consider many service factors for each department before a fair and informed decision can be made. While some of these criteria are objective, like dollar pricing for services, others, such as trust or flexibility, have to subjectively be quantified for comparative purposes. To do this, a simple *rating metric* can be used (i.e., a scale from "1" representing "poor rating" up to a "9" for a "good rating"). By adding ratings together over several criteria, a *score metric* for each alternative examined can be determined. A group of rating/scoring methodologies, which make use of subjectively derived metrics is called a *multi-criteria scoring method* (MCSM).

MCSMs allow for making a choice, from a set of alternatives using a set of two or more criteria (Alder 2000; Renkema and Berghout 1997). The alternatives must be mutually exclusive with discrete choices (i.e., no fractional choices of more than one alternative). Selecting one outsource provider from a set of several is an example of a mutually exclusive choice with discrete choice alternatives. To use MCSMs, the criteria used in the decision choice must also be rated in some numerical fashion. Any numbering rating scale such as 1 to 9, or 1 to 100, can be created and used in MCSMs. The choice of a rating scale is left up to the decision maker.

There are different versions of MCSMs that exist in the literature (Render and Stair 2000). They can be categorized into two basic types: un-weighted MCSMs and weighted MCSMs. In *un-weighted MCSMs* the ratings are simply summed up to achieve a score, which can be used to denote the desired choice of alternatives. Under this method the criteria are equally weighted (e.g., a rating of 1 for flexibility is equal in weight to a rating of 1 for trust). Assume the rating metric used in Table 5.2 is on a scale from "1" representing a poor rating to "9" for a good rating. The Total Score row (note the bold values in Table 5.2) represent a summation of the four column ratings for each of the criterion used in the selection process. Since the larger score denotes the best score, the un-weighted MFSM choice would be Alternative C with a score of 23.

To summarize the steps in the un-weighted MCSM:

1. Identify all alternative choices.
2. Identify all relevant criteria.
3. Construct a MCSM table with individual columns for each alternative, rows for each criterion, and a final row labeled Total Score.
4. Rate each alternative using a scale of choice (e.g., 1 to 9), where the lower value on the scale represents a less preferred value and the higher value represents a more preferred value for each criterion.

Table 5.3

MCSM Table for Weighted Outsource Provider Selection Problem

Selection criteria	Criterion weight	Outsource provider A	Outsource provider B	Outsource provider C
1. Flexibility	0.5	5	1	9
2. Trustworthiness	0.1	5	5	2
3. Price	0.2	4	3	6
4. Delivery	0.2	5	6	6
Total Score	**1.0**			

5. Place the ratings by row and column in each cell that makes up the table.
6. Sum the ratings in each column (i.e., each alternative) to generate a score and place these values in the Total Score row at the bottom of the table.
7. Select the alternative with the largest total score value.

The selection of Outsource Provider C in Table 5.2, based on the un-weighted MCSM score, implies each of the four criteria in the decision process are equally weighted in the decision process. It is more likely in real-world problems that criteria have differing weights. For example, the criterion "price" may be three or four times as important as "flexibility." Determining a mathematical *criterion weight* (i.e., a mathematical weight reflecting the importance of criterion relative to the others) can be derived subjectively or objectively with other quantitative methods. These criterion weights are usually expressed as decimals (or percentages) and must add up to 1.0 (or 100 percent).

For illustration purposes assume one is faced with the same three alternatives and four criteria problem in Table 5.2, but now a criterion weight for each of the four criteria has been assigned as shown in Table 5.3. The origin of the criterion weights in Table 5.3 is subjectively "guessed-at" by the champion of the outsourcing project team, who feels the criterion of "*flexibility*" in an outsource provider is five times as important as the criterion of "*trust*." Assume that "*price*" and "*delivery*" *criteria* are twice as important as "*trust*."

Taking the criterion weights and multiplying them by each of the related alternative ratings in each row presented in Table 5.3 modifies the rating of the criterion for each alternative to reflect the proportioned importance. These are the boldface values in the criteria rows in Table 5.4. Next sum them by column for each alternative in Table 5.4 to result in a Total Score value which again is used for the final alternative choice of an outsource provider based on the largest total score. In this *weighted MCSM* example, again select the Outsource Provider C, since its Total Score of 7.1 is larger than the other two alternatives.

A procedure for determining the criterion weights using both subjective judgment and an objective process might include the following steps:

1. Determine the different criteria to be weighted.
2. Allow everyone in a group of decision makers to allocate a fixed number of points (e.g., 100 points per person) over the different criteria from Step 1. These should be viewed as "votes" representing the importance of each criterion (i.e., the

Table 5.4

Computation for the Weighted MCSM Outsource Provider Selection Problem

Selection criteria	Criterion weight	Computations for outsource provider A	Computations for outsource provider B	Computations for outsource provider C
1. Flexibility	0.5	0.5 x 5 = **2.5**	0.5 x 1 = **0.5**	0.5 x 9 = **4.5**
2. Trustworthiness	0.1	0.1 x 5 = **0.5**	0.1 x 5 = **0.5**	0.1 x 2 = **0.2**
3. Price	0.2	0.2 x 4 = **0.8**	0.2 x 3 = **0.6**	0.2 x 6 = **1.2**
4. Delivery	0.2	0.2 x 5 = **1.0**	0.2 x 6 = **1.2**	0.2 x 6 = **1.2**
Total Score	1.0	**4.8**	**2.8**	**7.1**

more the votes by everyone, the higher the criterion weight will be).

3. Add up the points for group members and divide the total points for each criterion by the total points allowed for the group as a whole. The resulting ratios represent the criterion weights for a MCSM model.

For example, suppose there are four criteria and a group of five executives determining the weights. Each of the five executives is given 100 points to allocate over the four criteria. Summing the five executives' allocations, then dividing each by 500 points results in the criterion weights.

To summarize the steps in the weighted MCSM procedure:

1. Identify all alternative choices.
2. Identify all relevant criteria.
3. Identify, judgmentally derive, or compute criterion weights for each criterion.
4. Construct an MCSM table with individual columns for each alternative and one additional column labeled Criterion Weight, rows for each criterion, and a final row labeled Total Score.
5. Rate each alternative using a scale of choice (e.g., 1 to 9), where the lower value on the scale represents a less preferred value, and the higher value

represents a more preferred value for each criterion.

6. Place the ratings by row and column in each cell that makes up the table.
7. Place the criterion weights in the Criterion Weight column.
8. Multiply the criterion weights by each of the ratings across each row, and place those values in each of the rating cells of the table.
9. Sum these computed ratings by column (i.e., each alternative) to generate a total score and place these values in the Total Score row at the bottom of the table.
10. Select the alternative with the highest total score.

As Franceschini et al. (2003) have pointed out, the rating and scoring metrics of MCSM make a powerful tool for O-I decision making. They can be used with all the shaded areas in Figure 5.1, since each area can involve multiple criteria and alternative choices.

Metric Accuracy and the Delphi Method

Opinions based on personal judgment can vary a great deal across a group of executives or directors. When averaged, a group's ratings of each alternative on each criterion may reflect a group consensus, or it may not. The greater the variability in the group members' ratings, the greater the possibility for a misleading result. Conversely, the less the variability, the more likely the estimate represents a true consensus.

To estimate the variability in the group of values used in the point estimate, common variation statistics, range, and standard deviation statistics are computed to provide some indication of the variability in the metrics (Anderson et al. 2002, 83–87):

$$\text{Range} = \text{Highest value in the group} - \text{Lowest value in the group} \qquad (1)$$

$$\text{Standard deviation} = \sqrt{\frac{\sum (x_i + \bar{x})^2}{n-1}} \qquad (2)$$

where x_i are the i individual values from the group of size n, and $\bar{x}$ is the average value of the group. For particular parameters that have a large range or standard deviation values, additional effort to improve the accuracy by reducing the variability in the metrics might be indicated. Relative value size for these variation statistics varies based on accuracy desired. As a basic rule, range or standard deviation values that are more than 25 percent of the resulting average value may be a questionable parameter in some MCSM analyses.

One method ideal for combining multiple assessments into a single value is called the Delphi method. The *Delphi method* is a decision-making procedure for structuring a group-compromising process to deal with complex problems (Reid and Sanders 2005, 257–258). The Delphi method can be characterized as a controlled debate, which ensures a group is allowed to voice opinions equally and bring the opinions to conformity. The steps into a Delphi method for purposes of the parameter assessment problem are presented in Table 5.5.

The Delphi method is a systematic approach, which evokes collective opinion and offers several beneficial features, including:

1. Reduces the effect of dominant group members.
2. Reduces peer pressure by allowing group members to use independent judgment.
3. Allows ideas and concepts to be introduced to the group and evaluated without prejudice.
4. Reduces divergent opinions.

The Delphi method can be used for a wide range of decision-making applications (Laudon and Laudon 2004, 471–472). This methodology is also ideal when multiple experts are brought together to generate an *expert judgment* (i.e., an expert's opinion) on a particular decision point (Anderson et al. 2002, 776). Opportunities for the Delphi method's application in O-I are considerable, since most of the O-I planning process involves multiple groups, including experts, the board of directors, and each level of an organization's management.

External Benchmarking and Gap Analysis

Some organizations are less interested in internal executive opinions and more interested in external opinions, such as those from customers or industry-wide expert perceptions. Firms must know how well they are competing in order to identify strengths, weaknesses, opportunities, risks, and to plan appropriately. These strategic components of planning are very important because they directly relate to the opportunities international O-I has to offer.

Virtually all of the methodologies presented in this chapter require some comparisons upon which to render a decision. *Benchmarking* is an explicit comparative analysis involving the selection of a standard of excellence for processes, services, or

Table 5.5

Steps in Using the Delphi Method to Reach Consensus on Parameters

Steps	Description
1. Select a group of board members, executives, or experts to determine the parameters for a MCSM problem.	These group members should be knowledgeable or have expertise on the parameters, criteria, and problem situation under study. They should also be kept anonymous.
2. Send each group member a questionnaire requesting opinions concerning identification of parameters.	The questionnaire should clearly state all necessary parameters required (e.g., time frame on which to return the questionnaire; the level in the firm—strategic, tactical, or operational; etc.).
3. Collect the questionnaires from the group, document results, analyze, and prepare a report.	See what parameter values are in common with each group member. Create distributions to define the frequency of selection by group members for each parameter. Prepare a report that summarizes the selections and the frequency of selection by all members in the group. Provide basic averaged values and statistics.
4. Send the report and a revised questionnaire to all group members.	Ask the group members to use the information in the report to update and possibly revise selections of parameters. Ask group members, whose suggested parameters are in the minority, to explain why they do not feel the need to change and conform to the majority.
5. Repeat steps 3 and 4 until the group agrees on all parameters	Permit the group members to see whether or not their selections are being supported by others in the group. Eventually, the majority will form a consensus and changes in parameters will no longer occur. It is important to allow the minority group members to share reasons why they chose not to change their opinions, since this can sometimes sway others.

practices that represent the best any individual, group, or organization can perform (Reider 2000). The standard of excellence is usually referred to as an *industry best practice* (Schwartz and Gibb 1999, 73). *External benchmarking* refers to going outside the organization to determine excellence (Chase et al. 2004, 289; Cox and Thompson 1998). The *benchmark* is used as a target or goal to be achieved (i.e., the best practice in the industry). Since O-I planning is based on goals (i.e., strategic, tactical, etc.), benchmarking is a useful methodology to support O-I. Benchmarking can be used as a one-time process to identify an opportunity or an O-I provider. It can also be used as a long-term program of continuous improvement to keep an O-I provider knowledgeable of a firms' best practice expectations. If an O-I provider knows that some

O-I competitive provider is doing a better job in one or more of the example measures in Table 5.6, they are more likely to meet or exceed the performance of the competitor. In this way benchmarking is used not only to identify areas for improvement, but also to motivate continuous improvement.

External Benchmarking Procedure

To use benchmarking as a methodology for O-I, it is best to formalize it as either a *management project* (short duration, for a one time decision) or a *management program* (for continuous decision making). Regardless of the use, a procedure for external benchmarking usually includes the following steps (Schniederjans et al. 2004, 290–294; Shah and Singh 2001; Spendolini 1992; Zee 2002, 142–164):

Table 5.6

Benchmarking Measures for O-I

O-I areas for	Benchmark measures
Provider services	–Response time to requests for services –Average customer (external and internal) satisfaction score –Average number of defects per transaction –Quality measures or ratings by operations staff, auditors, customers, suppliers, vendors, etc. –On-time delivery rate
Provider costs	–Late charges paid to third-party outsourcers –Average number of days required to train personnel during O-I transition –Cost per project, per transaction, per department –Total cost overruns –Percentage of business lost due to provider failure –Penalty costs of provider employee turnover

1. *Establish a benchmarking team.* Benchmarking requires oversight for successful implementation. This *benchmark team* might include members inside and outside the firm. The teams should also include technical specialists in areas that will be benchmarked (e.g., accountants for accounting benchmarks). The team may consist of outside experts who specialize in benchmarking or who are knowledgable of a particular decision domain. The team may also be established by level of management (i.e., a team of just upper-, middle-, or lower-level managers) in situations where benchmarking is specifically applied to deal with problems at a particular level of management.

2. *Identify and document the activities, processes, or functional areas requiring improvement.* Use performance measures for all business activities, like financial and non-financial measures, subjective criteria from customer surveys or identified through the firm's strategic internal organizational analysis. Many of these measures are computed routinely and should not require a great deal of collection effort. Even actitivities, processes, or functional areas that may not appear to be a problem should have performance measures. If functional areas are not assessed through continuous performance measures, this would indicate a business weakness.

3. *Identify measurable industry best performance or an industry standard of excellence.* Benchmarking requires identification of some measure of best performance. Such outstanding firms in an industry can be identified by reviewing research reports in the literature (i.e., journal publications, trade magazines, association publications, etc.). One such journal is the *International Journal of IT Standards and Standardization Research.* Other sources of information on benchmarking include governmental bodies, trade associations, academic institutions, and online sources (see www.betterm anagement.com). O-I organizations such as the *FS Outsourcing Company* (www.fsoutsourcing.com) mentioned in Chapter 4 and *Outsourcing Benchmarking Association* (www.obenchmarking.com) can provide measures for outsourcing industry comparisons. These performance measures should be collected and used as benchmarks for comparison.

4. *Collect data on current operations and compare with benchmarks.* The measures collected on current operations should be compared with those industry best performance benchmarks or an industry leader. The greater the difference, the more important the performance area needs to be improved or outsourced.

5. *Establish a set of recommended changes.* Long-term, short-term, and multiple strategies of

change and implementation should be defined. From these alternatives, the "best" of the best should be selected and undertaken.

6. *Follow-up.* To ensure success, management techniques, such as "gap analysis" (see next section), should be employed. Performance measures that help identify problems, both current and proposed, should be posted where personnel can see them. Management must communicate progress made toward the stated benchmark goals, and continue to offer suggestions on approaches to improve. Also, industry best performance measures should be updated periodically as standards change over time.

Benchmarking can be applied to any of the shaded regions in Figure 5.1 as it relates to O-I planning (Franceschini et al. 2003). One of the more recent applications of benchmarking is in the use of selecting outsourcing providers. Since outsource providers can be measured on service criteria, such as the provider's propensity to change their prices or their general success with other client firms, outsourcing industry benchmarks can be used to help identify and select possible outsource providers. (We will discuss benchmarking for provider selection again in Chapter 7.)

Gap Analysis

A graphical aid called gap analysis can be used to communicate areas where the firm does not meet a benchmark. *Gap analysis* permits a comparative presentation of a business unit's performance in achieving benchmarks or other goals. Building on the principle of *visual management* (i.e., the concept that the individual's business performance should be displayed for all to see), upper management can have a *gap chart* constructed that compares an organization's actual performance with the performance they desire to achieve (i.e., the benchmark).

This gap chart can be developed in different ways. One approach is to use judgmentally generated measures from rating/scoring metric questions. A procedure for gap analysis might include the following steps:

1. *Determine the criteria to be measured.* This is usually the benchmarked areas in a firm.
2. *Collect measures on current or actual performance.* A survey instrument can be used to poll the opinions of a target group related to the business areas of concern. These measures can be determined using some rating/scoring metrics. For the most part averaged values for all the target group members are used. The target group might include customers, employees, managers, and outside experts.
3. *Collect measures on desired performance.* These are usually the benchmark measures scaled in the same way as the actual performance measures.
4. *Draw the gap chart.* The gap chart will list the criteria selected in Step 1 on the vertical axis and the rating measures along the horizontal axis.
5. *Plot the "actual" and the "desired" score metrics.* Plot the actual averaged scores from the targeted group as points and connect the points with a continuous line, from top to bottom. Plot the desired score metrics the same way.
6. *Compare the "gap" between each point.* The greater the gap, the greater the difference between the actual perception of the criteria and what is desired.

For example, in Table 5.7 operational-level managers might want to poll employees on various performance monitoring criteria to determine

Table 5.7

Operational Management Questions Used in the Construction of a Gap Chart to Measure Outsource Provider Performance

Outsource provider performance measure	Survey question
Service quality	How would you rate the service quality of our outsource provider? Poor Average Perfect 1 2 3 4 5 6 7 8 9 10
Operations	How would you rate the speed with which our outsource provider's warehouse responds to order changes? Poor Average Perfect 1 2 3 4 5 6 7 8 9 10
Marketing	How would you rate our outsource provider's marketing service department representative? Poor Average Perfect 1 2 3 4 5 6 7 8 9 10
Communications support	How would you rate the effectiveness of the outsource provider's information systems support for your communications? Poor Average Perfect 1 2 3 4 5 6 7 8 9 10
Cost effectiveness	How would you rate the price charged by our outsource provider for services rendered? Poor Average Perfect 1 2 3 4 5 6 7 8 9 10

if an outsource provider is meeting expected performance goals. The survey, given to operational-level employees, permits them an opportunity to comment, via a rating metric, on the current or "actual performance" of the outsource provider. Any kind of rating scale or continuous scale can be used as was explained in the previous rating/scoring metric section of this chapter. This survey will establish the "actual" service status being provided based on the operational-level employees opinions. The collected benchmarks from an industry's best practice leader can then

Figure 5.2　**Gap Chart of Outsource Provider Monitoring Example**

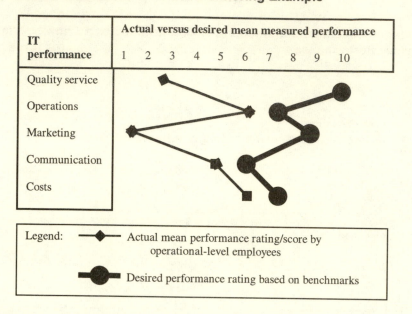

be plotted as the organization's desired or target performance. By taking the mean of the ratings as a score for each survey question, the mean scores can then be plotted on a gap chart as presented in Figure 5.2. The difference between the plotted, actual, and desired points on the chart represents the "gap" between where the organization's operational-level employees currently perceive the firm and where they want to be. The greater the gap, the greater the need for corrective action to bring the performance measure toward a desired target of performance. In the case of an O-I provider in Figure 5.2, it might mean penalties (if the O-I agreement and both parties have agreed to such penalties) or simply an opportunity to remind the outsource provider what is important to the client firm. Clearly in Figure 5.2, there are big gaps in the performance of quality service and marketing from what the client firm benchmarked.

Like most visual management approaches, gap analysis should be part of a continuous improve-ment process, which can be used for strategic, tactical, and operational-level planning activities. It can have application to all of the shaded areas in Figure 5.1 where rating/scoring metrics can be applied to compare the performance of multiple criteria.

Measuring International O-I Risks

To measure a risk, one must first identify its type. In a general sense there are country-wide risks or *macroeconomic risks*, which are out of the control of a client firm. They include events such as natural disasters (e.g., earthquakes, floods, etc.), wars, currency exchange rate changes, interest rate changes, and changes in national wage levels, to mention a few. Selecting one country's outsource provider over another means selecting a preferred country where the client firm's business activities will be located. Differing macroeconomic risk levels exist for each country.

One of the best methodologically based approaches for assessing a country's risk (i.e., viewing the risk of a country as a whole) is found in the many risk ratings easily obtained from publications like *The Economist, Euromoney,* and the *Institutional Investor.* These ratings are based on many risk factors and the rating/scoring metrics discussed earlier in this chapter. For example, *Euromoney* combines nine categories of risk assessment factors (i.e., political risk, economic risk, economic data, debt indicators, debt in default, credit ratings, access to bank finance, access to short-term finance, access to capital markets, and discount on forfeiting) in a weighted MCSM model (Cavusgil et al. 2002, 29–30). The *Institutional Investor* uses a rating scale from 0 to 100 to poll leading international banks, money management firms, and economists to determine risk scores by country (Cavusgil et al. 2002, 31). These publications and others provide projected risk ratings, which are useful for longer-term international O-I decisions.

Because of the multi-criteria nature of models used in selecting countries, most of the country selection models are based on MCSM methodologies. One typical modeling technique proposed decades ago by Kugel (1973) incorporates all of the same international O-I risk factors (i.e., economics, culture, politics, and demographics) introduced in Chapter 3. In this model multiple categories for dozens of criteria related to a country are listed with rating/scoring metric scales, which permit each of the criteria to be judged by executives or experts. A tabular scoring approach, like that in the weighted MCSM method, is used to arrive at a final score for each country, based on perceived risk avoidance and opportunities. Similar methods, such as Coplin and O'Leary (1983), which focus on just political risk assessment, continue to appear in the literature. An example of the types of questions and rating/scoring that these tabular methods incorporate are presented in Table 5.8. An extension of Kugel's approach, where the scaling system is incorporated into a computerized,

multi-objective optimization model can be seen in Hoffman and Schniederjans (1994) and Dawley et al. (1999). (We will discuss optimization models in Chapter 8.) These models permit a larger amount of selection criteria and countries to be analyzed at one time. By utilizing an optimization method many unique tradeoffs between risk factors are easily explored (e.g., a tradeoff of culture risk for economic risk). It can also incorporate a means for examining the accuracy of the rating/scoring metrics to provide a more valid result over the simpler tabular methods.

In some international O-I decisions, a general risk index for a country is not specific enough to be useful. Client firms interested in one or more specific types of international risk factors in making a country decision, which can also be the outsource provider decision, may want to focus research and assessment efforts on economic, political, cultural, or demographic international risk factors.

Economic Risk Factor Assessment

When an international O-I decision is based chiefly on economic results, other risk factors (i.e., culture, politics, and demographics) may not be worth the additional research or data collection efforts. While this should rarely be the case (i.e., excluding the other factors from the analysis), sometimes the importance of a country's economic opportunities so dominates a decision, other factors are rendered superfluous. Economic risk factors can be expanded from the few presented in Chapter 3 into at least five different categories (i.e., capital, labor, natural resources, infrastructure and technology) as listed in Table 5.9 (Austin 1990, 40–56; Cavusgil et al. 2002, 22–37; Rhinesmith 1993, 107–130). Each of these risk factor categories can be subdivided by various types of criteria, each requiring some means of measurement for use in a MCSM model.

Table 5.8

Typical Rating/Scoring Questions for Tabular Model Risk Assessment

International O-I risk factor	Survey question
Politics: Taxation legislation	How would you rate the riskiness of this country's taxation system regarding international outsourcing? High risk Average Low risk 1 2 3 4 5 6 7 8 9 10
Politics: O-I legislation	How would you rate the riskiness of this country's legislation against the practice of outsourcing in this country? High risk Average Low risk 1 2 3 4 5 6 7 8 9 10
Politics: Revenue policy legislation	How would you rate the riskiness of this country's legal restrictions on repatriation of capital and profits? High risk Average Low risk 1 2 3 4 5 6 7 8 9 10
Politics: Tariff legislation	How would you rate the riskiness of this country's current level of tariffs for our O-I plans? High risk Average Low risk 1 2 3 4 5 6 7 8 9 10 How would you rate the chance that this country's current level of tariffs is going to change over the planning horizon of the proposed international O-I agreement? High risk Average Low risk 1 2 3 4 5 6 7 8 9 10 How would you rate the riskiness of this country's current level of nontariff barriers to O-I? High risk Average Low risk 1 2 3 4 5 6 7 8 9 10
Politics: Government stability	How would you rate the riskiness of this country's fiscal and monetary policy? High risk Average Low risk 1 2 3 4 5 6 7 8 9 10 How would you rate the riskiness of this country's labor policy? High risk Average Low risk 1 2 3 4 5 6 7 8 9 10

Table 5.9

Economic Risk Factor Categories

Economic risk factor category	Factor criterion	Measurement system: Range of risk scale	Questions on possible risk to O-I
Capital	Domestic financial institutions	Rating: strong to weak	Does the outsource provider have access in the country to the capital needed to finance operations?
Capital	Inflation	Rating: high to low	Will the devaluation of currency make renegotiation of the O-I agreement necessary?
Capital	Income skewedness	Rating or percentages: normal to disproportional	Is there an unfairness in employee income levels, such that a risk of major redistribution might threaten the current wage structures necessary for O-I success?
Capital	Trade deficits	Dollars or rating: high to low	Are the trade deficits so great between the provider and client countries that devaluation or revaluation will change the expected benefits of the O-I agreement?
Labor	Skilled and unskilled labor capital	Rating or counts: available to not available	Does the outsource provider have the necessary skilled and unskilled labor available to accomplish agreement obligations?
Natural resources	Availability	Rating or units: high to low	Does the outsource provider have the necessary natural resources available to meet agreement obligations?
Infrastructure	Transportation/physical	Rating: good to poor	Is the transportation system in the provider country adequate to meet the client's shipping and logistic needs?
Infrastructure	Information system	Rating: good to poor	Are the information and telecommunication systems in the provider country adequate to meet the client firm's communication needs?
Technology	Technology levels	Rating: good to poor	Does the provider country have a level of technology sophistication necessary to support the O-I agreement?

These factors and criteria also raise questions on possible risks for client firms in any international O-I decision situation.

Secondary sources, or published information provided by private or public sources, can help identify economic factor risks when selecting an outsource provider in a foreign country. Some of these sources of economic information include using a country's *gross domestic product* (GDP) as an indicator of growth potential for markets in an outsource provider's country. While it is usually beneficial to find countries with growing GDP, a client firm that is fearful the outsource provider may market the client's product in the local foreign market might use GDP as an indicator of risk. Also, world trade statistics are useful in judging the intensity (or lack thereof) of trade activity for countries. Sources of GDP and world trade statistics information can be obtained from the *World Bank,* the *United Nations Conference on Trade and Development,* and the *National Trade Data Bank* of the *U.S. Department of Commerce.* Additional information can be obtained from universities and business schools, international business consultants, trade associations, and major finance and investment houses or banks.

Table 5.10

Politics Risk Factor Categories

Politics risk factor category	Factor criterion	Measurement system: range of risk scale	Questions on possible risk to O-I
Legalities	Legal system ease of use	Rating: difficult to easy	Is the legal system in the provider country difficult for a client firm to use? Is it too costly or too complex?
Legalities	Legal system fairness	Rating: unfair to fair	Does the outsource provider country have a legal system that favors the provider at the expense of the client firm?
Ideology	Coherence of people in country	Rating: high to low coherence	If the coherence is low (or high), will that help or harm the outsource provider's business performance? Might nationalistic sentiments create problems or lead to discriminatory regulations against the client firm?
Ideology	View of government's role in society	Rating: high to low	If the provider needs a strong government to ensure safe operations, will expectations of the role of the government permit help if needed?
Instability	Political instability	Rating: high to low	Might local government officials be ousted, rendering the O-I agreements null?
Instability	Institution instability	Rating: high to low	Are the country's political parties, bureaucracies, and other institutions unstable?
Instability	Government enforcement instability	Rating: high to low	Will sufficient enforcement personnel and regulations be in place to ensure compliance?

Politics Risk Factor Assessment

Like economic risk factors, politics risk factors can be assessed using rating/scoring methods with weighted or unweighted MCSM methods. International O-I investment decisions are actually considered one of the safest means for minimizing political risk, which firms undertake in an international business venture, such as O-I (Fatehi 1996, 495–496). Listed in Table 5.10 are samples of the many risk factor criteria, which should be considered in an international O-I decision (Austin 1990, 57–62; Caslione and Thomas 2002, 184; Coplin and O'Leary 1983; Fatehi 1996, 432–434; Rodrigues 1996, 53–56).

Culture Risk Factor Assessment

Culture is difficult to define, much less to assess its risk in an international O-I decision. Rating/ scoring methods are commonly used involving university experts and international consultants in determining cultural risk evaluations. Table 5.11 lists the categories with related criteria and possible risk questions, which requires answers in order to understand the risky nature of the O-I decision (Austin 1990, 62–68; Carroll and Gannon 1997, 36–56; Milgate 2001, 161–175).

Demographic Risk Factor Assessment

Demographic risk factors may have little impact in the short term on any international O-I agreement, but because longer-term *business process outsourcing* (BPO) agreements are currently on the rise ("Global BPO Market . . ." 2004), consideration of potential demographic risk factors need to be anticipated and incorporated into any O-I plan or decision. Rating/

Table 5.11   **Culture Risk Factor Categories**

Culture risk factor category	Factor criterion	Measurement system: range of risk scale	Questions on possible risk to O-I
Social norms	Trustworthiness	Rating: high to low	Can we trust the provider to abide by the O-I agreement? Can we trust the employees not to pilfer a product before it is shipped to customers?
Social norms	Value placed on quality work	Rating: high to low	Are the employees working for the provider culturally motivated to do a quality job?
Social norms	Religious attitudes	Rating: high to low	Will the perceived religious background of the client firm's managers clash with those of the provider firm?
Social norms	Individualism	Rating: high to low	Will a high level of individualism in the provider's society prevent conformity with the client's business policy, as required in the agreement?
Social norms	Time orientation	Rating: high to low	Will the time orientation in the provider's society permit employees to defer gratification of their wants and needs in order to achieve the client firm's long-term goals?
Social norms	Uncertainty avoidance	Rating: high to low	Will a high level of risk-avoidance in the provider's society inhibit aggressive marketing efforts necessary for client firm success?
Social norms	Terrorists	Rating: high to low	Will the tolerance of known terrorist organizations in the provider's country risk the lives of the client firm managers during plant visits?
Language	Understandability	Rating: high to low	Will the client firm be able to effectively communicate orders, plans, and expectations in the language of the provider's country?
Gender roles	Expectations	Rating: very distinct to less distinct	Will the client managers' beliefs about gender roles clash with the traditional gender roles in the provider's country?

scoring methods can be used with socio-economic university experts and international consultants as common resources for the assessed risk evaluation. Those listed in Table 5.12 are just a few of the many risk factor criteria, which should be considered in the international O-I decision (Austin 1990, 68–75; Cavusgil et al. 2002, 17–22; Fatehi 1996, 432–434; Rodrigues 1996, 53–56).

As can be seen from the problem leading questions in Table 5.12, a problem with migration can lead to a problem of urbanization or a political problem. This is the same *interactive chain-effect* of risk factors mentioned in Chapter 3. An additional example of the interactive chain-effect is presented in Figure 5.3.

While it is difficult to itemize and plan for the interaction of all risk factors, one way they can be managed is to identify and attempt to minimize the impact of risk factors, the primary international risk factors, thus lessening possible interactive chain-effects. Had the client firm in Figure 5.3 taken anticipatory steps in the selection and planning of an O-I agreement, as it related to the primary demographic risk factor, it might have avoided all subsequent interactive chain-effects.

Table 5.12

Demographic Risk Factor Categories

Demographic risk factor category	Factor criterion	Measurement system: range of risk scale	Questions on possible risk to O-I
Population	Growth	Actual population numbers or rating: decline in growth	Will rapid population growth lead to labor unrest that prevents the provider from fulfilling the O-I agreement?
Population	Age	Actual population distribution or rating: old to young	Will the younger average age of people in the provider's country mean that the labor skills to satisfy the O-I agreement are unavailable?
Urbanization	Dispersal of population	Rating: high to low	Will the lack of large metropolitan areas in the provider's country inhibit production/service activities required by the O-I agreement?
Migration	Population movement	Rating: high to low migration	Will the rapid migration of labor, typical of a provider's country, cause labor problems?
Migration	Rural-urban migration	Rating: high to low migration	Will the business opportunities that the O-I agreement creates in the provider country cause rural workers to move to urban centers? Might this migration create political problems for the client firm?
Migration	Neighboring country migration	Rating: high to low migration	Will the business opportunities that the O-I agreement creates in the provider country cause an influx of workers to the provider's country? Might this influx create political problems?

Figure 5.3   **Example of Interactive Chain-effect for O-I Risk Factors**

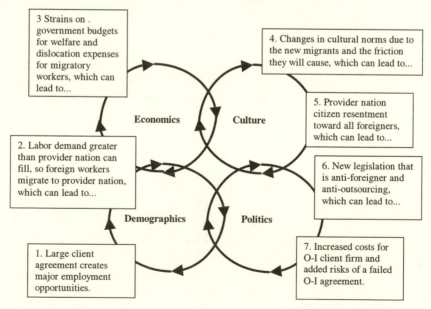

Summary

This chapter introduced a variety of different metric-based methodologies useful in international O-I planning steps. These methodologies included polling executive opinion and boards of directors, rating/scoring metrics, multi-criteria decision making, the Delphi method, external benchmarking, and gap analysis. A discussion of how international risk factors can be assessed was also presented.

As we have seen in this and prior chapters, the initial decision to utilize international O-I as a strategy for business success must be carefully analyzed. The next chapter will examine initial decision methodologies that can aid in the strategic O-I decision.

Review Terms

Benchmark
Benchmark team
Benchmarking
Business process outsourcing (BPO)
Criterion weight
Delphi method
Executive polling
Expert judgment
External benchmarking
Gap analysis
Gap chart
Gross domestic product (GDP)
Industry best practice
Interactive chain-effect
Macroeconomic risks
Management program
Management project
Multi-criteria scoring methods (MCSM)
O-I metrics
Outsourcing-insourcing (O-I)
Rating metric
Score metric
Secondary source
Unweighted MCSM
Visual management
Weighted MCSM

Discussion Questions

1. Which group, either executives or board members, would be more useful as a source of metric measuring information for an O-I decision? Explain reasoning.
2. If the parameters used in a MCSM are questionable, should the MCSM be used to make an international O-I decision?
3. What is the purpose of the Delphi method?
4. Why is external benchmarking important to the strategic planning steps of international O-I planning?
5. Gap analysis is considered a visual management technique. Why?
6. How can international O-I risks be measured?
7. What are interactive chain-effects for O-I risk factors?
8. Why do you think rating/scoring methods are a major methodological approach used in international O-I risk factor assessment?

Concept Questions

1. What is a rating metric? How can it be used? Explain.
2. What is the difference between weighted and unweighted MCSMs?
3. How are the weights in a weighted MCSM model determined?
4. How can inaccurate measurements of decision-making metrics be determined?
5. What are some of the benefits of the Delphi method?
6. What are examples of O-I measures of benchmarking for provider services?
7. What are examples of O-I measures of benchmarking for provider costs?
8. What are the basic elements that make up a gap chart?

9. What are macroeconomic risks?
10. Where can secondary source risk information on countries be obtained?
11. What are some of the economic risk factor criteria? How should they be measured?
12. What are some of the politics risk factor criteria? How should they be measured?
13. What are some of the culture risk factor criteria? How should they be measured?
14. What are some of the demographic risk factor criteria? How should they be measured?

Methodology Problems

1. A client firm has narrowed its choice of outsource provider to two firms located in differing countries. The firm wants to decide which one of the two countries is the better choice based on risk avoidance criteria. Polled executives have established four criteria. The resulting ratings for the two countries are presented in the table below, where 1 is a lower risk and 3 is a higher risk. Using the unweighted MCSM model, which country would you select? Show supportive computations.

Selection criterion	England	Canada
1. Price of service from outsourcer	2	3
2. Nearness of facilities to client	3	1
3. Level of technology	1	3
4. History of successful outsourcing	1	2

2. Using the same ratings given in Problem 1, assume the executives have determined four criteria weightings: Price with a weight of 0.1, Nearness with 0.6, Technology with 0.2, and History with 0.1. Using the weighted MCSM model, which country would you select? Show supportive computations.

3. A client firm is trying to decide which one of four countries they should research for possible outsource providers. The first step is to select a country based on cultural risk factors, because these are critical to eventual business success with the provider. They have reviewed outsource provider directories and found that the four countries below have an ample number of providers from which they can choose. To aid in the country selection step, they enlisted the aid of a local university cultural expert, who provided ratings of the various criteria in the table below. The resulting ratings are on a 1 to 10 scale, where 1 is a low risk and 10 is a high risk. Using the unweighted MCSM model, which country would you select based on risk avoidance? Show supportive computations.

Culture selection criterion	Mexico	Panama	Costa Rica	Peru
Trust	1	2	2	1
Society value of quality work	7	10	9	10
Religious attitudes	3	3	3	5
Individualism attitudes	5	2	4	8
Time orientation attitudes	4	6	7	3
Uncertainty avoidance attitudes	3	2	4	2

4. Using the same ratings given in Problem 3, assume the university expert has determined six criteria weightings: Trust with a weight of 0.4, Quality with 0.2, Religious with 0.1, Individualism with

0.1, Time with 0.1, and Uncertainty with 0.1. Using the weighted MCSM model, which country would you select? Show supportive computations.

5. A group of four client firm board of directors is assigned the task of assessing on a 1 to 10 rating scale, where 1 is a low risk and 10 is a high risk, the economic risk factors for a MCSM model. In the table below are the four individual board members' best guessed rating estimates. Average the ratings to determine a mean value for each of the six criteria. Compute the range statistics for each (i.e., subtract the lowest rating criterion from the largest to determine the range statistic). Comment on the accuracy of each parameter. Which parameter is the least accurate? The most accurate? Explain.

Economic criterion	Board member 1	Board member 2	Board member 3	Board member 4
Trade deficits	2	3	5	4
Skilled and unskilled labor capital	6	6	6	8
Availability	1	3	7	2
Transportation/physical	3	3	3	4
Information system	5	4	3	4
Technology levels	2	9	8	8

6. A client firm has decided to use a weighted MCSM model for O-I planning. While five different political criteria have been selected, the members of an O-I team need to establish MCSM weights. To do this, three members of the team were selected. They were each given 100 points to allocate (more points represent higher risk). These allocations are presented in the table below. Using the procedure for determining weights, what are the weights for the five criteria?

Politics criterion	Board member 1	Board member 2	Board member 3
Legal system use	10	20	10
Legal system fairness	30	20	40
Political instability	40	20	40
Institution instability	10	20	5
Government enforcement instability	10	20	5

7. A client firm wants to construct a gap chart to determine how well the current outsource provider is performing. This gap chart will measure three performance criteria: quality, delivery, and costs. The benchmarks for the three criteria are industry rating averages based on a 1 to 10 scale, with 1 being the best possible rating and 10 the worst. The industry averages for the three criteria are as follows: 9 for quality, 8 for delivery, and 10 for costs. Three operational level managers who are actively involved in the outsourcing project rated the provider firm on the same criteria, and their ratings are shown in the table below. Compute the necessary gap chart statistics and plot them on a gap chart. Comment on the results of the gap chart.

Gap chart criterion	Manager 1	Manager 2	Manager 3
Quality	6	8	7
Delivery	8	8	8
Costs	4	9	9

8. A board of directors has decided that a business process outsource (BPO) is appropriate for the company's needs in the long run. The board

wants to establish a gap chart to determine which functional area to outsource in this BPO. The gap chart will have five functional areas rated on a 1 to 10 scale (i.e., 1 is a poor rating indicating poor performance and 10 is a good rating). Industry ratings for typical functional areas are: Accounting 7, Finance 8, Information systems 9, Manufacturing 7, and Marketing 9. Four board members rated the five functional areas in the table below. Compute the necessary gap chart statistics and plot them on a gap chart. Comment on the results of the gap chart.

Functional criterion	Board member 1	Board member 2	Board member 3	Board member 3
Accounting	4	5	4	4
Finance	3	3	5	6
Information systems	1	1	3	2
Manufacturing	4	6	7	2
Marketing	2	5	6	9

References

Adler, R. W. "Strategic Investment Decision Appraisal Techniques: The Old and New." *Business Horizons* (November–December 2000): 15–22.

Anderson, D. R.; Sweeney, D. J.; and Williams, T. A. *Statistics for Business and Economics.* 8th ed. Mason, OH: South-Western, 2002.

Austin, J. E. *Managing in Developing Countries: Strategic Analysis and Operating Techniques.* New York: Free Press, 1990.

Carroll, S. J., and Gannon, M. J. *Ethical Dimensions of International Management.* Thousand Oaks, CA: Sage Publications, 1997.

Caslione, J. A., and Thomas, A. R. *Global Manifest Destiny.* Chicago: Dearborn Trade Publishing, 2002.

Cavusgil, S. T.; Ghauri, P. N.; and Agarwal, M. R. *Doing Business in Emerging Markets.* Thousand Oaks, CA: Sage Publications, 2002.

Chase, R. B.; Jacobs, F. R.; and Aquilano, N. J. *Operations Management for Competitive Advantage.* 10th ed. Boston: Irwin/McGraw-Hill, 2004.

Coplin, W. D., and O'Leary, M. K. *Introduction to Political Risk Analysis.* Croton-on-Hudson, NY: Policy Studies Associates, 1983.

Cox, A., and Thompson, I. "On the Appropriateness of Benchmarking." *Journal of General Business* 23, no. 3 (Spring 1998): 1–20.

Dawley, D. D.; Schniederjans, M. J.; Hoffman, J. J.; and Irwin, J. G. "Goal Programming and International Expansion in the Hospital Industry." *Journal of Managerial Issues* 11, no. 3 (Fall 1999): 259–279.

Fatehi, K. *International Management: A Cross-Cultural and Functional Perspective.* Upper Saddle River, NJ: Prentice Hall, 1996.

Franceschini, F.; Galetto, M.; Pignatelli, A.; and Varetto, M. "Outsourcing: Guidelines for a Structured Approach." *Benchmarking: An International Journal* 10, no. 3 (2003): 246–261.

"Global BPO Market to Touch $682.5 Billion, Says IDC." *Outsourcing Intelligence Bulletin: FSO Magazine* 4, no. 6 (May 9–16, 2004), editor@fsoutsourcing.com.

Hoffman, J. J., and Schniederjans, M. J. "A Two-Stage Model for Structuring Global Facility Site Selection Decisions: The Case of the Brewing Industry." *International Journal of Operations and Production Management* 14, no. 4 (1994): 79–96.

Kugel, Y. "A Decisional Model for the Multinational Firm." *International Management Review* 13, (1973): 3–14.

Laudon, K. C., and Laudon, J. P. *Management Information Systems.* 8th ed. Upper Saddle River, NJ: Prentice-Hall, 2004.

Milgate, M. *Alliances, Outsourcing, and the Lean Organization.* Westport, CT: Quorum Books, 2001.

Reid, R. D., and Sanders, N. R. *Operations Management.* 2nd ed. New York: John Wiley and Sons, 2005.

Reider, B. *Benchmarking Strategies: A Tool for Profit Improvement.* New York: John Wiley and Sons, 2000.

Render, B., and Stair, R. M. Supplement 11 to *Quantitative Analysis for Management.* Upper Saddle River, NJ: Prentice Hall, 2000.

Renkema, T. J., and Berghout, E. W. "Methodologies for Information Systems Investment Evaluation at the Proposal Stage: A Comparative Review." *Information and Software Technology* 39 (1997): 1–13.

Rhinesmith, S. H. *A Manager's Guide to Globalization.* Homewood, IL: Business One Irwin, 1993.

Rodrigues, C. *International Management: A Cultural Approach.* Minneapolis/St. Paul: West Publishing, 1996.

Schniederjans, M. J.; Hamaker, J. L.; and Schniederjans, A. M. *Information Technology Investment: Decision-Making Methodology.* Singapore: World Scientific Publishing, 2004.

Schwartz, P., and Gibb, B. *When Good Companies Do Bad Things.* New York: John Wiley and Sons, 1999.

Shah, J., and Singh, N. "Benchmarking Internal Supply Chain Performance: Development of a Framework." *The Journal of Supply Chain Management* (Winter 2001): 37–47.

Spendolini, M. J. *The Benchmarking Book.* New York: American Management Association, 1992.

Zee, H. V. *Measuring the Value of Information Technology.* Hershey, PA: Idea Group Publishing, 2002.

6

Financial Methodologies for the Initial Outsourcing-Insourcing Decision

---

Learning Objectives After completing this chapter you should be able to:

- Describe how present value analysis discounts investment alternatives to aid in the initial outsourcing decision.
- Describe how break-even analysis and return on investment can be used to aid in the initial outsourcing decision.
- Describe how internal rate of return and accounting rate of return can be used to aid in the initial outsourcing decision.
- Describe how payback period method and cost/benefit analysis can be used to aid in the initial outsourcing decision.

Introduction

The *outsourcing-insourcing* (O-I) planning methodologies in the last chapter were general in nature and could be used in most planning steps. This chapter narrows the focus on a collection of methodologies chiefly used in the initial decision and planning steps of O-I, denoted in the darkened boxes in Figure 6.1.

Many agreements between an outsource provider and a client firm involve fixed payments to the provider for a particular service. Since the client firm determined what it would pay for the service before considering an outsourcing strategy, the regimentation of payments to the provider allows the client firm to know with some degree of certainty what to expect in terms of cash flow over a future planning horizon. The relatively high degree of certainty of cash flows is a unique benefit

of O-I investment decisions, and it permits use of a variety of financial methodologies.

Boards of directors undertaking strategic planning are given financial information on which to base most important decisions, particularly the international O-I decision. There are literally dozens of financial decision-making methodologies useful in such an investment decision (Minoli 1995, 85–102; Schniederjans et al. 2004, 81–154). Several of the more commonly used financial methodologies will be examined, including, present value analysis, break-even analysis, return on investment, internal rate of return, accounting rate of return, payback period method, and cost/benefit analysis. As recommended by Adler (2000) and Franceschini et al. (2003), some of these financial methodologies generate cost information that can aid in strategic planning. They also can be used to establish tac-

Figure 6.1   **Application of This Chapter's Methodologies in International O-I Planning**

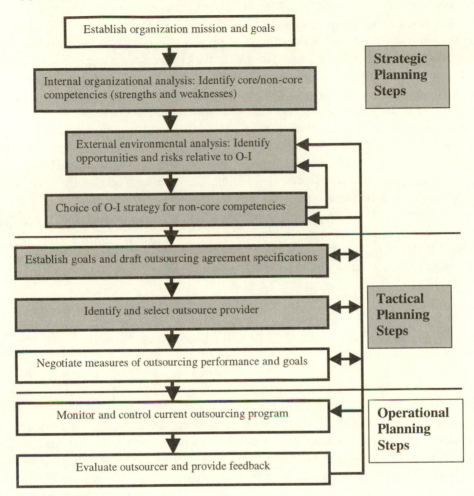

tical goals and select international O-I providers by middle-level managers.

Present Value Analysis

Present value analysis is basically a methodology whereby today's value of future cash flows are compared to the cost of the investment (Birrer and Carrica 1990; Friedlob and Schleifer 2002; Minoli 1995, 89). The value of future cash flows discounted for the forgone interest of an alternative investment is referred to as the *present value* (PV) of the investment. As a rule, if the present value of an investment is greater than the cost of the investment today, then it should be undertaken because it adds value. Present value analysis is based on the reasoning that a dollar today is worth more than receiving a dollar tomorrow because it can be invested and accrue interest. This methodology is used where cash flows result from a cost reduction or cost avoidance as is the case in international O-I decision situations (Minoli 1995, 89). Indeed, many international O-I decisions come down to an examination of cost savings per month or quarter over a period of years. These cash flows to the client firm have to be brought back into the present time of the decision. Present value analysis is also used to evaluate independent investments individually or to select among a set of mutually exclusive investments. Mutually exclusive outsourcing investment decisions, such as choosing between outsource providers at the tactical planning level or between an outsourcing and an insourcing strategy at the strategic level of planning, are examples of how this methodology can aid O-I decision making.

The present value of an investment can be computed as follows (Schniederjans et al. 2004, 117–119):

$$PV = \frac{C_1}{1+r} + \frac{C_2}{(1+r)^2} + ... + \frac{C_n}{(1+r)^n} \qquad (1)$$

where $C_1 ... C_n$ are the expected cash flows for n time periods, and r is the interest rate or *cost of capital* to the firm, also called the discount rate. The *discount rate* is the interest rate that could be earned by investing in alternative investments of comparable risk.

The value for the PV is best computed by a financial hand calculator or by computer spreadsheet software. For example, by using *Microsoft*® 2003 *Excel*® and clicking "Insert," then "Function," an "Insert Function" window opens. Select the category "Financial," then scroll down and select the "PV" function. Clicking on this function reveals a window with open boxes that allows for entering the r discount rate, n number of cash flow periods, and C the amount of the cash flow (ignore the other two open windows, they will default to zero). The formula in this software is set up such that you must put a minus sign in front of cash flow values.

For example, suppose a board of directors wants to determine the possible savings from adopting an international O-I strategy. Looking at the insourcing costs of doing the work versus an outsource provider, an estimated $2 million average cash flow savings per year for five years is possible by adopting an outsourcing strategy. Assume the client firm's cost of capital, or discount rate, is 12 percent. What is the PV of this outsourcing venture? To answer this question, plug the values of 0.12, 5, and –2,000,000 into the equation below (or into Excel®—remember the 2 million must be negative):

$$PV = \frac{2,000,000}{1+0.12} + \frac{2,000,000}{(1+0.12)^2} + \frac{2,000,000}{(1+0.12)^3} +$$

$$\frac{2,000,000}{(1+0.12)^4} + \frac{2,000,000}{(1+0.12)^5} \qquad (2)$$

The value of the future stream of $10,000,000 (i.e., 5 years at $2 million per year) is actually worth only a little over $7 million. Without comparison to some other alternative it is difficult to know if this is a worthwhile investment. The use of the present value formula is chiefly limited to comparing one alternative investment with another. If computing the PV of cash savings from an O-I strategy has a higher PV then select the O-I strategy. In most cases PV is used in combination with other methodologies to incorporate the time-value of an investment.

Net Present Value

Net present value (NPV) is an extension of PV analysis and can be used as a stand-alone decision methodology (i.e., NPV does not have to be compared to other alternatives as PV does). NPV is the present value of cash flows minus the initial investment cost. NPV can be computed as follows (Schniederjans et al. 2004, 119):

$$NPV = C_o + \frac{C_1}{1+r} + \frac{C_2}{(1+r)^2} + ... + \frac{C_n}{(1+r)^n} \qquad (3)$$

where C_o is the initial investment and is always expressed as a negative value, $C_1 ... C_n$ are the expected cash flows, r is the discount rate, and n is the number of time periods. This model is based on the assumption that an investment should return a net positive cash flow after the expense of investment and discounting for the interest rate opportunity costs are considered. For independent investments, the following rules can be used to guide the investment decision:

1. If NPV is greater than zero, then make the investment.
2. If NPV is equal to or less than zero, then do not make the investment.

The value for the NPV can be computed using the formula in equation (3) or with *Microsoft*® 2003 *Excel*® by clicking "Insert," then "Function," and "Insert Function" windows open. Select the category, "Financial," then scroll down and select the "NPV" function. Clicking on this function reveals a window with open boxes that allow for entering the r discount rate and as many C cash flow amounts as desired in the problem. Future income flows are positive values in this software application and costs are negative flows. Also, this software allows unequal amounts of cash flow. If the initial value is an up-front payment, then that amount will have to be manually subtracted from the *Excel*® generated value after it is computed.

To illustrate the use of NPV, let us assume an outsourcing team is trying to select one of two possible outsource providers, Provider A or Provider B. The costs of the contractual arrangements with the two outsource providers are different and thus affect the firm's cash flow differently every year during the four years of the agreement. Suppose Outsource Provider

A requires a $1 million initial payment (to help them acquire necessary start-up technology) and a fixed year-end payment of $500,000. Outsource Provider B requires a $700,000 initial payment and a fixed year-end payment of $600,000. Entering into an agreement with Outsource Provider A will result in estimated yearly cash flows to the client firm of $900,000, $1,000,000, $850,000, and $550,000. Entering into an agreement with Outsource Provider B will result in estimated yearly cash flows to the client firm of $1,200,000, $700,000, $700,000, and $600,000. Assume the year-end payment has been subtracted from the cash flows. If the client firm's discount rate is 10 percent, which of the two outsource providers offers the best financial deal? To answer this problem requires computing the NPV for cash flows to the client firm from both outsource providers. The NPVs can be calculated using *Excel*® as suggested above and subtracting the amount of the initial payment, or by using the NPV formula. Here is what the NPV formula looks like when we plug in the values for Provider A:

$$NPV = -1,000,000 + \frac{900,000}{1+0.10} + \frac{1,000,000}{(1+0.10)^2} +$$

$$\frac{850,000}{(1+0.10)^3} + \frac{550,000}{(1+0.10)^4}$$

$$= -1\,000,000 + 2,658,903.08$$

$$= \$1,658,903.08 \qquad (4)$$

And for Provider B:

$$NPV = -700,000 + \frac{1,200,000}{1+0.10} + \frac{700,000}{(1+0.10)^2} +$$

$$\frac{700,000}{(1+0.10)^3} + \frac{600,000}{(1+0.10)^4}$$

$$= -700\,000 + 2,605,149.92$$

$$= \$1,605,149.92 \qquad (5)$$

From the NPV computations, both providers are going to result in a positive NPV. Since Outsource

Provider A has a larger NPV, the estimated final NPV payoff is greater. As such the client outsourcing team should select Provider A.

One complication impacting the use of NPV involves comparing differing investments with unequal time horizons or unequal investment lives. An investment with a life of ten years might produce very different results than an investment with a five-year planning horizon. Several techniques exist to account for the problem of unequal alternative investment lives. The simplest way is to adjust the project lives so that they are the same length by using the longer-term investment values for the short-term alternative. For example, suppose a choice between two alternative outsourcing agreements must be made based on the NPV of the two investments' estimated costs and cash flow in Table 6.1. Since Outsource Agreement A is only for two years, it clearly will be at a disadvantage if all four years of the cash flow are added when computing the NPV of Outsource Agreement B. To correct this problem assume the same third and fourth years' cash flows (i.e., $600,000 per year) are possible under both agreements, since an outsourcing agreement can be extended or made continuous in most situations. This would allow all four years of both agreements to be equally compared in NPV analysis. Alternatively, assume that the outsourcing agreement cash flows might be replicated. Thus, in Year 3 of Table 6.1, the cash flow would be $300,000 (i.e., 1st Year of $800,000 minus a second initial cost of $500,000) and a Year 4 of $1 million (i.e., repeating Year 2). Either of these assumptions can be used to cause the equalization of NPV computations over the same time horizon.

As a side note, we should point out that present value analysis may need to consider inflation, though in many situations inflation is already accounted for by the interest or discount rate. For additional information on these computational

Table 6.1

Data for NPV Problem with Unequal Investment Lives

Cost or cash item	Outsource agreement A	Outsource agreement B
Initial Cost ($)	500,000	500,000
Cash Flow Year 1 ($)	800,000	850,000
Cash Flow Year 2 ($)	1,000,000	700,000
Cash Flow Year 3 ($)	0	600,000
Cash Flow Year 4 ($)	0	$600,000

procedures see Brealey and Myers (2000) and Copeland and Weston (1988).

Break-Even Analysis

Break-even analysis for O-I investments involves the comparison of quantifiable costs with quantifiable and non-quantifiable benefits (Droms 2003; Minoli 1995, 89). In break-even analysis, a break-even point is determined where the total value of benefits equals the total costs. *Non-quantifiable benefits* are intangible—that is, a monetary value cannot be assigned to them. Break-even analysis of O-I investment decisions uses subjective assessment of intangible benefits.

Steps for break-even analysis, assuming that all costs and benefits have been identified and assigned a value, are as follows:

1. Compute the present value (PV) of costs over the planning horizon of the project. This should include any up-front or down payment costs and all future cash payments.
2. Calculate the PV of all quantifiable benefits over the planning horizon of the project.

Table 6.2

Costs and Benefits of an O-I Strategy

Cost or benefit item	Year 0	Year 1	Year 2	Year 3	Year 4
Costs:					
Up-front cost ($)	800,000				
Annual cost ($)		200,000	200,000	200,000	200,000
Benefits:					
Reduced costs of production ($)		450,000	450,000	450,000	450,000
Improved product quality		—	—	—	—

3. Subtract the value from Step 2 from the PV of costs from Step 1. The result is referred to as *net costs*. If the value is negative (i.e., the PV of benefits are equal to or higher than the PV of costs) stop here, and accept the investment. If the net costs are positive, go to Step 4.
4. Subjectively evaluate the worth or value of the intangible benefits.
5. Make a decision. The value of intangible benefits must equal the positive net costs for the O-I investment to break even. If the intangible benefits exceed net costs, then the investment should be undertaken. If not, reject the O-I investment.

To illustrate the use of break-even analysis in O-I planning, let us consider a sample problem. Suppose a board of directors must decide whether or not to outsource as a strategy. The costs and benefits of the proposed O-I strategy have been evaluated by executives and experts and have been entered in Table 6.2. The *initial cost* of the O-I agreement, which will allow the provider to hire new personnel, is $800,000. The *annual cost* for the provider services is $200,000 for each of four years. Assume the discount rate for the PV calculations is 11 percent. The anticipated benefits are reduced costs of production for the client firm of $450,000 per year for each of the four years, and an intangible benefit of improved product quality.

First, compute the PV of the quantifiable costs using the figures from Table 6.2:

$$PV = 800,000 + \frac{200,000}{1+0.11} + \frac{200,000}{(1+0.11)^2} +$$

$$\frac{200,000}{(1+0.11)^3} + \frac{200,000}{(1+0.11)^4}$$

$$= 800\,000 + 620,489.14$$

$$= \$1,420,489.14 \tag{6}$$

Next, compute the PV of the quantifiable benefits using the figures from Table 6.2:

$$PV = \frac{450,000}{1+0.11} + \frac{450,000}{(1+0.11)^2} +$$

$$\frac{450,000}{(1+0.11)^3} + \frac{450,000}{(1+0.11)^4}$$

$$= \$1,396,100.56 \tag{7}$$

The net cost for the proposed O-I strategy is $24,388.58 (i.e., $1,420,489.14 − $1,396,100.56). With no criteria to consider other than the net cost, the O-I strategy would not be selected because the

PV of tangible costs exceeds the PV of the tangible benefits. But the intangible benefit of improved quality should be considered at this point in the break-even analysis. If the board of directors believes the improvement in product quality that will result from using an outsource provider is worth $24,388.58 or more, they should invest in the outsourcing strategy. If not, they should reject it.

One limitation of break-even analysis as presented above is that it may not account for all risk factors. How can international O-I risk factors be incorporated into break-even analysis? One way is to adjust the discount rate used in the PV computations to take into account the non-beneficial risks that may be present. By decreasing the discount rate for the costs in equal proportion (or in relationship) to perceived international risk, the PV of costs would be increased, making the investment less attractive. Another way is to increase yearly costs by some percentage to reflect added risk. Either way will increase the PV of costs, making the O-I investment less likely, or more accurately reflective of the net cost situation of the decision. (Risk factor inclusion in this and other financial methods will be discussed in the last section of this chapter.)

Return on Investment

Return on investment (ROI) is an investment methodology whereby the rate of return of an investment is compared to the *opportunity cost of capital* (i.e., the expected return forgone by investing in outsourcing rather than in an equally risky alternative investment in the capital market) (Friedlob and Schleifer 2002; Gouge 2003, 78–79; Minoli 2003, 90; Plewa and Friedlob 2001). Opportunity costs have been utilized in outsourcing decision models by Kee and Robbins (2003). Increasingly, as observed by McDougall (2004) and Chorafas (2003, 178), banks are expecting international outsourcing projects to generate an

attractive ROI. It has, therefore, become a common business performance measure for outsourcing projects and is viewed as a successful strategy in business planning (Jurison 1995).

ROI is calculated as the profit divided by the cost of the investment. If the return from the investment is greater than the opportunity cost of capital then the investment is worth more than it costs and should be undertaken. The rules for the ROI methodology are as follows:

1. If ROI is greater the opportunity cost of capital, then make the investment.
2. If ROI is equal to or less than the opportunity cost of capital, then do not make the investment.

To illustrate the use of ROI, assume the estimated total cost of an outsourcing agreement is $1.5 million for a one year project of introducing, installing, and training the client firm's personnel in using a state-of-the-art technology, in which it is assumed this outsource provider is a leader. The resulting cost reduction impact of this training at the end of the first year alone will be $2 million. Assume this investment has similar risks to that of a security in the capital market with a return of 15 percent. ROI is computed as follows:

$$\text{ROI} = \frac{\text{Profit}}{\text{Investment cost}}$$

$$= \frac{2,000,000 - 1,500,000}{1,500,000} = .33 \text{ or } 33\% \qquad (8)$$

Since the ROI of the investment is 33 percent, which is greater than the opportunity cost of capital of 15 percent, the outsourcing agreement should be accepted. The problem with this methodology is that the ROI is true only if cash flows are realized in two periods or less. When there are more than two periods, it is questionable whether this method of calculating return yields the true return considering the time-value of money (as with PV analysis). In O-I decision situations with two or more time periods, some researchers suggest using the "internal rate of return." As a result of this limitation ROI tends to be used in concert with other methodologies (Northrop 2003).

Internal Rate of Return

Internal rate of return (IRR), also called *discounted-cash-flow rate of return*, is the discount rate that seeks to achieve a zero NPV for a project. IRR is an extension of the NPV methodology where the IRR is the rate that equates the present value of the cash flows with the initial investment (Bancroft and O'Sullivan 1993; Chorafas 2003, 178; Friedlob and Schleifer 2002; Minoli 1995, 89). IRR can be used to evaluate independent or mutually exclusive O-I investment opportunities. When selecting one alternative investment among a mutually exclusive set, the investment with the highest IRR is selected, with some limitations. IRR is computed as follows:

$$\text{NPV} = C_o + \frac{C_1}{1+\text{IRR}} + \frac{C_2}{(1+\text{IRR})^2} + ...$$
$$+ \frac{C_n}{(1+\text{IRR})^n} = 0 \qquad (9)$$

where C_o is the initial investment and is always expressed as a negative value, $C_1 \ldots C_n$ are the expected cash flows, *IRR* is the internal rate of return necessary to make the equation equal to zero, and n is the number of time periods. The C values in equation (9) can be either positive or negative, depending on whether the cash is flowing in (i.e., positive value) or out (i.e., negative value).

Determining the IRR in equation (9) can be done manually as a trial-and-error process by plugging estimates for IRR into the above equation, adjusting them as necessary to achieve a NPV equal to zero. Alternatively it is much easier to use financial calculators or a spreadsheet system like *Microsoft®*

2003 *Excel®*. Regardless of how it is computed, the following rules can be used to guide the investment decision:

1. If IRR is greater than the opportunity cost of capital, then make the O-I investment.
2. If IRR is equal to or less than the opportunity cost of capital, then do not make the O-I investment.

Now examine an O-I sample IRR problem. A client firm's board of directors determined they can hire an international outsource provider to cover their information systems functions. The cost to the client firm is a one time, up-front cost of $1 million. The information systems operating costs saved on this O-I investment will be a year-end savings over the next three years of $500,000, $400,000, and $200,000, respectively. If the client firm's opportunity cost of capital is 9 percent, should they invest in this O-I deal?

Using *Microsoft®* 2003 *Excel®* and clicking "Insert," then "Function," the "Insert Function" window opens. Select the category "Financial," then scroll down and select the "IRR" function. Clicking on this function reveals a window with two open boxes. It is necessary to place the four cost values in a spreadsheet, and then refer to their location in the first box that asks for the payment estimates. In the second box place a guess. The software generates the estimated value once the stream of negative and positive cash flows is referenced. In this problem the resulting necessary interest rate to make the NPV of this O-I investment zero is 0.05726 or 5.726 percent. Since this IRR is less than the 9 percent opportunity cost of capital for the client firm, it should not be undertaken based on these cost values.

There are some limitations in the use of IRR. First, there can be more than one IRR that equates the NPV of investment to zero. Second, Descartes' "rule of signs" states there may be as many different solutions to a polynomial as there are changes of sign. So in situations where the sign of the cash flow changes, there may be as many different solutions as there are sign changes. Third, there may be situations where no IRR equates the NPV of an investment to zero. Finally, when the opportunity cost of capital is not equal for all cash flows, the question of which opportunity cost of capital should be utilized to evaluate the alternatives is another limitation of the IRR methodology. In these situations the NPV method is much more reliable than IRR in offering the best solution.

Despite these limitations, IRR is a commonly used investment methodology and can be helpful in O-I investment decisions. Some of the advantages of using the IRR methodology include it considers the time value of money, all cash flows, and yields a percentage, which boards of directors or executives can easily understand. Some of the disadvantages include the need to estimate opportunity cost of capital that can yield multiple rates of return, which in turn can yield misleading conclusions for mutually exclusive projects. Also, the methodology assumes cash flows may be reinvested at a return equal to IRR, which may not be a useful comparison in all O-I decision situations.

Accounting Rate of Return

Accounting rate of return (ARR) or the *book rate of return*, is the average annual income from an investment divided by average annual book value of the initial investment cost (Friedlob and Schleifer 2002). ARR is similar to any return measuring income or cash flows as a proportion of the initial investment amount. The ARR is compared to a "cutoff rate of return." The *cutoff rate of return* is a goal or designated rate established to determine the attractiveness of alternative investments. ARR can be computed as follows:

$$\text{ARR} = \frac{\text{Average annual net income}}{\text{Average annual book assets}} \quad (10)$$

For the formula in (10) the *average annual net income* is computed by subtracting depreciation from cash flow. *Average annual book assets* are computed by subtracting accumulative depreciation from the gross book value of the asset. These values appear on the financial statements of an organization and are different than those utilized in other methods because other methodologies use estimated cash flows attributable to an O-I investment versus book accounting values. This difference may limit the use of ARR, because most O-I agreements are not considered as a fixed investment, but an operating expense whose costs are applied against current operating cash flow. Yet, many O-I agreements involve the exchange of technology and other assets. Therefore, this methodology might have greater application.

To illustrate the use of this methodology consider a sample problem. Suppose a board of directors is evaluating an outsourcing proposal for their information security system. They must decide whether or not to invest in the proposed provider's security services or continue to insource the work. There is a one time payment (i.e., the investment) for these services of $90,000, and it is depreciated on a straight-line basis over three years. The ARR must be equal to or greater than the cutoff rate of return for other investments, which is 10 percent. The annual net income for the book assets is presented in Table 6.3. The average annual net income based on the net income values in Table 6.3 is $10,000 (i.e., ($20,000 + 0 + 10,000)/3).

The annual book assets are presented in Table 6.4. Average annual book value of assets is computed by determining the net book value of assets, which is the gross book value of assets less cumulative depreciation. As shown in Table 6.4,

Table 6.3

Annual Net Income for Sample Problem

Accounting item	Year 1	Year 2	Year 3
Cash inflow ($)	50,000	30,000	40,000
Depreciation ($)	30,000	30,000	30,000
Net income ($)	20,000	0	10,000

Table 6.4

Annual Book Value of Assets for Sample Problem

Accounting item	Year 0	Year 1	Year 2	Year 3
Gross book value of asset ($)	90,000	90,000	90,000	90,000
Cumulative Depreciation ($)	0	30,000	60,000	90,000
Net book value of asset ($)	90,000	60,000	30,000	0

the cash inflow less depreciation gives the net income for each year of the O-I investment. The resulting average annual book assets is $45,000 (i.e., ($90,000 + 60,000 + 30,000 + 0)/4).

The accounting rate of return in this problem is 22.2 percent (i.e., 10,000/45,000 = .222). Since the accounting rate of return is larger than the cutoff rate of 10 percent, the O-I investment should be undertaken.

The ARR is limited in that it does not consider the time value of money. In addition, it is dependent on the type of depreciation method utilized and the decisions concerning capitalization versus expenses (e.g., the use of straight-line depreciation verses accelerated depreciation). Book values can also be affected by the decisions accountants make as to whether a cost associated with an O-I investment is an operating expense, which is usually the case, or part of the capital investment. As a rule, if a cost is considered part of the capital investment instead of an operating expense, all else being constant, then average annual net income and average annual book assets should both increase, therefore, increasing the ARR. Alternatively, if the opposite is true and a cost is considered an operating expense instead of a capital expenditure, then the ARR ratio should decrease. Despite these limitations, ARR has been specifically identified as a useful decision-making methodology in outsourcing decisions (Minoli 1995, 92).

Payback Period

Payback period is a methodology useful in evaluating O-I investments where the payback period of an investment is compared to some pre-specified length of time referred to as the "cutoff period" (Ferguson 2003; Johnson 1999). The *payback period* is the amount of time required to recover the cost of the initial investment. The *cutoff period* is a pre-specified length of time in which an investment must recover its initial investment in order to be considered acceptable. The decision rule for the payback period methodology is:

1. If the payback period is shorter than the cutoff period, make the investment.
2. If the payback period is equal to or longer than the cutoff, do not make the investment.

Payback period methodology can also be used to compare multiple alternatives, where the shorter the payback, the better the alternative choice.

Payback period methodology involves selecting a suitable cutoff period and determining the payback period for each alternative investment. Key to using this methodology for single investment decisions is to establish benchmarks for payback periods. Each type of alternative investment in O-I has its own ideal payback period. In short-term O-I contracts the payback period might need to be a matter of months. In continuous O-I agreements, the length of the payback may be many years. Such payback period estimation of benchmarks is usually performed on expectations from the O-I industry. As mentioned in Chapter 5, O-I benchmarks can be obtained from a variety of sources including the *Outsourcing Benchmarking Association* (www.obenchmarking.com).

To illustrate the use of the payback period methodology consider the following problem. Suppose a board of directors must select one O-I proposal from a set of two alternatives (i.e., Alternatives A and B). The outsource agreement is for the installation and training of the client firm's personnel on the use of a technology that has a life of only five years. Table 6.5 presents the initial investment cost and expected profit or cash flows associated with the two alternative proposals. The initial cost is a one time payment, and the cash flows will be discontinued at the end of the expected five year life of the technology. Assuming a cutoff period of two years, which proposal should be selected?

To answer this question sum cash flow values from Table 6.5 as presented in Table 6.6. The payback period for Alternative A is 3 years and for Alternative B is 2 years. Accordingly, Alternative B would be the only choice, since it recovers the initial investment within the cutoff period.

Unfortunately, the payback method has a major limitation. This methodology equally weighs all cash flows, irrespective of the time period they are received. It ignores the time value of money. As a result, cash flows received in the future are worth less than those received earlier, so their possible discounted values are lost. If we were to use NPV on the problem above with a discount rate of 10 percent or less, the solution would favor Alternative A instead of B. Also, many O-I investment projects return little during the early periods of

Table 6.5

Cost and Cash Data for Payback Period Sample Problem

Cost or cash flow item	Alternative A	Alternative B
Initial cost ($)	1,000,000	950,000
Cash flow year 1 ($)	450,000	500,000
Cash flow year 2 ($)	450,000	450,000
Cash flow year 3 ($)	300,000	200,000
Cash flow year 4 ($)	250,000	200,000
Cash flow year 5 ($)	300,000	100,000

implementation or during the primary payback period. Yet they may return significantly more in periods subsequent to the payback period, which are not considered using this methodology.

One way to combat the disadvantages of the payback period methodology is to select an appropriate cutoff period. Another way to avoid the time value of money and discount the cash flows before calculating the payback period is called the "*discounted payback period.*" The *discounted payback period* is the number of periods necessary to recover the initial cost, using the present value of the cash flows.

Cost/Benefit Analysis

Cost/benefit analysis involves comparing the present value of benefits associated with an investment to the present value of the costs of the investment. It can be used for *ex ante* (i.e., before O-I project to make the decision), *medias res* (i.e., during the O-I project), and *ex post* (i.e., after O-I project is finished and a post analysis is called for) evaluations. Cost/benefit analysis is a widely used decision-making methodology to evaluate an independent investment and to select one from a set of independent or dependent investments (Brown et al. 2003; Domberger 1998, 71–72; Schniederjans

Table 6.6

Payback Period Computations for Sample Problem

Cost or cash flow item	Alternative A	Sum of cash flow for Alternative A	Alternative B	Sum of cash flow for Alternative B
Initial Cost ($)	1,000,000	—	950,000	—
Cash flow year 1 ($)	450,000	450,000	500,000	500,000
Cash flow year 2 ($)	450,000	900,000	450,000	950,000
Cash flow year 3 ($)	300,000	1,200,000	200,000	1,150,000
Cash flow year 4 ($)	250,000	1,450,000	200,000	1,350,000
Cash flow year 5 ($)	300,000	1,750,000	100,000	1,450,000

et al. 2004, 140–154; Weimer and Vining 2004).

Basically, cost/benefit analysis involves identifying costs and benefits for each alternative investment, discounting the costs and benefits back to the present, and selecting the best alternative according to pre-specified criteria. A cost/benefit analysis can be performed in four steps: defining the decision alternatives, identifying and quantifying costs and benefits, comparing alternatives and choosing a criteria for the decision choice, and performing sensitivity analysis.

Step 1. Define the Decision Alternatives: Defining the decision alternatives involves investigating the needs and requirements of an O-I investment and determining possible alternatives. A well-defined decision alternative includes specification of the objectives to be achieved and a plan to attain those objectives. Many of the common objectives in international O-I agreements were described in the first four chapters of this textbook (e.g., reduce costs, improve customer service, etc.), and most focus on dealing with identifying non-core competencies as strategic weaknesses, which a firm needs to enhance. This part of problem definition also involves generating all possible alternative courses of action that can strengthen non-core competencies with both outsourcing and insourcing. This might also involve narrowing

the list by eliminating unacceptable alternatives, which do not meet basic budgetary constraints, or for perceived economic, political, cultural, or demographic risk reasons.

Step 2. Identification and Quantification of Costs and Benefits: Once the O-I decision has been defined and appropriate alternatives identified, the next stage in the analysis is to determine all relevant costs and benefits associated with each. All relevant effects, whether positive or negative should be taken into consideration and assigned a dollar value. A cost is any expenditure incurred with each alternative. Costs may be tangible or intangible. Many O-I decisions are driven by *tangible costs*, such as labor costs. *Intangible costs* are effects that cannot readily be assigned a dollar value. Table 6.7 lists some of the typical costs, discussed in previous chapters, of undertaking an international O-I project.

A *benefit* is a positive consequence of an O-I project. Benefits often arise from making improvements in the way an organization performs non-competency tasks. Table 6.8 shows examples of possible benefits discussed in prior chapters.

One methodological approach to identifying costs and benefits, both tangible and intangible, involves using executive polling methods discussed in Chapter 5. This approach could simply involve

Table 6.7

Potential Costs of an O-I Project

Tangible	Intangible
Price charged by outsource provider for services	Difficulties in managing O-I relationship
Charges for altering the O-I agreement	Negative impact on employees
Reward payments for exceptional effort	Organizational restructuring
Extra legal staff to prepare agreement	Labor resistance to change
Risk of negative exchange rate change	Transition-time loss of productivity
Risk of provider failing to deliver product on time	Loss of control
Risk of unprofitable operations	Security risk issues

Table 6.8

Potential Benefits of an O-I Project

Tangible	Intangible
Cost savings	Improved asset utilization
Gain outside expertise	Improved organizational flexibility
Improved service/operations	Improved customer satisfaction
Focus on core competencies	Enhanced organizational learning
Gain outside technology	Mitigation of operating risk
Increased profits	
Improved markets	

giving executives a checklist of possible costs and benefits and asking them to indicate those that apply to a particular outsourcing proposal.

Once possible costs and benefits are identified, they must be converted into dollars for eventual comparative purposes. The tangible costs and benefits usually are expressed in terms of dollars with little complication. Cost items, like the price a provider charges the client firm in Table 6.7 or a benefit item like cost savings listed in Table 6.8, are already converted into dollars and only require a simple estimation of a fixed time horizon to adjust for the cost/benefit analysis.

The intangible costs and benefits are another matter. Several approaches can be used to deal with or quantify the intangible costs and benefits. One approach is to simply ignore them. It may be acceptable to leave intangibles out of the analysis, because of the complexity in assigning them a dollar value. Also, research on their impact in the O-I decision may reveal intangibles do not have much of an effect and can be left out of the analysis without affecting the final decision.

One approach that can be used to assess intangible costs or benefits is to utilize a "surrogate measure." A *surrogate measure* can be the value of a similar cost or benefit, which is more easily assigned a monetary value. For example, suppose a firm historically experiences labor strikes, whereby costs can be assessed per day lost due to labor disputes. They could use this figure as an estimate of labor resistance to outsourcing. An example of estimating benefits could include the relationship between improved customer service (e.g., a drop in the number of customer complaints and increased sales) and increased profit potential resulting from greater sales.

Another approach to estimating the value of intangible costs and benefits is to use a survey to determine their value. Survey methods are used extensively in cost/benefit analysis to determine the value of a cost or benefit (Brown et al. 2003). Building on the survey used to identify individual cost/benefit items in the previous step of the analysis, an additional survey could be designed to measure in dollars what an improvement in asset utilization might mean to a department. Rough estimates from a group of users can be averaged together to provide a reasonable "guess" as to a benefit's true contribution in dollars to an organization. The quantification of costs and benefits of intangibles coupled with a survey method is at best a "guess," but with a large enough sample of estimators the combined valuing of intangibles can collectively emerge with a reasonable useful cost/benefit estimate.

Step 3. Compare Alternatives and Choose a Criterion for Decision: Costs and benefits that occur in subsequent time periods should be discounted to current dollars. While in some instances, aggregate costs and benefits can be compared without considering the time value of money, it is recommended that cash flows be discounted. This could be accomplished using present value (PV) analysis of the stream of cash flows within the context of particular criterion chosen for the O-I decision. There are several criteria that can be selected for the decision choice, including maximizing the ratio of benefits to costs, maximizing net present value of net benefits, and the shortest payback period.

The *benefit/cost ratio* is the present value of benefits divided by the present value of costs. This ratio can be computed as follows:

$$\text{Benefit / cost ratio} = \frac{\sum_{t=0}^{n} \dfrac{B_t}{(1+r)^t}}{\sum_{t=0}^{n} \dfrac{C_t}{(1+r)^t}} \qquad (11)$$

where B_t is the cash flow value of benefits in t time periods, C_t is the cash flow value of costs in t time periods, r is the discount rate, and n is the number of periods that benefits and costs occur. The value of B_t and C_t where t is equal to zero represents up-front or down payment cash flows. For example, in many international O-I investment situations technology is transferred from the client firm to the outsource provider accruing an initial cash flow back to the client firm. In other O-I situations, the outsource provider may require an up-front payment (representing a cost to the client firm) to give them the necessary start-up capital for recruiting personnel or buying technology to support the O-I agreement.

The interpretation of this ratio is simple. Unless the ratio is above one, the costs will exceed benefits, and in the case of a single proposal, it should be rejected. In situations where there is more than one alternative being considered, the larger the resulting benefit/cost ratio, the more desirable or beneficial the alternative choice will be.

To illustrate the use of benefit/cost ratio, let us suppose an outsourcing team made up of middle-level managers has been empowered to choose an outsource provider. The team has narrowed the final selection down to two firms (i.e., Outsource Provider A or B), which are located within the same country as the client firm. The team previously prepared a "request for proposal" (discussed in Chapter 4). Based on the responses of the two outsource providers, a listing of possible costs and benefits were identified. The listing of these costs and benefits, along with estimated dollar values, are presented in Tables 6.9 and 6.10. Note in Tables 6.9 and 6.10, different outsource providers can offer differing benefits. This should not matter as long as they are expressed or quantified in terms of monetary values for the client firm.

Totaling the costs and benefits on the tables and assuming the discount rate of eight percent,

Table 6.9

Costs and Benefits of Outsource Provider A

Costs (all numbers in $1,000):	C_0	C_1	C_2	C_3	C_4	C_5
Initial up-front cost	1,000	500	500	500	500	500
Allowance for missing deadlines	—	100	100	100	100	100
Extra legal staff	100	100	100	100	100	100
Total Costs	**1,100**	**700**	**700**	**700**	**700**	**700**
Benefits:	B_0	B_1	B_2	B_3	B_4	B_5
Increased productivity	—	1,000	1,000	1,000	1,000	1,000
Increased market share	—	1,000	1,000	1,000	1,000	1,000
Total Benefits		**2,000**	**2,000**	**2,000**	**2,000**	**2,000**

Table 6.10

Costs and Benefits of Outsource Provider B

Costs (all numbers in $1,000):	C_0	C_1	C_2	C_3	C_4	C_5
Initial up-front cost	700	600	600	600	600	600
Allowance for missing deadlines	—	100	100	100	100	100
Extra legal staff	100	100	100	100	100	100
Total Costs	**800**	**800**	**800**	**800**	**800**	**800**
Benefits:	B_0	B_1	B_2	B_3	B_4	B_5
Increased productivity	—	800	800	800	800	800
Reduced workforce savings	—	1,000	1,000	1,000	1,000	1,000
Gain unique outside technology	—	300	300	300	300	300
Total Benefits		**2,100**	**2,100**	**2,100**	**2,100**	**2,100**

the desired PVs for the benefit/cost ratio can be computed. The PVs for the costs and benefits for Outsource Provider A are:

$$\text{PVcosts}_{\text{for A}} = \frac{1,100,000}{(1+0.08)^0} + \frac{700,000}{1+0.08} + \frac{700,000}{(1+0.08)^2} +$$

$$\frac{700,000}{(1+0.08)^3} + \frac{700,000}{(1+0.08)^4} + \frac{700,000}{(1+0.08)^5}$$

$$= \$3,894,867.03 \tag{12}$$

$$\text{PVbenefits}_{\text{for A}} = \frac{2,000,000}{1+0.08} + \frac{2,000,000}{(1+0.08)^2} +$$

$$\frac{2,000,000}{(1+0.08)^3} + \frac{2,000,000}{(1+0.08)^4} + \frac{2,000,000}{(1+0.08)^5}$$

$$= \$7,985,420.074 \tag{13}$$

The PVs for the costs and benefits for Outsource Provider B are

$$\text{PV costs} \atop \text{for B} = \frac{800,000}{(1+0.08)^0} + \frac{800,000}{1+0.08} + \frac{800,000}{(1+0.08)^2} +$$

$$\frac{800,000}{(1+0.08)^3} + \frac{800,000}{(1+0.08)^4} + \frac{800,000}{(1+0.08)^5}$$

$$= \$3,994,168.030 \tag{14}$$

$$\text{PV benefits} \atop \text{for B} = \frac{2,100,000}{1+0.08} + \frac{2,100,000}{(1+0.08)^2} +$$

$$\frac{2,100,000}{(1+0.08)^3} + \frac{2,100,000}{(1+0.08)^4} + \frac{2,100,000}{(1+0.08)^5}$$

$$= \$8,384,691.078 \tag{15}$$

Having calculated the present value of the costs and benefits for each provider, insert the values into the numerator and denominator of the benefit/cost ratio from equation (12) as presented in Table 6.11. Since the benefit/cost ratio for Outsource Provider B is larger than for A, B should be selected.

A second criterion (instead of the benefit/cost ratio) is to select the alternative having the largest net present value of net benefits. The *net present value of net benefits* is calculated as the present value of benefits minus the present value of costs discounted to the present. The net present value of net benefits can be computed as:

$$\text{Net Present Value} = \frac{B_0 - C_0}{(1+r)^0} + \frac{B_1 - C_1}{(1+r)^1} + ... + \frac{B_n - C_n}{(1+r)^n} \tag{16}$$

where B is the value of benefits, C is the value of costs, r is the discount rate, and n is the number of periods that benefits and costs occur. Using the same outsourcing sample problem information from Tables 6.9 and 6.10, the NPVs for both outsource providers can be computed. The NPV for Outsource Provider A is:

$$\text{NPV(A)} = \frac{0 - 1100}{(1+.08)^0} + \frac{2,000 - 700}{(1+.08)^1} + \frac{2,000 - 700}{(1+.08)^2}$$

$$+ \frac{2,000 - 700}{(1+.08)^3} + \frac{2,000 - 700}{(1+.08)^4} + \frac{2,000 - 700}{(1+.08)^5}$$

$$= \$4,090,523.048 \tag{17}$$

Table 6.11

Benefit/Cost Ratios for Outsource Sample Problem

	Outsource Provider A	Outsource Provider B
Benefit/ Cost Ratios	B/C = $\frac{7,985,420}{3,894,867}$ = 2.05	B/C = $\frac{8,384,691}{3,994,168}$ = 2.10

The NPV for Outsource Provider B is:

$$\text{NPV(B)} = \frac{0 - 800}{(1+.08)^0} + \frac{2,100 - 800}{(1+.08)^1} + \frac{2,100 - 800}{(1+.08)^2}$$

$$+ \frac{2,100 - 800}{(1+.08)^3} + \frac{2,100 - 800}{(1+.08)^4} + \frac{2,100 - 800}{(1+.08)^5}$$

$$= \$4,390,523.048 \tag{18}$$

Based on these NPVs, Outsource Provider B is the better choice. Note using this methodology, it is clear only the initial cost of $300,000 (i.e., $1,100,000–$800,000) differentiates the two outsourcing proposals.

The third criterion is the *payback period,* which was previously discussed in this chapter. Again in the outsource provider selection problem, the information in Tables 6.9 and 6.10 can be used, particularly the total costs and total benefits rows. By netting the totals the cumulative net cash flows for both outsource provider proposals can be determined and are shown in Table 6.12. As can be seen in this table, both proposals paid back the initial cost by the first year. While Provider B's proposal was initially $300,000 less expensive, it therefore, consistently afforded more money to the client firm than Provider A's proposal. There is no clear choice based on this criterion for this sample problem.

Step 4. Perform Sensitivity Analysis: We can define *sensitivity analysis* as a methodology useful in determining the reliability of a decision generated from a cost/benefit analysis. If the cost

Table 6.12

Payback Period Data for Outsourcing Sample Problem

Cost or cash flow item (all numbers in $1,000)	Provider A net cash flows	Cumulative net cash flow from A	Provider B net cash flows	Cumulative net cash flow from B
Initial cost	1,100		800	
Year 1 cash flow	1,300	1,300	1,300	1,300
Year 2 cash flow	1,300	2,600	1,300	2,600
Year 3 cash flow	1,300	3,900	1,300	3,900
Year 4 cash flow	1,300	5,200	1,300	5,200
Year 5 cash flow	1,300	6,500	1,300	6,500

and benefit values used in a given cost/benefit analysis are known with certainty, the resulting O-I decision will be fully reliable. Unfortunately, many cost and benefit values used in cost/benefit analysis, especially those for intangible costs and benefits, are only estimates of true values and undoubtedly contain some error. The degree of error in estimates determines the reliability of the final decision yielded by the analysis. We can determine some degree of error in the estimates by performing a sensitivity analysis.

There are many variations in performing sensitivity analysis, but a common way is to select costs, benefits, or other parameters and vary them in order to examine their impact on an existing solution. The analysis may involve selecting high and low values of a parameter, plugging them into the model and assessing the impact on a decision. This is important in making O-I decisions because many O-I agreements have *sliding-rates* (i.e., a range of rates that can be charged based on service activity). For example, an outsource agreement might allow a provider to charge from $1,000 to $1,200 per hour to cover service calls for an information service help desk depending on the requests for service. In a cost/benefit analysis, that range would be converted to a point estimate, representative of the possibilities of cost. The mid-

point of the range, or $1,100 (i.e., between $1,000 and $1,200) could be selected as a parameter to estimate possible charges for service from this provider. As a means of checking the sensitivity of the solution, it should be run again, using the low value of $1,000 and once again with the high value of $1,200 to see if resulting changes alter the existing solution. If the solution does not change, then the parameter is not sensitive, so possible error will not impact the outcome of the original choice. On the other hand, if varying the parameter changes the solution, it is clear this parameter is important. Greater estimation efforts should be given to improve the final estimate used in the analysis. This could mean re-writing the agreement to limit the range or obtaining expert opinions to guide the final parameter selection more accurately.

There are other sensitivity analysis methods available for examining the accuracy of parameters and decisions based upon them. For a more in-depth discussion see Sassone and Schaffer (1978).

An International Context Risk Rejoinder

As a general rule in dealing with risks, particularly risks that exist in international business, boards of directors and middle-level managers may establish a "*risk management program.*" In any *risk management program*, once risks have been identified, they can be managed by selecting a strategy that:

1. seeks to avoid the risk,
2. accepts the risk,
3. seeks to reduce the risk, or
4. transfers the risk to someone else.

Avoid a risk by making a less risky decision when it is appropriate and when the risk is not greater than the threshold to accept it. Accepting the risk, seeking to reduce it, or even trying to transfer it to the outsource provider are all strategies, which invite risk into the decision, and therefore mandate inclusion of it in the analysis. Indeed, if a client firm tries to transfer risk to an outsource provider, they may actually be accepting the risk, since the failure of the provider will impact the client firm. As a result, it is critical to assess and factor international O-I risks into financial computations used to determine outsourcing strategies.

Making a decision to let an international outsourcing firm undertake some of the business activities for a client firm invites almost all of the same risks organizations take in becoming international. Many of the risk factor assessment methodologies suggested in Chapter 5 can be used to determine specific international economic, political, cultural, and demographic risk values useful in making parameter adjustments in the financial methodologies presented in this chapter. To illustrate how risk can be factored into the financial analysis methodologies presented in this chapter, consider a board of directors, utilizing the Delphi method (from Chapter 5) with a group of experts, having assessed a percentage to reflect the economic riskiness of entering into an international outsourcing agreement with two outsource provider firms located in different countries (e.g., Mexico and Canada). Assume the higher the risk

factor percentage, the greater the risk in undertaking the outsourcing agreement, where risk is expressed in decimal form for each alternative, and ranges from 0.00 (no risk) to 1.00 (very high risk). For purposes of illustration, this particular international risk factor is determined by looking at the possibility of an exchange rate change between the client firm and the two countries in question. Specifically, what are the chances the exchange rate will cause a need for revision in what is paid to the client firm? By averaging the Mexican peso and the Canadian dollar against the client firm's currency, an average percentage of currency change can be determined. The Mexican Provider A firm has an assessed risk factor of 0.06 percent, indicating there is a 0.06 percent possibility that an unfavorable exchange rate of currency will take place. The Canadian Provider B firm has an assessed risk factor of 0.02 percent, indicating there is a 0.02 percent possibility that an unfavorable exchange rate of currency will occur. Also, the client firm chooses to use the payback method in their decision. How can this international risk factor be incorporated in a payback method analysis?

One simple way to factor risk into the payback method is to reduce the cash flow benefits of the two providers in proportion to the risk. (Note: there are many possible alternative ways of using risk factors, like those with greater or lesser impact on the cost parameters.) If a reduction in a cash (i.e., cost or benefit) parameter is indicated, the formula below can be used if the risk factor is expressed in decimal form on a range from 0.00 (no risk) to 1.00 (very high risk):

$$\text{Risk factor adjustment} = \frac{C_1}{1 + \text{risk}} + \frac{C_2}{1 + \text{risk}} +$$

$$.... + \frac{C_n}{1 + \text{risk}} \qquad (19)$$

Table 6.13

Payback Period Risk Adjustment Computations for Sample Problem

Cost or cash flow item	Mexican Outsource Provider A	Risk factor adjustment (0.06)	Sum of cash flow for Outsource Provider A	Canadian Outsource Provider B	Risk factor adjustment (0.02)]	Sum of cash flow for Outsource Provider B
Initial Cost ($)	1,000,000	—	—	1,200,000	—	—
Cash flow year 1 ($)	500,000	$\frac{500,000}{1+0.06}$ =471,698.11	471,698.11	800,000	$\frac{800,000}{1+0.02}$ =784,313.72	7,843,13.72
Cash flow year 2 ($)	500,000	$\frac{500,000}{1+0.06}$ =471,698.11	943,396.22	600,000	$\frac{600,000}{1+0.02}$ =588,235.29	1,372,549.01
Cash flow year 3 ($)	300,000	$\frac{300,000}{1+0.06}$ =283,018.86	1,226,415.08	100,000	$\frac{100,000}{1+0.02}$ =98,039.22	1,470,588.23
Cash flow year 4 ($)	200,000	$\frac{200,000}{1+0.06}$ =188,679.24	1,415,094.32	100,000	$\frac{100,000}{1+0.02}$ =98,039.22	1,568,627.45

A risk factor above 1.00 is possible, but implies the cash flow should be reduced to an amount less then half of its original estimated value. Assume the estimated cash flows for the two international outsource providers (i.e., A and B) are presented in Table 6.13. The "risk factor adjustment" columns show the computations for the cash flow adjustments. As can be seen in Table 6.13, with the adjustments, Provider B is able to pay back the initial cost in two years versus Provider A's three-year payback period. Note without the risk adjustment to the cash flows to Provider A, its payback would have occurred in two years. So in this problem the risk adjustment did have an impact on the final choice.

Most of the parameters in the financial methodologies presented in this chapter can be adjusted for perceived risk. Table 6.14 lists common parameters used in the models in this chapter and offers suggestions as to how the parameters could be adjusted to reflect international risk factors encountered in a typical O-I arrangement.

Alternative Unit Break-Even/Risk Methodology

In situations where a client firm's unit production is identified as a possible candidate for outsourcing, the O-I decision is a classic subcontracting, "buy-or-make" decision that firms have faced since the beginning of business history. One of the classic buy-or-make methodologies that can be applied here is a total cost break-even model, where "to buy" means outsourcing and "to make" means insourcing. Reid and Sanders (2005, 113–114) present a break-even model by first defining total cost under insourcing as:

Table 6.14

Suggested Adjustments to Financial Parameters for International Risk

Financial parameter	Perceived direction risk	Suggested adjustment on financial parameter
Benefit cash flow (B_t)	Higher	Lower cash flow
Benefit cash flow (B_t)	Lower	Increase cash flow
Cost cash flow (C_t)	Higher	Increase cash flow
Cost cash flow (C_t)	Lower	Lower cash flow
Discount rate (r)	Higher	Raise discount rate
Discount rate (r)	Lower	Lower discount rate
Time period (t)	Higher	Increase time periods
Time period (t)	Lower	Decrease time periods

$$TC_{in} = FC_{in} + (VC_{in} \times Q_{in}) \qquad (20)$$

where TC_{in} is the total cost of an item produced by insourcing, FC_{in} is the total fixed cost of an item produced by insourcing, VC_{in} is the total variable cost of an item produced by insourcing, and Q is the total number of units produced by insourcing. Using this same approach total cost under outsourcing can be defined as:

$$TC_{out} = FC_{out} + (VC_{out} \times Q_{out}) \qquad (21)$$

where TC_{out} is the total cost of an item produced by outsource provider, FC_{out} is the total fixed cost of an item produced by outsource provider, VC_{out} is the total variable cost of an item produced by the outsource provider, and Q is the total number of units produced by outsource provider. At an ideal break-even point $Q_{in} = Q_{out}$ and $TC_{in} = TC_{out}$, by letting $Q = Q_{in} = Q_{out}$ (i.e., Q becomes the unknown variable), the two equations (20 and 21) can be restated in terms of each other:

$$FC_{in} + (VC_{in} \times Q) = FC_{out} + (VC_{out} \times Q) \qquad (22)$$

By solving for the value of Q in (22) how many units must be outsourced or insourced can be determined in order to reach a break-even point in total costs from both possible sources:

$$Q = \frac{FC_{in} - FC_{out}}{VC_{out} - VC_{in}} \qquad (23)$$

The model in equation (23) assumes the value for Q cannot be negative, and if Q is negative the model becomes invalid. To use equation (23) for the O-I decision, a desired or expected demand in units a client firm seeks to achieve must be known. Denote this expected demand in units as Q^*. This value is the number of units needed to meet customer demand for a fixed period of time, usually a year. The decision rules for using the formula in equation (23) are depicted in Figure 6.2. As seen in the graph in Figure 6.2, if the value of Q from the model computation is less than Q^*, choose the source (i.e., either insource or outsource) that provides the lower fixed cost and the higher variable cost. If the value of Q from the model computation is more than Q^*, choose the source that provides the lower variable cost, because for each unit be-

Figure 6.2   **Decision Rules for Unit Break-even Model**

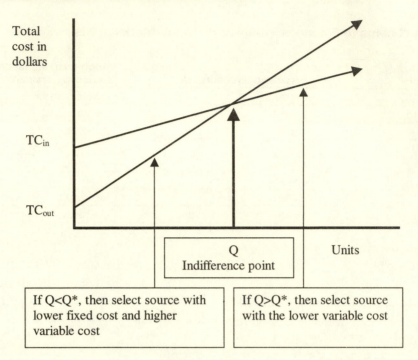

yond Q the firm will save the difference between the higher and lower variable costs per unit. If Q is equal to Q^*, then the decision maker can arbitrarily select outsourcing or insourcing.

Schniederjans and Zuckweiler (2004) believe the simple unit break-even model needs to have mathematical adjustments reflecting risk factors inherent in financial parameters when using international O-I as a strategy. They incorporate international risk factors in the model in equation (23) as mathematical adjustments as follows:

$$Q = \frac{\Sigma (FC_{in} \times RF_{in}) - \Sigma (FC_{out} \times RF_{out})}{\Sigma (VC_{out} \times RV_{out}) - \Sigma (VC_{in} \times RV_{in})} \quad (24)$$

where the sum (Σ) of the products of the various cost parameters and the respective probable occurrence (representing the riskiness) for all parameters in the model, RF_{in} is the probable occurrence (in decimal form) of the insourcing fixed cost parameter, RF_{out} is the probable occurrence of the outsourcing fixed cost parameter in international operations, RV_{in} is the probable occurrence of the insourcing variable cost parameter, and RV_{out} is the probable occurrence of the outsourcing variable cost parameter in international operations. The risk factors can be based on simple probabilities. (We will discuss probability estimation methods in Chapter 7.)

To illustrate the unit break-even model in equation (23) consider a simple, one product problem. Suppose a client firm is currently insourcing all of its single product production with a yearly fixed cost of $2 million (i.e., FC_{in}) and a variable cost per unit of $3 (i.e., VC_{in}). The client firm is approached by an outsource provider who can produce a product of equal quality for a yearly fixed cost payment of $1 million (i.e., FC_{out}) and a variable cost per unit of $4 (i.e., VC_{out}). The client firm is now facing a new yearly demand of 1.1 million units (i.e., Q^*). Should the client firm outsource or continue to insource production? Plugging the values in equation (23), the unit break-even point is as follows:

$$Q = \frac{FC_{in} - FC_{out}}{VC_{out} - VC_{in}} = \frac{2,000,000 - 1,000,000}{4 - 3}$$

$$= 1,000,000 \text{ units} \qquad (25)$$

Since the computed $Q < Q^*$ or 1 million is less than the expected demand of 1.1 million units, the decision rules favor the outsource provider with the lower fixed cost and higher variable cost. Now suppose the client firm has learned that the fixed cost parameter for the outsource provider is now uncertain, such that there is a 20 percent chance fixed costs will be $1.2 million and an 80 percent chance they will be $750,000. How can this new risk information in the unit break-even model be incorporated? Using the *unit break-even/risk model* in equation (24), and assuming no other risk information is available on the other three parameters, this new modeling situation is expressed as:

$$Q = \frac{(FC_{in} \times RF_{in}) - (FC_{out} \times RF_{out})}{(VC_{out} \times RV_{out}) - (VC_{in} \times RV_{in})}$$

$$= \frac{(2,000,000 \times 1.0) - [(1,200,000 \times 0.2) + (750,000 \times 0.8)]}{(4 \times 1.0) - (3 \times 1.0)}$$

$$= 1,160,000 \text{ units} \qquad (26)$$

Since the computed $Q > Q^*$ or 1.16 million is greater than the expected demand of 1.1 million units, the decision rule using the unit break-even model now favors the insourcer in this risk revised problem.

While the unit break-even models in equations (22) or (23) are limited in considering one product at a time, these models can be expanded to include more than one product, and a new Q formula, such as that in equations (23) or (24), can be determined algebraically. It can also be used to handle any additional criteria assessed on the basis of product cost per unit. For firms looking to outsource the manufacturing of a single product or a group of products to an outsource provider, where cost is a major factor, this model may be appropriate. Considering how much cost minimization has been a driving force in the outsourcing industry, it may be an ideal initial decision in O-I methodology (McDougall 2004).

Summary

This chapter presented a collection of finance-based methodologies useful in the initial decision of using international O-I at the strategic and tactical levels of planning. The financial methods presented included present value analysis, break-even analysis, return on investment, internal rate of return, accounting rate of return, payback period method, and cost/benefit analysis. The chapter ended with a brief discussion on how international risk considered in using financial methodologies.

Every method presented in this chapter could be used to compare external outsourcing with internal insourcing, since both represent alternative or mutually exclusive financial investments. They are also useful in tactical outsourcing partner planning decisions. So critical is the outsourcing partner decision, it is mentioned it in every chapter. The entire next chapter is devoted solely to this step in the international O-I planning process.

Review Terms

Accounting rate of return (ARR)
Annual cost
Average annual book assets
Average annual net income
Benefit
Benefit/cost ratio
Book rate of return
Break-even analysis
Cost/benefit analysis
Cost of capital
Cutoff period
Cutoff rate of return
Discount rate
Discounted payback period
Discounted-cash-flow rate of return
Ex ante
Ex post
Initial cost
Intangible costs

Internal rate of return (IRR)
Medias res
Net costs
Net present value (NPV)
Net present value of net benefits
Non-quantifiable benefits
Opportunity cost of capital
Outsourcing-insourcing (O-I)
Payback period
Present value (PV)
Present value analysis
Return on investment (ROI)
Risk management program
Sensitivity analysis
Sliding rates
Surrogate measure
Tangible costs
Unit break-even/risk model

Discussion Questions

1. What is the primary reason that present value (PV) analysis is useful in investment decisions?

2. Why is a discount rate used in present value analysis?

3. What is a major limitation of the payback period methodology as it relates to outsourcing decisions?

4. How are surrogate measures used in cost/benefit analysis?

5. How can we incorporate international risk into the financial planning methodologies used for outsourcing decisions?

Concept Questions

1. What is the difference between present value (PV) and net present value (NPV)?

2. What are we trying to find the break-even point for when we do a break-even analysis?

3. What are the decision criteria in the return on investment (ROI) methodology?

4. What is the difference between internal rate of return (IRR) and accounting rate of return (ARR)?

5. What steps does a cost/benefit analysis involve?

6. What are the criteria for making a decision using cost/benefit analysis?

Methodology Problems

1. A board of directors wants to determine how much they can save by adopting an international O-I strategy. Looking at the costs of insourcing the work versus using an outsource provider, they

estimate $5 million average cash flow savings per year for three years from the outsourcing strategy. Assume the client firm's cost of capital, or discount rate, is ten percent. What is the PV of this outsourcing venture?

2. An outsourcing team wants to calculate the savings to be realized by adopting an international O-I strategy. Looking at the costs of insourcing the work versus outsourcing it, they estimate $10 million average cash flow savings per year for four years is possiblefrom outsourcing. Assume the client firm's cost of capital, or discount rate, is nine percent. What is the PV of this outsourcing venture?

3. An outsourcing team is trying to select one of two outsource providers, Provider A or Provider B. The costs of contractual arrangements with the two outsource providers are different and affect the client firm's cash flow uniquely for every year of the three years the agreement is expected to run. Suppose Provider A requires a $3 million initial payment and a fixed year-end payment of $250,000, while Provider B requires a $1.5 million initial payment and a fixed year-end payment of $300,000. For years one through three, an agreement with Provider A will result in estimated yearly cash flows to the client firm of $1.2 million, $1.5 million, and $2 million, respectively. For years one through three, an agreement with Provider B will result in estimated yearly cash flows to the client firm of $2 million, $1.5 million, and $1 million, respectively. Assuming that the client firm's discount rate is twelve percent, use the criterion of net present value to determine which of the two outsource providers is offering the better financial deal.

4. Suppose a board of directors must decide whether to undertake an outsourcing strategy. The costs and benefits of the proposed O-I strategy have been evaluated by executives and are presented in the table below. The initial cost of the O-I agreement, which pays for the provider to hire new personnel, is $1 million, with an annual cost for the provider services of $250,000 for each of four years. Assume the discount rate is twelve percent. The anticipated benefits are reduced costs of production for the client firm of $750,000 per year for each of the four years, and there is an intangible benefit of improved product quality. Using break-even analysis, what would the benefit of "improved company image" have to be worth to make this project acceptable?

Cost or benefit item	Year 0	Year 1	Year 2	Year 3	Year 4
Costs (per thousand):					
Up-front cost ($)	1,000				
Annual cost ($)		250	250	250	250
Benefits:					
Reduced costs of production ($)		750	750	750	750
Improved company image		—	—	—	—

5. Assume the estimated total cost of an outsourcing agreement is $2 million for a one-year project. It is expected that the resulting benefits to the client firm at the end of the first year will be $3 million. If this investment has a risk similar to that of a security in a capital market with a return of 20 percent, would it be a worthwhile investment according to the return on investment (ROI) methodology?

6. A firm must pay an up-front fee of $5 million for a one-year outsourcing project. It is expected that the resulting benefits to the client firm at the end of the first year will be $6 million. If this investment has a risk similar to that of a security in a

capital market with a return of 10 percent, would it be a worthwhile investment according to the return on investment (ROI) methodology?

7. If the opportunity cost of capital is 15 percent and the internal rate of return (IRR) on an O-I investment is 16.5 percent, should the O-I investment be made?

8. If the opportunity cost of capital is 12 percent and the internal rate of return (IRR) on an O-I investment is 11.5 percent, should the O-I investment be made?

9. If the average annual net income on an O-I project is $12 million and the average annual book assets are $24 million, what is the accounting rate of return (ARR) for this project?

10. Given the values in the table below, what is the accounting rate of return (ARR)?

Accounting item		Year 1	Year 2	Year 3
Cash inflow ($)		60,000	30,000	50,000
Depreciation ($)		30,000	30,000	30,000
Net income ($)		30,000	0	20,000
Accounting item	Year 0	Year 1	Year 2	Year 3
Gross book value of asset ($)	90,000	90,000	90,000	90,000
Cumulative depreciation ($)	0	30,000	60,000	90,000
Net book value of asset ($)	90,000	60,000	30,000	0

11. If the cutoff rate for an outsourcing project is an accounting rate of return (ARR) of 12 percent, and the computed ARR is 15 percent, should the project be undertaken?

12. A client firm has a payback period benchmark of three years on all of its projects. The estimated payback period for an outsourcing project turns out to be 3.1 years. Should the firm accept or reject this project?

13. Given the cost/cash flows for the three alternatives in the table below, which alternative

should be selected if the payback period must be within 3 years?

Cost or cash flow item	Alternative A	Alternative B	Alternative C
Initial cost ($)	1,000,000	950,000	850,000
Cash flow year 1 ($)	500,000	400,000	400,000
Cash flow year 2 ($)	200,000	300,000	450,000
Cash flow year 3 ($)	200,000	200,000	200,000
Cash flow year 4 ($)	250,000	200,000	100,000
Cash flow year 5 ($)	300,000	100,000	100,000

14. If the sum of the discounted benefits for an outsourcing project is $500,000, and the sum of the discounted costs is $300,000, is this an attractive project based on its benefit/cost ratio?

15. A client firm is trying to choose one of two O-I providers using cost/benefit analysis. Below are cost and benefit data for Provider A:

Costs (all numbers in $1,000):	C_0	C_1	C_2	C_3	C_4
Initial up-front cost	800	400	300	400	300
Overtime pay allowance	—	100	100	100	100
Total Costs	800	500	400	500	400
Benefits:	B_0	B_1	B_2	B_3	B_4
Increased productivity	—	900	800	700	600
Decreased costs	—	900	500	500	500
Total Benefits		1,800	1,300	1,200	1,100

Below are cost and benefit data for Provider B:

Costs (All numbers in $1,000):	C_0	C_1	C_2	C_3	C_4
Initial up-front cost	900	500	500	500	500
Overtime pay allowance	—	100	100	100	100
Total Costs	900	600	600	600	600
Benefits:	B_0	B_1	B_2	B_3	B_4
Increased productivity	—	1,200	500	500	500
Decreased costs	—	900	500	500	500
Total Benefits	—	2,100	1,000	1,000	1,000

Using the benefit/cost ratio as a criterion for selection, which outsource provider should the client firm choose? Do not discount cost or cash flows.

16. (Refer to the cost and benefit data in the tables for problem 15.) Using the net present value of net benefits as a criterion for selection, which outsource provider should the client firm choose? Assume a discount rate of 10 percent.

17. Suppose a client firm is currently insourcing all of its single product production, with a yearly fixed cost (FC_{in}) of $5 million and a variable cost per unit (VC_{in}) of $2. The client firm is approached by an outsource provider that can manufacture the product with equal quality for a yearly fixed cost payment (FC_{out}) of $2 million and a variable cost per unit (VC_{out}) of $6. The client firm is now facing a yearly demand (Q^*) of two million units. Using the unit break-even model, should the client firm outsource or continue to insource the manufacture of this product?

18. Suppose a client firm is currently insourcing all its single product production with a yearly fixed cost of $7 million and a variable cost per unit of $3. The client firm has published a request for information and found an outsource provider that can manufacture the product with equal quality for a yearly fixed cost payment of $3 million and a variable cost per unit of $8. The client firm is now facing a yearly demand of 1.5 million units. Using the unit break-even model, should the client firm outsource or continue to insource the manufacture of this product?

References

Adler, R. W. "Strategic Investment Decision Appraisal Techniques: The Old and New." *Business Horizons* (November–December, 2000): 15–22.

Bancroft, G., and O'Sullivan, G. *Quantitative Methods of Accounting and Business.* 3rd ed. St. Louis: McGraw-Hill, 1993.

Birrer, G. E., and Carrica, J. L. *Present Value Applications for Accountants and Financial Planners.* New York: Greenwood Publishing Group, 1990.

Brealey, R. A., and Myers, S. C. *Principles of Corporate Finance.* 6th ed. New York: McGraw-Hill, 2000.

Brown, R., Campbell, H., and Brown, R. P. *Benefit-Cost Analysis.* Cambridge: Cambridge University Press, 2003.

Chorafas, D. N. *Outsourcing, Insourcing and IT for Enterprise Management.* Houndmills, Great Britain: Palgrave/MacMillan, 2003.

Copeland, T. E., and Westland, J. F. *Financial Theory and Corporate Policy.* Reading, MA: Addison-Wesley, 1988.

Domberger, S. *The Contracting Organization: A Strategic Guide to Outsourcing.* Oxford: Oxford University Press, 1998.

Droms, W. G. *Financial and Accounting for Nonfinancial Managers.* 5th ed. Boulder, CO: Perseus Publishing, 2003.

Ferguson, S. *Financial Analysis of M&A Integration.* Homewood, IL: McGraw-Hill, 2003.

Franceschini, F.; Galetto, M.; Pignatelli, A.; and Varetto, M. "Outsourcing: Guidelines for a Structured Approach." *Benchmarking: An International Journal* 10, no. 3 (2003): 246–261.

Friedlob, G. T., and Schleifer, L. *Essentials of Corporate Performance Measurement.* New York: Wiley, 2002.

Gouge, I. *Shaping the IT Organization.* London: Springer, 2003.

Johnson, H. *Maximizing the Value of the Firm.* Essex, England: Pearson Education, 1999.

Jurison, J. "The Role of Risk and Return on Information Technology Outsourcing Decisions." *Journal of Information Technology* 10, no. 4 (1995): 239–247.

Kee, R. C., and Robbins, W. A. "Public Sector Outsourcing: A Modified Decision Model." *Journal of Government Financial Management* 52, no. 2 (Summer 2003): 46–52.

McDougall, P. "The Offshore Equation: Is Offshoring Worth the Heat? The Financials are Compelling, and the Benefits May Well Ripple Throughout the Economy." *Information-Week* (Sept. 6, 2004), www.informationweek.com/story/showArticle.jhtml?articleID=46800044&tid=16008.

Minoli, D. *Analyzing Outsourcing.* New York: McGraw-Hill, 1995.

Northrop, R. "Hidden Cost of ROI." *Intelligent Enterprise* 6, no. 10 (2003): 46–48.

Plewa, F. J., and Friedlob, G. T. *Understanding Return on Investment.* New York: Wiley, 2001.

Reid, R. D., and Sanders, N. R. *Operations Management.* New York: Wiley, 2005.

Sassone, P. G, and Schaffer, W. *Cost-Benefit Analysis: A Handbook.* New York: Academic Press, 1978.

Schniederjans, M. J.; Hamaker, J. L.; and Schniederjans, A. M. *Information Technology Investment: Decision-Making Methodology.* Singapore: World Scientific Publishing, 2004.

Schniederjans, M. J., and Zuckweiler, K. "A Quantitative Approach to the Outsourcing-Insourcing Decision in an International Context." *Management Decision* 42, no. 8 (2004): 974–986.

Weimer, D. L., and Vining, A. R. *Policy Analysis: Concepts and Practice.* Upper Saddle River, NJ: Prentice-Hall, 2004.

7

Methodologies for Selecting Outsourcing-Insourcing Partners

Learning Objectives   After completing this chapter you should be able to:

- Describe preliminary considerations, including risk factors, involved in selecting an O-I partner.
- Describe international risk factors to consider in selecting an outsource provider.
- Explain how benchmarking can be used as an ex ante method of selecting an outsource provider.
- Explain how benchmarking can be used as an ex post method of selecting an outsource provider.
- Explain how decision theory methods can be used to help select an outsource provider.
- Explain the difference between the use of the expected value criterion and the use of the expected opportunity loss criterion in decision making.
- Explain how the Laplace criterion can be used to make decisions under uncertainty.
- Explain how the maximax criterion can be used to make decisions under uncertainty.
- Explain how the maximin criterion can be used to make decisions under uncertainty.
- Explain how the Hurwicz criterion can be used to make decisions under uncertainty.
- Explain how the minimax criterion can be used to make decisions under uncertainty.
- Explain how the centroid method can be used to select an outsource provider when the client firm needs to minimize distance between itself and the provider.

Introduction

The importance of selecting outsourcing-insourcing partners should not be underestimated (Hamblen 2002). Other than the decision to use outsourcing as a strategy in the first place, there is no more important decision than finding the right provider

(Mamaghani 2000; Michell and Fitzgerald 1997). That is why Chapter 4 discussed partner selection in international O-I and suggested a risk assessment methodology to aid in selecting an outsourcing partner. Chapter 5 demonstrated how rating/scoring metrics with multi-criteria scoring methods could be used to select outsource providers, while Chapter 6

Figure 7.1   **Application of This Chapter's Methodologies to International O-I Planning**

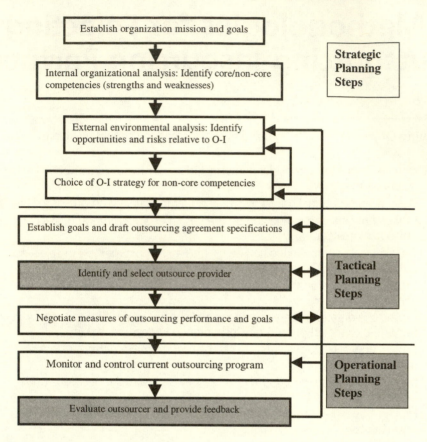

illustrated various financial methodologies that may be employed for this purpose. While these methodologies can apply to a broad range of decision-making situations, this chapter will focus entirely on the tactical step in O-I planning, and specifically the selection of an outsource provider. In addition, some of the methodologies suggested in this chapter can be used at the operational level of planning, where a client firm might wish to conduct a comparative analysis to evaluate a current outsource provider or select a new one. These areas of application to the international O-I planning process are presented in Figure 7.1.

To begin with, we will expand on the discussion from Chapter 5 of the use of benchmarking as a means of selecting outsource providers. We will also discuss the use of decision theory and distance-minimizing methodologies from the field of *operations research* as techniques helpful in selecting providers. Operations research uses mathematical modeling to solve business and engineering problems.

Consistent with the international O-I planning process diagrammed in Figure 7.1, assume that a firm has sent out and received *requests for information* (RFI) (a topic discussed in Chapter 4). An RFI explains the need for an outsource partner and the capabilities required of the provider. Proposals sent by outsource providers in response to the

RFI allow the client firm to select one outsource provider from a set of alternative providers.

Preliminary Selection Considerations and Risk Factors

Choosing an outsource provider involves screening out less attractive candidates. The preliminary screening steps for reviewing proposals from outsource providers involve assessing each provider's ability to satisfy the client firm's objectives, qualifying providers, and assessing the risk of arrangements with each provider.

Screen Out Providers That Do Not Satisfy the Primary Objectives in the RFI

Because many outsource providers have limited production capacity, a given provider may not be able to meet all of the objectives (e.g., timeliness, cost, etc.) detailed in the RFI. If some outsource providers can satisfy all of the client's objectives, then those that cannot should be screened out. In situations where no provider has the production capacity to handle the job as defined in the RFI, the client firm may have to provide extra support (i.e., funding, human resources, technology, etc.) to increase the capacity of one or more of the outsource providers.

Screen Out Providers That Do Not Qualify

A variety of criteria can be used to determine if a particular outsource provider is qualified. The criteria chosen are dependent on the client firm and its needs, but can be categorized to include broad qualification areas of a provider's experience, capabilities, financial offer, and strategies. Examples of criteria and issues considered include those listed in Table 7.1 (Cullen and Willcocks 2003, 127–129; Kern and Willcocks 2001, 385; Milgate 2001, 189–191). Any of the select criteria issues raised in Table 7.1 might cause a provider to be screened out from further consideration.

Table 7.1

Categories of Outsource Provider Selection Criteria

Outsource provider criteria category	Select criteria
Experience	– experience working in similar arrangements – experience working in the same or a similar industry – experience in working with a similar organization
Capability	– production capacity to meet objectives – financial strength – human resources – scope breadth and depth – flexibility for changing service levels
Risk management	– willingness to share risks – willingness to take part in dispute resolution – in termination of the agreement
Financial offer	– price/fee structure for services – penalty/reward system – termination charges – price/fee for altering agreement
Transition strategy	– transition plan and timetable – staff transfer/hire opportunities – proposed degree of responsibility during transition – disruption costs – asset turnover
Operations strategy	– proposed supply-chain structure – proposed technology availability – service improvement plans
Monitoring strategy	– reporting requirements – customer satisfaction assessment – benchmarking system in place

They can be viewed as general criteria that should be addressed by the outsource provider in any reputable project offering. Their absence from a proposal may

Table 7.2

Risk Factors to Consider in the Outsource Provider Selection Process

Risk factors in selecting a provider	Risk factors issues
Provider characteristics	–reputation (good or bad) –experience (high or low) –political connections (good or bad)
Legal	–legal judgments against the firm –fines or suspensions for breaches of rules or laws –government investigations or charges –outstanding litigation (what for?)
Ownership	–identity of the majority owner –ownership agreements on patents or technology
Personnel	–who are the current directors, executives? –who are the past directors, executives? –who are the auditors? –who are recent consultants?
Client firm property rights protection	The likelihood of dissemination of core technology or business processes, or the expatriation of employees with valued knowledge
Compatibility of business philosophies	Differences in business philosophies lead to disagreements on operating strategies, policies, practices, and methods
Motivation	Why has the provider entered into an outsourcing arrangement? It should include a variety of mutually beneficial reasons including risk sharing, economies of scale, competitive leverage, cost savings, and greater efficiency.
Reliability	The intentions and ability to provide what is promised between the client and provider must be based on more than personal gain. It must also be based on the provider's honesty, trustworthiness, and reasonableness.
Financial resources	–review financial statements –review loans –review financial commitments to other business and outsourcing agreements –credit rating –history of receivership or liquidations –for international outsource firms the *U.S. Department of Commerce World Traders Data Reports* (WTDR) is a source of financial and trade information
Production resources	Both for manufactured goods and services, an outsourcing provider of both goods and services must have the production capacity to deliver on their promises. To determine an outsource firm's capacity, the client firm should inspect the outsource firm's manufacturing facilities and investigate incentives governments may offer the outsource firm.
Organizational resources	The experience level of staff assigned by an outsource provider to a project is important. A review of absenteeism, training support and workforce size is prudent, particularly for labor-intensive outsourcing agreements

(continued)

Table 7.2 *(continued)*

Technical resources	Does the outsource provider have the technology and research staff to do the job? Client firms should review outsourcers' technology, including its age and capacity, as well as their R&D and engineering staffs.
Marketing resources	Does the outsource provider have the necessary marketing staff or access to markets needed to fulfill the outsourcing agreement? Client firms should review outsourcers' prior projects, access to markets, and current marketing staff and specialties.

be a signal of concern, or at the very least, a point that should be raised by the client firm.

Screen Out Higher Risk Providers

Continuing with this textbook's theme of risk avoidance, it is important to formally include risks inherent in any outsourcing selection process. In general there are many different types of risks client firms run when selecting an outsource provider. To minimize these risks, the firm must first be aware of them. While not an exhaustive listing, Table 7.2 presents a variety of risk factors and related issues that might be applicable to most outsource selection processes (Cavusgil et al. 2002, 112–125; Cullen and Willcocks 2003, 127). This listing can be helpful in identifying possible risks that, once exposed, might be useful in screening out candidates, which pose greater levels of risk than others. Risk measuring systems, like the simple one proposed in Chapter 4, may have application in weighing differences for a comparative selection analysis.

Any international outsource provider selection has additional risk factors beyond those in Table 7.2 that should be considered (Cavusgil et al. 2002, 93–100). Examples of some of these international risk factors are presented in Table 7.3.

The three screening steps above may be all that is necessary to arrive at the selection of a single outsource provider. On the other hand, there are so many outsource providers, in so many different areas of the world, the selection process can seem overwhelming. To help reduce efforts, there are several selection methodologies that provide a systematic approach to the outsource provider selection process. One that requires little computation is "benchmarking."

Benchmarking and O-I Partner Selection Decisions

Benchmarking can be used both as a tactical, selection method for new outsource providers (i.e., ex ante) and as an operational comparative monitoring methodology (i.e., ex post) to ensure a current outsource provider is the best choice for a client firm. It can also be used to evaluate existing insourcing performance to determine if outsourcing is necessary.

Benchmarking as an Ex Ante Selection Method

The procedure for external benchmarking presented in Chapter 5 consists of the following steps:

1. Establish a benchmarking team.
2. Identify and document the activities, processes or functional areas requiring improvement.
3. Identify measurable industry best performance or industry standard of excellence.
4. Collect data on current operations and compare with benchmarks.
5. Establish a set of recommended changes.
6. Follow up.

Table 7.3

International Risk Factors to Consider in the Outsource Selection Process

Risk factors in selecting an international provider	Risk factors issues
Licensing rights	If the client gives the outsource provider a temporary license to use the client's intangible assets like a patent, trade secrets, or knowledge it will be important to know how these client rights are protected in the provider's country.
Technology transfer	When a client firm lends tangible assets like technology to a provider on a temporary basis it will be important to know how these technologies are protected in the provider's country.
Clearing transactions	*Clearing* (i.e., the process of clearing accounts for deposits and withdrawals for trade) issues in the foreign country must be considered in the timing of cash flow and in light of governmental restrictions on amounts and timing of the transfer of funds.
Offset arrangements	*Offset arrangements* (i.e., a portion of outsourced business must be produced/conducted in both the client and provider countries) in outsourcing agreements are common but can make some projects prohibitively costly or otherwise unfeasible.
Countertrade arrangements	*Countertrade arrangements* (i.e., an exchange of goods and services between the client and provider instead of financial payments) can limit the profitability of an outsourcing agreement but are commonly expected in countries where limitations on exporting currency exist..
Turnkey projects	*Turnkey projects* (i.e., outsource firm creates a new business process and turns it over to the client firm for continued use) are very common in outsourcing agreements. Some governments, though, require a continued return on investment for their country's providers, thus limiting the potential for this type of outsourcing and introducing risk to future profits for the client firm..
Management contracts	International management contracts give client firms the right to manage some aspects of the outsource provider's operations. This can limit the risk to the client firm but also restrict it to outsource firms that will cede some control to the client firm.

As explained in Chapter 5, this six-step process positions a client firm to determine if they have tasks that an outsource firm can perform and establishes the type of information necessary for the client firm to write up a *request for proposal* (RFP) (discussed in Chapter 4). It may be that insourcing can meet the benchmarks. However, if it cannot, then outsourcing becomes an option. The benchmarks help establish measurable criteria on which outsource providers can be compared and selected. In Step 3 above, the process of finding measurable *industry best performance* or *industry standards of excellence* requires research on industry practices. Sources of general industry performance standards abound on the Internet. Table 7.4 presents a listing of current benchmarking sources by type of function, including outsourcing. Many sources of benchmarks are more specific to a particular type of industry and even a particular individual business process. Examples for the Telecommunications industry are presented in Table 7.5 (page 132).

The Web site of the *Global Organization Structure Benchmarking Association,* www.gobenchmarking.com, lists benchmark sources for dozens of industries ranging alphabetically from airlines to water utilities. The Web site also lists sources of benchmarks for specific business processes ranging alphabetically from abandoned property management to utility managers.

Table 7.4

Sources of Benchmarking Standards

Name of association	Web site	Types of benchmarks
Shared Services Accounting and Finance Benchmarking Association	www.ssbenchmarking.org/accounting.html	Accounting and finance
Shared Services Human Resources Benchmarking Association	www.ssbenchmarking.org/humanresources.html	Human resources
Shared Services Information Technology Benchmarking Association	www.ssbenchmarking.org/infotech.html	Information systems
Global Organization Structure Benchmarking Association	www.gobenchmarking.com	International business
Outsourcing Benchmarking Association	www.obenchmarking.com	Outsourcing
Shared Services Procurement Benchmarking Association	www.ssbenchmarking.org/procurement.html	Procurement
Six Sigma Operations Benchmarking Association	www.6sigmaops.com	Production and operations

Once the benchmarks are obtained, they can be used to compare specific outsource proposals tendered to the client firm. Those outsource proposals that seek to achieve the benchmarks can be used to identify the best candidates from those that cannot compete. An example of a source of pricing benchmarks is provided in the META Group's *2004 Outsourcing Pricing Guide*. The information presented is based on META Group research in the areas of outsourcing and price benchmarking. Each profile provides an overview of what to expect when considering an outsourcing arrangement in that area, including basic services and pricing ("Eighty Percent Financial . . ." 2004).

Benchmarking as an Ex Post Selection Method

As we can see in Figure 7.1, one of the last operational level planning steps in international O-I is to evaluate an outsource provider. This step is prudent to ensure that the current outsource provider gives the client firm a market competitive performance equal to anything available from other outsource providers. It is a reasonable expectation that an outsource provider will meet or exceed industry benchmark standards over the period of time the agreement is in force. Indeed, this requirement may be formally stated in the outsourcing agreement. Outsourcing firms that cannot compete or choose not to meet or exceed benchmark expectations should be replaced by outsource providers who will.

Monitoring the current outsource provider is an essential part of the international O-I planning process. By monitoring current and ever changing benchmarking standards a client firm can assure itself of industry best performance either from the current outsource provider or, if not, begin the process of finding a new partner. What types of out-

Table 7.5

Sources of Business Process Benchmarks for the Telecommunications Industry

Industry	Business Process	Web site	Types of benchmark available
Telecommunications	Customer service	www.tbig.org/tcsba.html	—cost reduction —best practices —complaint handling —help desk management —shared services processes
Telecommunications	Human resources	www.tbig.org/thrba.html	—cost reduction —best practices —service recovery —corporate governance —corporate security
Telecommunications	Procurement and supply chain	www.tbig.org/tpscba.html	—cost reduction —best practices —complaint handling —help desk management —corporate security
Telecommunications	Sales force effectiveness	www.tbig.org/tsfeba.html	—cost reduction —best practices —service recovery —help desk management —corporate security

sourcing measures might be useful as benchmarks? A listing of typical outsource measures of provider performance that serve to evaluate the provider is presented in Table 7.6 (Cullen and Willcocks 2003, 72; Baldwin et al. 2000, 7–84; Greaver 1999, 173–174). As Lacity and Hirschheim (1993) and Kern and Willcocks (2001, 24–30) suggest, everything should be measured that may have an impact on the success of the client-provider relationship. These measures can be checked against benchmarked performance to evaluate the benefits of continuing an outsource provider agreement. The use of the *gap chart* methodology (discussed in Chapter 5) can be used to display differences. On a routine basis it also acts as an ideal monitoring system. The benchmark measures should be included in the outsourcing agreement and agreed to by both parties. In addition, the means of measurement, including whose job it is to measure, who must report, and timing due dates for reporting should also be agreed upon. On a more positive note, they can also be used to motivate a current outsource provider by demonstrating where improvements are possible.

Decision Theory Methods for Partner Selection Decisions

Anderson (2003) proposed an outsource provider selection method that consists of several steps incorporating the two steps shaded in Figure 7.1:

Table 7.6

Some Measures of Outsource Provider Performance to Be Used in Benchmarking

Area of application	Items
Financial	–gives value for money
	–provides transparency, allowing client firm to identify problems
	–honesty in reporting
	–stability
Relationship	–mutual respect and trust
	–willingness to work with client firm
	–flexibility
	–responsive to client's changing needs
	–ongoing monitoring and evaluation
	–continuous improvement
Customer service	–overall customer satisfaction
	–timeliness of response to customers
	–follow-up response to customers' claims
	–courteousness to customers
	–customer waiting time
	–emergency inquiry response time
Operations	–technology downtime
	–safety incidents and worker compensation claims
	–number of customer orders processed per time period
	–number of customer orders completed on time/still open
	–number of unscheduled maintenance calls
	–superior performance
Human resources	–training hours per employee
	–employee turnover
	–positive attitude

1. Conduct a business analysis to determine client firm needs/outsource requirements.
2. Establish outsource provider evaluation criteria.
3. Create an objective scoring model.
4. Evaluate outsource provider solutions.
5. Justify costs from the outsource proposals.
6. Select a provider.
7. Implement a repeatable provider selection process.

The idea of this selection method involves more than choosing an outsource provider (Step 6), it also requires evaluation of the provider on a continuous basis (Step 7). Anderson (2003) suggests building weighting systems into a scoring methodology reflects the types of risk present in the decision process and results in a better outsource provider decision. Such a decision could be used for both ex ante and ex post purposes.

The recognition of risk is critically important in the provider selection decision. There are two categories of risks possible: extrinsic and intrinsic. The *extrinsic risk* factors in this situation are the external factors often unique to a particular firm or its practices/policies that can be identified and should be included in the analysis. There can be hundreds of these possible risk factors. An example is a client firm risking its reputation for high quality products by doing business with an outsource provider that has a reputation for poor quality. Where extrinsic risk factors are identifiable and measurable, they should be brought into the selection analysis as additional selection criteria. Since these types of risk factors have been presented in several prior chapters, this chapter will focus on the intrinsic risk factors. The *intrinsic risk* factors are often related to the degree of information on which a decision will be based. They can be viewed as the possible errors in the parameters used in a decision model to render a decision. When there is less than perfect information, which is always the case in outsource provider selection decisions, decision theory scientists claim the firm faces a "risk" decision making situation. Decision theory methodologies incorporate and consider intrinsic risk within the context of a decision model.

Decision theory (DT) is a collection of methodologies and principles used to make single, alternative choice decisions (i.e., where the decision is to select one alternative from a set of others) (Meredith et al. 2002, 221–269; Savage 2003, 183–220; Schniederjans et al. 2004, 234–250). Before using these DT methodologies the basic elements of the DT model must be understood so as to identify and correctly formulate problems.

Decision Theory Model Elements

There are three elements in all DT problems: alternatives, states of nature, and payoffs:

1. *Alternatives* (sometimes called "choices" or "strategies") are the independent decision variables in the DT model. They represent the alternative strategies or choices of action a decision maker must select. When only one choice is allowed, it is called a *pure choice problem.* This discussion will be limited to pure choice DT problems, since the outsource provider selection is usually the selection of only a single provider at one time.
2. *States of nature* are independent events assumed to occur in the future. For example, business market conditions, like a boom or bust economy or high-sales or low-sales markets, are considered states of nature.
3. *Payoffs* are dependent parameters assumed to occur given a particular selected alternative and a particular state of nature. Payoff values may be any value (e.g., positive, negative, or zero, dollars of profit, dollars of cost, ratings scores, etc). Since ratings or scores can be used, the weighted scor-

Table 7.7

Generalized Statement of the DT Model

Alternatives	States of nature			
	1	2	...	n
1	P_{11}	P_{12}	...	P_{1n}
2	P_{21}	P_{22}	...	P_{2n}
:	:	:	:	:
m	P_{m1}	P_{m2}	...	P_{mn}

ing methodology proposed by Anderson (2003) is applicable to the DT model.

We combine the three primary elements above into a *payoff table* to formulate the DT model of a problem. The general statement of a DT model is presented in Table 7.7.

In Table 7.7 the DT model has m alternatives and n states of nature or a differing number of states of nature and alternatives. It is common in the outsource provider selection problem to have many alternative providers with only a few differing market scenarios (e.g., high sales versus low sales) conditions that might impact the selection decision. Also, the P_{ij} (where i=1, 2, . . . , m; j=1,2, . . . , n) payoff values are listed by row and column denoting if a particular outsource provider is selected and a particular state of nature occurs, the decision maker will be rewarded with the specific P_{ij} payoff. The alternatives are always listed in DT model formulations as rows and the states of nature always as columns. What complicates the problem is that the exact payoff is dependent on the nature of the decision environment that the decision maker faces.

Types of Decision Environments

Consistent with DT, there are three primary types of decision environments: certainty, risk, and uncertainty:

1. *Certainty decision environment:* Under this environment the decision maker knows clearly what the alternatives are to choose and the payoffs that each choice will bring with certainty if the alternative is chosen. Even in highly defined contractual outsourcing agreements, a certain state of nature or a certain payoff cannot be assured. Therefore, discussion of this type of DT model will be excluded.

2. *Risk decision environment:* Under this environment some information on the states of nature is available, but is less than perfect. For example, a client firm might be facing either a high customer service demand market or a low demand market for computer help desk services. The selection of an outsource provider capable of handling these different types of markets can vary, and the costs to provide the extra computer help desk services (e.g., staffing, hours of labor, technology support, etc.) can have a substantial impact on profitability. The client firm may, based on prior history, have a good idea as to whether they will have a high or low demand situation, but they will not know with certainty. As such it faces a risk situation where the likelihood of a particular high or low demand situation occurring can only be assessed with a probability or chance of occurrence. This partial information, represented by a probability estimate, is characteristically a risk decision environment situation.

3. *Uncertainty decision environment:* Under this environment no information about the likelihood of states of nature occurring is available. A particular payoff occurring can only be assumed if a given state of nature occurs. For example, in outsourcing situations where a firm has no prior history with a new product or service, or the firm is a start-up company without any history, but is considering using outsourcing as a strategy for handling marketing or production activities, there is no information on the possible state of nature. This would be an uncertainty decision environment.

The three types of decision environments can be viewed as a linear continuum ranging from complete knowledge (i.e., under certainty), to partial knowledge (i.e., under risk), and finally to no knowledge of the states of nature occurring (i.e., under uncertainty). With each of these environments, there are different criteria and a variety of methodologies to derive payoff information on which a decision can be made.

Decision Theory Model Formulation Procedure

The procedure for formulating a DT model can consist of the following steps:

1. Identify and list as rows the alternatives from which to choose.
2. Identify and list as columns the states of nature that can occur.
3. Identify and list payoffs in the appropriate row and column.
4. Formulate the model as a payoff table.

To illustrate this procedure, let us consider an outsource provider selection problem where a client firm's outsourcing team wants to decide between two outsource providers, Provider A and Provider B. The outsourcing project, which will last only one year, is an in-house training program that will introduce a new computer system. It is a one-year agreement proposal. What the client firm will receive (i.e., the payoffs) depends on the customer demand conditions (i.e., states of nature) that define the expected service levels during the year and the outsource provider selected. The two possible customer demand conditions in this problem are "High Demand" or "Low Demand." If the client firm uses Outsource Provider A and experiences a "High Demand" condition, the net benefit to the client firm is $4 million for the year. If the client firm experiences a "Low Demand" condition with Outsource Provider A, they will only net $1 million for the year. If the client firm chooses Outsource Provider B and experiences a "High Demand" condition, they will net $6 million for the year. If the client firm experiences a "Low Demand" condition with Outsource Provider B, the client firm will incur a loss equal to the firm of $2 million for the year. What is the DT model formulation for this problem?

Using the four-step DT procedure, formulate this model accordingly:

1. *Identify and list as rows the alternatives from which to choose.* There are two alternatives: Outsource Provider A and Outsource Provider B. Only one will be chosen, which makes this a pure choice problem.
2. *Identify and list as columns the states of nature that can occur.* In this problem there are two states of nature: High Demand and Low Demand. So this results in a 2 by 2 payoff table.
3. *Identify and list the payoff in the appropriate row and column.* The payoffs are in customer sales, where the $4, $1, $6, and $-2 million values are the payoffs.
4. *Formulate the problem/model as a payoff table.* The payoff table formulation of the complete model is presented in Table 7.8.

Once a DT model is formulated, the payoff table can be used to analyze the payoffs and render a decision. The methodologies that are used to generate a solution using the DT model vary by the type of decision environment. Since a certainty decision environment is highly unusual in international O-I decision making, the focus will be on decision making under risk and uncertainty.

Table 7.8

DT Formulation of the Outsource Provider Selection Problem

	States of nature	
Alternatives	High demand	Low demand
Provider A	4	1
Provider B	6	−2

Decision Making Under Risk

There are different criteria to aid in making decisions when the decision maker knows the problem is a "risk" situation where the states of nature are probabilistic. It should be noted the sum of these probabilities over all the states of nature must add to one. Like a flip of a coin, only two states of nature are possible (i.e., a head or a tail), the probability of each is 0.50, and adding the probabilities of both possible outcomes equals one.

Probabilities for states of nature come from "objective" or "subjective" sources. *Objective source probabilities* include observation of historical behavior. Research on outsourcing projects reveals about half fail (Hall 2003). When objective methods are used to determine probabilities, assume the following three conditions:

1. The probability of past events will follow the same pattern in the future.
2. The probabilities are stable in the process that is being observed.
3. The sample size is adequate to represent past behavior.

If these assumptions are not realistic, an alternative way of determining probabilities involves use of *subjective source probabilities.* This entails having experts make their best guess at what a probability should be for the states of nature. Using this approach to probability assessment relies on the assumption that the experts are knowledgeable of the behavior for which they are assessing probabilities, and their judgment is reasonably accurate.

Once the probability information on the states of nature has been determined, criteria can be selected to guide the computations in order to generate a solution from the DT model. Of the many different criteria that can be used to aid in making decisions in a risk environment consider the following two criteria: expected value and expected opportunity loss.

Expected Value Criterion

The *expected value* (EV) *criterion* is determined by computing a weighted sum of the payoffs for each alternative. The EV criterion can be computed using the following steps:

1. Attach the probabilities for each state of nature to the payoffs in each row in the payoff table.
2. Multiply the probability in decimal form by each payoff and sum by row. These values are the expected payoffs for each alternative.
3. Select the alternative with the best expected payoff. The best alternative will depend on the values used in the computations.

To illustrate this criterion revisit the outsource provider selection model previously formulated. Say the probability of "High Demand" is 30 percent, and the probability of "Low Demand" is 70 percent. The existence of states of nature probabilities make this problem a risk decision environment. To compute the expected values the percentage probabilities are changed to decimal values and

Table 7.9

Expected Value Solution for the Outsource Provider Selection Problem

	States of nature		
Alternatives	**High demand (30%)**	**Low demand (70%)**	**Expected payoff**
Provider A	4(0.30)+	1(0.70)=	$1.9 million
Provider B	6(0.30)+	−2(0.70)=	$0.4 million

multiplied by their respective payoff values. In Table 7.9 the EVs of each alternative are the sum of products in the rows and are presented in the last column of the payoff table. Since the payoff values are in net profit, the larger the expected value, the better the solution choice is for the client firm. As can be seen in Table 7.9, the best payoff (i.e., maximum expected net profit) is for the Outsource Provider A alternative at $1.9 million.

Expected Opportunity Loss Criterion

The *expected opportunity loss* (EOL) *criterion* is based on avoiding loss. The decision using this criterion seeks to minimize the *expected opportunity loss* (i.e., what one stands to lose if the best decision for each state of nature is not selected). The procedure for computing the values on which this criterion is based involves the following steps:

1. Determine the opportunity loss values for not making the best decision in each state of nature. The best payoff under each state of nature is found by subtracting all the values in that column from that best payoff (including itself). The result is *opportunity loss* and represents what one stands to lose if the alternative selected is not the best payoff for that state of nature. The

opportunity loss values can be structured into an opportunity loss table represented by the same framework as the DT payoff table.

2. Attach the probabilities to the opportunity loss values and compute expected opportunity loss values for each alternative by adding the products of the probabilities and multiplying by the respective opportunity loss values by row.

3. Select the alternative with the minimum expected opportunity loss value computed in Step 2.

Now apply these steps to the DT outsource provider selection problem. In Step 1 we have to determine the opportunity loss values. In Table 7.10 the DT outsource model is restated. Note the values in parentheses are the best payoff for each state of nature (i.e., 6 is better than 4 for high demand, and 1 is better than a -2 for low demand).

By taking the best values in each column and subtracting them from other values in the column, obtain the opportunity loss values for each cell in the opportunity loss table in Table 7.11. As expected, the best values result in a 0 opportunity loss, since they were the best values. The opportunity loss of 3 for Outsource Provider B with low demand reflects the actual loss of $2 million (i.e., -2) plus the loss of $1 million that was forgone by giving up the best choice in that column (i.e., 1).

Having determined the opportunity loss values, now move on to Step 2 where the probabilities are attached to the opportunity loss values. Compute expected opportunity loss values for each alternative by adding the products of the probabilities and multiplying their respective opportunity loss values by row. These computations are presented in Table 7.12.

Based on the expected values in Table 7.12, one can now perform Step 3 of the EOL procedure and

Table 7.10

Best Payoffs for Each State of Nature in the Outsource Provider Selection Problem

Alternatives	States of nature	
	High demand (30%)	Low demand (70%)
Provider A	4	(1)
Provider B	(6)	-2

Table 7.11

Opportunity Loss Table for Outsource Provider Selection Problem

Alternatives	States of nature	
	High demand	Low demand
Provider A	$6 - 4 = 2$	$1 - 1 = 0$
Provider B	$6 - 6 = 0$	$1 - (-2) = 3$

complete the decision process. The goal is to select the choice that minimizes EOL, so this would be Outsource Provider A (i.e., losing an expected $0.6 million is better than losing an expected $2.1 million).

Decision Making Under Uncertainty

Decision making under uncertainty means that the decision maker has no information on which state of nature will occur. Client firms with no experience in outsourcing may find this situation common. The client may know what the payoffs might be, given a state of nature occurring, but they may not have any specific information about which state of nature will actually happen. In this decision situation, as with risk, many different criteria can be used. Five criteria commonly used

Table 7.12

Expected Opportunity Loss Values for Outsource Provider Selection Problem

	States of nature		
Alternatives	**High demand (30%)**	**Low demand (70%)**	**Expected opportunity loss**
Provider A	2(0.30) +	0(0.70) =	$0.6 million
Provider B	0(0.30) +	3(0.70) =	$2.1 million

Table 7.13

Laplace Solution for Outsource Provider Selection Problem

	States of nature		
Alternatives	**High demand (50%)**	**Low demand (50%)**	**Expected values**
Provider A	4(0.50) +	1(0.50) =	$2.5 million
Provider B	6(0.50) +	−2(0.50) =	$2.0 million

are Laplace, maximin, maximax, Hurwicz, and minimax.

Laplace Criterion

The *Laplace criterion* assumes that since no information is available on any state of nature, each is equally likely to occur. Based on the *Principle of Insufficient Information*, assign an equal probability to each state of nature, and then compute an expected value for each alternative using the same procedure as that for the expected value risk criterion. The computational procedure for the Laplace criterion can include the following steps:

1. Attach an equal probability to each state of nature. For example, if there are two states of nature, the probability of each state is 50 percent.
2. Compute an expected value for each alternative as in the "expected value" criterion.
3. Select the alternative with the best expected value computed in Step 2.

To illustrate these criterion steps, again revisit the DT outsource provider selection problem. In Step 1 identify there are two states, which results

in an assumed equal (i.e., 50 percent each) probable occurrence. Attaching these probabilities to the outsourcing problem in Table 7.13 in Step 2, compute the expected values for both alternative providers. Consistent with Step 3, select Outsource Provider A with the larger expected net profit.

Maximax Criterion

The *maximax criterion* assumes a totally optimistic approach to decision making. Since there is no information on what state of nature will occur, why not assume an optimistic outcome? It involves selecting the maximum of the maximum payoffs possible in the payoff table, hence the name "max-i-max." The maximax choice is based on the following steps:

1. Select the maximum payoff for each alternative.
2. Select the alternative with the maximum payoff of the maximum payoffs from Step 1.

Look at this solution criteria applied to the outsource provider selection problem. As can be seen in Table 7.14, the maximum payoffs for each of the two alternatives are $4 million and $6 mil-

Table 7.14

Maximax Solution for Outsource Provider Selection Problem

	States of nature			
Alternatives	High demand	Low demand	Max payoff	Max of the max
Provider A	4	1	4	
Provider B	6	–2	6	$6 million

Table 7.15

Maximin Solution for Outsource Provider Selection Problem

	States of nature			
Alternatives	High demand	Low demand	Min payoff	Max of the min
Provider A	4	1	1	$1 million
Provider B	6	–2	–2	

lion, respectively. Of these, the $6 million payoff is the maximum payoff, so the maximum of the maximums is $6 million, which can be achieved by the selection of the Outsource Provider B alternative.

Maximin Criterion

The *maximin criterion* is a semi-pessimistic approach, which assumes the worst state of nature is going to occur, so make the best of it. To do so, take the maximum payoff choice from the minimum payoffs expected. The maximin selection is based on the following steps:

1. Select the minimum payoff for each alternative.
2. Select the alternative with the maximum payoff of the minimum payoffs from Step 1.

The solution to the outsource provider problem using this criterion is presented in Table 7.15. As can be seen, the minimum payoffs for each of the two alternatives are $1 million and $-2 million, respectively. Of these the $1 million payoff is the maximum payoff, so the maximum of the minimums is $1 million, indicating the selection of the Outsource Provider A alternative.

Hurwicz Criterion

The *Hurwicz criterion* is a compromised approach between the maximin and maximax approaches. In this criterion the decision maker must subjectively weigh the degree of optimism for the future of the decision. The *coefficient of optimism* is used for this weighting and is represented on a scale from 0 to 1. The closer the coefficient of optimism is to 1, the more optimistic the decision maker is about the future. The *coefficient of pessimism* is one minus the coefficient of optimism. Both of these coefficients are used in the computation of the expected payoffs of the alternatives. The Hurwicz selection is based on the following steps:

1. State the value for the coefficient of optimism.
2. Determine the maximum and minimum payoffs for each alternative.
3. Multiply the coefficient of optimism by the maximum payoff, multiply the coefficient of pessimism by the minimum payoff, and add these values to derive the expected value for each alternative.
4. Select the alternative with the best expected payoff from Step 3.

To apply this criterion to the outsource provider

Table 7.16

Max and Min Payoffs for Use with Hurwicz's Method

Alternatives	States of nature		Max payoff	Min payoff
	High demand	Low demand		
Provider A	4	1	4	1
Provider B	6	−2	6	−2

selection problem, Step 1 requires a designation of the coefficient of optimism. Assume only slight optimism, and as such, set this coefficient at only 0.55. For Step 2 of Hurwicz's method determine the maximum and minimum payoffs for each alternative. These four payoffs are presented in Table 7.16. In this problem, all of the payoff values are conveniently used, but what if there are more than two states of nature? What would be done with those payoffs left out of the computations? Nothing! They are left out and only the max and min values are considered. Otherwise, this would simply be an expected value analysis.

In Step 3 of Hurwicz's method multiply the coefficient of optimism by the maximum payoff, multiply the coefficient of pessimism (i.e., 1–0.55) by the minimum payoff, and add these values together to derive the expected value for each alternative. The computations for this step are presented in Table 7.17.

Finally, in Step 4, as can be seen from the expected values in Table 7.17, the best expected payoff is Outsource Provider A at $2.45 million net profit.

Minimax Criterion

The *minimax criterion* is similar to the expected opportunity loss criterion in that both seek to avoid loss. The procedure for computing the values based on the minimax criterion consist of the following steps:

1. Determine the opportunity loss values for not making the best decision in each state of nature. This is accomplished by selecting the best payoff under each state of nature and subtracting all the values in that column from that best payoff. The opportunity loss values should be structured into an opportunity loss table.
2. Determine the maximum opportunity loss values for each alternative.
3. Select the alternative with the minimum opportunity loss value from those maximum values determined in Step 2.

Step 1 for the minimax criterion is the same as Step 1 in the EOL criterion, as presented in Table 7.11 and again below in Table 7.18. In Step 2 determine the maximum opportunity loss from those in the opportunity loss table. The maximum opportunity loss values are shown in the third column of Table 7.18. Finally, in Step 3, select the alternative with the smallest of the maximums. In our problem, this is Outsource Provider A, with a maximum opportunity loss of $2 million.

Note some of the criteria above generate differing answers to the same problem. How can one criterion suggest one alternative and others suggest a different alternative? How can one determine which alternative is the best if there are differing solutions? The answer depends on the selection of criteria that a decision maker chooses to guide the decision. If a person is an optimist, they might choose a maximax approach to decision making, and if they are more pessimistic, they might choose the maximin approach. If they have a risk avoidance nature, they might choose expected opportunity loss criteria. Of course these criteria selection schemes may lead to bias, since selecting a particular criterion will favor a particular decision maker's orientation. The best decision comes from looking at all possible criteria and choosing one

Table 7.17

Hurwicz Solution for Outsource Provider Selection Problem

Alternatives	States of nature		Max payoff (0.55)	Min payoff (1 − 0.55)	Expected values
	High demand	Low demand			
Provider A	4	1	4(0.55) +	1(0.45) =	$2.45 million
Provider B	6	−2	6(0.55) +	(−2(0.45)) =	$2.40 million

Table 7.18

Minimax Solution for Outsource Provider Selection Problem

Alternatives	States of nature		Maximum opportunity loss	Minimum of the maximums
	High demand	Low demand		
Provider A	6 − 4 = 2	1 − 1 = 0	2	$2 million
Provider B	6 − 6 = 0	1 − (−2) = 3	3	

that is generally viewed as the best choice (e.g., most of the criteria indicated that Outsource Provider A is a better choice than Outsource Provider B). Clearly, one can use any criterion at all to justify a particular position on a decision. Indeed, using a wide variety of criteria is perhaps the best way of using decision theory methodologies.

Geographic Distance Selection Methodologies

In some outsource partner selection decisions the geographic location of the potential partner is a critical factor for success. This may be due to costs of shipping great distances, communication problems, or nearness to customer markets, thus reducing shipping costs or delivery time. Regardless, distance from the client firm to the outsource provider may be a primary consideration in the outsource provider selection decision.

Depending on the type of problem a client firm is facing, a number of methodologies exist to support distance-related issues. Table 17.19 lists several methodologies useful in making selections from a set of alternative outsource providers. These methodologies originate from the field of operations research. Their procedural steps, as well as software, can be found in any basic textbook in this field of study (Hiller et al. 2002; Render et al. 2002). By way of illustration of these methodologies, look at the centroid method.

The Centroid Method

The *centroid method*, or *center of gravity method* (Chase et al. 2004, 413–415), considers existing facilities (like warehouses or production plants), distances between them (in miles or kilometers), and the volume of goods shipped to and from those facilities. This method seeks to compute geographic coordinates for a potential, single new facility (or outsource provider in this case) that will minimize linear distance (and resulting transportation costs) between existing facilities and the new facility location. This method computes the two-dimensional coordinates of a point where the

Table 17.19

Methodologies Useful in Considering Distance Criteria in Outsource Provider Selection

Name of methodology	Description and application to outsouce provider selection
Centroid method	Useful in selecting a geographic location for an outsource provider that would minimize linear distance between a group of existing client production facilities or markets. (We will discuss this model further in this section.)
Shortest-route method	Useful in selecting outsource providers that would minimize distance along a route of existing production facilities or markets. This is a situation where you have a specific origin point (e.g., client firm) and a specific destination (e.g., the market for the client's finished product). This would be a continuous line of points from the origin to the final destination, much like a truck route where stops would be made by the truck along the continuous line. Those outsource providers whose location is along the route would be the eligible candidates for selection.
Minimal spanning-tree method	Useful in selecting a particular outsource provider one at a time when considering a network of existing production/market locations that are a fixed distance from each other. What this methodology does is to find the routing where a set of fixed points can be reached with minimum distance when the network of all points are considered. By substituting candidate outsource provider locations into the network, one at a time, a final minimum distance in reaching all the points in the network is computed and can be compared for each candidate. The outsource provider whose location can be included in the network with the least total distance would be the best candidate.
Transportation method	Useful in selecting a particular outsource provider one at a time when considering a network of existing production/market locations that are a fixed distance from each other. Unlike minimal spanning-tree, this is a network where shipments are made from multiple distinations to multiple locations while seeking to minimize total transportation distance or costs. By substituting one outsource provider into the network and using the method to determine the total minimized distance, the best overall network can be determined along with the outsource provider that best fits within the network.

linear distance between existing facilities and the expected volume of transportation activity is minimized. The formulas for the two coordinates, which are based on the X-Y coordinates of a graph are:

$$C_x = \frac{\Sigma \, d_{ix} V_i}{\Sigma \, V_i} \qquad (1)$$

$$C_y = \frac{\Sigma \, d_{iy} V_i}{\Sigma \, V_i} \qquad (2)$$

where C_x is the X (i.e., horizontal axis) coordinate for the new outsource provider location, C_y is the Y (i.e., vertical axis) coordinate for the new outsource provider location, d_{ix} is the X coordinate of the existing ith location, d_{iy} is the Y coordinate of the existing ith location, and V_i is the volume of goods moved to or from the ith location.

This methodology can be used in either national or international outsourcing, though it does not consider real-world constraints, like oceans, rivers, or any geographic limitation. It simply finds the minimum distance point on an X-Y coordinate graph called a *grid map* (i.e., a two-dimensional X-Y graph listing distances, usually in miles, between locations). To illustrate this methodology

Figure 7.2 **Grid Map of Existing Markets with Coordinates for Centroid Method Problem**

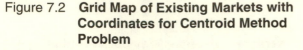
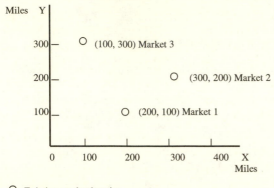

○ Existing market location

Figure 7.3 **Centroid Method Solution for Outsource Provider Selection Problem**

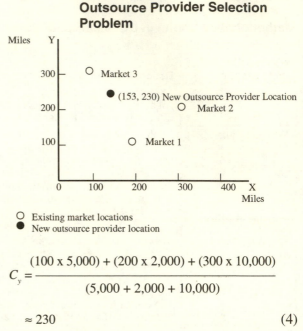

○ Existing market locations
● New outsource provider location

consider the following outsource provider selection problem.

Suppose a client firm has three existing markets for its products (i.e., Markets, 1, 2, and 3) on the grid map in Figure 7.2. The volume of goods moved to or from each market on a daily basis are: Market 1 has a daily goods volume of 5,000 units, Market 2 has a daily goods volume of 2,000 units, and Market 3 has a daily goods volume of 10,000 units. The client firm would like to determine the ideal location for an outsource provider to serve these markets that would minimize the distance from all three markets. Given the grid map in Figure 7.2, what are the coordinates for the location of the new outsource provider?

The grid coordinates of existing facilities are taken from the X and Y axes. In this problem $d_{1x} = 200$, $d_{2x} = 300$, $d_{3x} = 100$, $d_{1y} = 100$, $d_{2y} = 200$, $d_{3y} = 300$, $V_1 = 5,000$, $V_2 = 2,000$, and $V_3 = 10,000$. Using the formulas from equations (1) and (2), the following (X, Y) coordinates for the new facility can be computed:

$$C_x = \frac{(200 \times 5,000) + (300 \times 2,000) + (100 \times 10,000)}{(5,000 + 2,000 + 10,000)}$$

$$\approx 153 \tag{3}$$

$$C_y = \frac{(100 \times 5,000) + (200 \times 2,000) + (300 \times 10,000)}{(5,000 + 2,000 + 10,000)}$$

$$\approx 230 \tag{4}$$

The resulting X-Y coordinates for the new outsource provider are (153, 230), as presented in Figure 7.3. Note in the Figure 7.3 grid map how the heavier volume at Market 3 appropriately pulled the new outsource provider location closer, and at the same time pushed it further away from Markets 1 and 2.

Locating a site for an outsource provider does not guarentee one will actually be available at a particular X-Y coordinate site on the map. In most cases the location found using this method would be the first step in finding an outsource provider in the general area. The next step would require searching the general location to find candidates which may be close or would state in an RFI that they are willing to relocate to that position.

Summary

This chapter presented a variety of decision-making methodologies that can be used in the outsource provider selection decision. In addition to preliminary considerations in the O-I partner decision situation, other more structured methodologies were presented, including benchmarking, decision theory, and distance minimizing methodologies. For each methodology differing criteria were employed to show the opportunities and capabilities each methodology offered in the outsourcing decision. Benchmarking was shown to be useful in both ex ante and ex post decisions. Decision theory criteria included expected value, expected opportunity loss, Laplace, maximax, maximin, Hurwicz, and minimax. Distance minimizing methods, like the centroid method, were shown to be useful when geographic distance is a major factor in selecting an outsource provider.

Most of the methodologies and examples in this chapter are applicable to selecting an outsource provider rather than an insource agent of a firm. Yet many potential client firms usually balance outsource with insource portions of their business. This approach to outsourcing is logical, at least initially, until the client firm learns and becomes more comfortable with outsourcing as a viable business philosophy. This proportional decision situation is one of allocating business activities between outsourcers and insourcers. The next chapter focuses on proportional allocation methodologies.

Review Terms

Alternatives
Center of gravity method
Centroid method
Certainty decision environment
Clearing
Coefficient of optimism
Coefficient of pessimism
Countertrade
Decision theory (DT)
Expected opportunity loss (EOL)
Expected opportunity loss criterion
Expected value (EV)
Expected value criterion
Extrinsic risk
Gap chart
Grid map
Hurwicz criterion
Industry best practice
Industry standard of excellence
Intrinsic risk
Laplace criterion
Maximax criterion

Maximin criterion
Minimal spanning-tree method
Minimax criterion
Objective source probabilities
Offset
Operations research
Opportunity loss
Payoff table
Payoffs
Principle of insufficient information
Pure choice problem
Request for information (RFI)
Request for proposal (RFP)
Risk decision environment
Shortest-route method
States of nature
Subjective source probabilities
Transportation method
Turnkey projects
Uncertainty decision environment
World Traders Data Reports (WTDR)

Discussion Questions

1. Why is selecting an outsource provider a tactical decision?
2. Why consider international risk factors in the outsource provider selection decision?
3. Explain the difference between an ex ante and an ex post outsource provider selection decision?
4. Why consider risk and uncertainty decision environments in the outsource provider selection decision?
5. Why would a decision maker use expected opportunity loss in an outsource provider selection decision?
6. How does the Principle of Insufficient Information justify probabilities in an uncertain decision environment?
7. Which of the criteria for making a decision under uncertainty would you choose if you had to select an outsource provider? Justify your selection of a criterion.
8. Is it possible that the centroid method could generate a location for an outsource provider that makes no sense at all? Explain.

Concept Questions

1. What are preliminary outsource provider selection considerations?
2. What are preliminary outsource provider risk factors?
3. What is compared in a benchmarking process?
4. What are the basic elements that make up a DT model?
5. What is the procedure for formulating a DT model?
6. Which criteria are used when making a decision under a risk type decision environment?
7. Where can the probabilities used in a risk-type decision environment be obtained?
8. Which criterion uses expected value-type computations?
9. Which criteria are used when making a decision under uncertainty?
10. Which criteria of those described for decision making under uncertainty will most likely generate an optimistic outcome in a decision situation?
11. What is the relationship between the Hurwicz' coefficients of optimism and pessimism?
12. Can the centroid method be used in an international outsource provider selection decision?

Methodology Problems

The payoff table below applies to Problems 1 through 7. Assume they represent millions of dollars of payoff possible if each state of nature occurs and each provider is selected. Show all computational work to justify answers to the questions below.

	States of nature		
Alternatives	**High demand**	**Medium demand**	**Low demand**
Provider A	5	6	1
Provider B	4	−1	4
Provider C	3	6	7

1. Assume there is a risk decision environment. Assume the probabilities of the three states of nature occurring are: High demand 25%, Medium demand 50%, and Low demand 25%. Which outsource provider is the best

choice based on expected value criterion? If the probabilities change to 50%, 30% and 20%, respectively, will the prior selection change?

2. Assume there is a risk decision environment. Assume the probabilities of the three states of nature occurring are: High demand 15%, Medium demand 45%, and Low demand 40%. Which outsource provider is the best choice based on expected opportunity loss criterion?

3. Assume there is an uncertainty decision environment. Which outsource provider is the best choice based on the Laplace criterion?

4. Assume there is an uncertainty decision environment. Which outsource provider is the best choice based on the maximax criterion?

5. Assume there is an uncertainty decision environment. Which outsource provider is the best choice based on the maximin criterion?

6. Assume there is an uncertainty decision environment. Which outsource provider is the best choice based on the Hurwicz criterion? Assume the coefficient of optimism is 0.50.

7. Assume there is an uncertainty decision environment. Which outsource provider is the best choice based on the minimax criterion?

The payoff table below applies to Problems 8 through 10. Assume they represent millions of dollars of payoffs possible if each state of nature occurs, and each provider is selected. Show all computational work to justify answers to the questions below.

8. Assume there is a risk decision environment. Assume the probabilities of the three states of nature occurring are: High demand 10%, Medium demand 40%, and Low demand 50%. Which outsource provider is the best choice based on expected value criterion?

9. Assume there is a risk decision environment. Assume the probabilities of the three states of nature occurring are: High demand 25%, Medium demand 40%, and Low demand 35%. Which outsource provider is the best choice based on expected opportunity loss criterion?

10. Assume we have an uncertainty decision environment.

a. Which outsource provider is the best choice based on the Laplace criterion?
b. Which outsource provider is the best choice based on the maximax criterion?
c. Which outsource provider is the best choice based on the maximin criterion?
d. Which outsource provider is the best choice based on the Hurwicz criterion? Assume your coefficient of optimism is 0.70.
e. Which outsource provider is the best choice based on the minimax criterion?
f. Given the results of all five criteria, which outsource provider is the overall best choice? Explain your answer.

11. A client firm wants to decide which of three outsource providers (i.e., Outsource Providers A, B, or C) is offering the most profitable project. The outsourcing project will only last one year. The profits the client firm will receive depend on the customer demand levels during the year. There are three demand levels (X, Y, or Z). If the client firm uses Outsource Provider A and experiences X demand, the net profit to the client firm is expected to be $1 million for the year; if Y, then it is $4 million for the year; if Z, then it

| | States of nature | | |
| | High demand | Medium demand | Low demand |
Alternatives			
Provider A	10	5	2
Provider B	20	0	−12
Provider C	8	7	6
Provider D	0	9	12

is $7 million for the year. If the client firm uses Outsource Provider B and experiences X demand, the net profit to the client firm is expected to be $3 million for the year; if Y, then it is $2 million for the year; if Z, then it is $1 million for the year. If the client firm uses Outsource Provider C and experiences X demand, the net profit to the client firm is expected to be $3 million for the year; if Y, then it is $3 million for the year; if Z, then it is $4 million for the year. What is the DT model formulation for this problem?

12. A client firm is facing an outsource provider decision. An RFI was sent to several outsourcing firms. Two outsource providers responded (i.e., Outsource Provider A and B) with offers. The outsourcing project can last several years, but will have a year probationary period. The later years' rewards are contingent on successful performance during the first year. Because the client firm wants to ensure the best possible results, it will make the decision based on the first year's resulting impact on cost reduction. The possible cost reduction the client firm will receive depends on the customer demand levels during the year. There are three demand levels (X, Y, or Z). If the client firm uses Outsource Provider A and experiences X demand, the cost reduction to the client firm is expected to be $2 million for the year; if Y, then it is $3 million for the year; if Z, then it is $5 million for the year. If the client firm uses Outsource Provider B and experiences X demand, the cost reduction to the client firm is expected to be $2 million for the year; if Y, then it is $5 million for the year; if Z, then it is –$2 million for the year. Construct a DT model for this problem.

The grid map below applies to problems 13 and 14. Show all computational work to justify answers to the questions below.

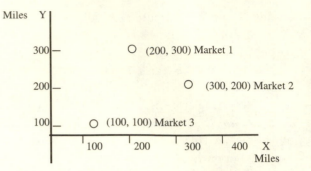

13. Assume only Market 1 and Market 2 locations apply to this problem. A client firm would like to locate an outsource provider near these two markets. The volume of business to or from Market 1 is 5,000 units per day and the volume of business to or from Market 2 is 8,000 units per day. Where should the outsource provider be located if minimizing distance and catering to volume are important in the location decision?

14. Assume all three market locations in the grid map above apply to this problem. A client firm would like to locate an outsource provider near all three of these markets. The volume of business to or from Market 1 is 3,000 units per day; the volume of business to or from Market 2 is 1,000 units per day; and the volume of business to or from Market 3 is 4,000 units per day. Where should the outsource provider be located if minimizing distance and catering to volume are important in the location decision?

References

Anderson, A. "A Structured Approach to Selecting Outsourcing Partners Reduces Risk and Improves ROI." *Communications News* 40, no. 8 (2002): 38–39.

Baldwin, L. H.; Camm, F.; and Moore, N. Y. *Strategic Sourcing: Measuring and Managing Performance*. Santa Monica, CA: Rand, 2000.

Cavusgil, S. T.; Ghauri, P. N.; and Agarwal, M. R. *Doing Business in Emerging Markets*. Thousand Oaks, CA: Sage Publications, 2002.

Chase, R. B.; Jacobs, F. R.; and Aquilano, N. J. *Opera-*

tions Management for Competitive Advantage. 10th ed. Boston: Irwin/McGraw-Hill, 2004.

Cullen, S., and Willcocks, L. *Intelligent IT Outsourcing.* London: Butterworth-Heinemann, 2003.

"Eighty Percent of Financial Firms to Outsource Operations by 2005, Says Report." *Outsourcing Intelligence Bulletin: FSO Magazine* 11, no. 2 (August 8–15, 2004), editor@fsoutsourcing.com.

Greaver, M. F. *Strategic Outsourcing.* New York: American Management Association, 1999.

Hall, M. "Outsourcing Deals Fail Half the Time." *Computerworld* 37, no. 44 (2003): 10.

Hamblen, M. "Sizing Up Outsourcers." *Computerworld* 36, no. 45 (2002): 48.

Hiller, F. S.; Lieberman, G.; and Lieberman, G. J. *Introduction to Operations Research.* 3rd ed. Boston: McGraw-Hill, 2002.

Kern, T., and Willcocks, L. P. *The Relationship Advantage: Information Technologies, Sourcing, and Management.* Oxford: Oxford University Press, 2001.

Lacity, M., and Hirschheim, R. *Information Systems Out-sourcing: Myths, Metaphors and Realities.* New York: Wiley, 1993.

Mamaghani, F. "Selecting an Outsourcing Vendor for Information Systems." *International Journal of Management* 17, no. 3 (2000): 334–344.

Meredith, J.; Shafer, S.; and Turban, E. *Quantitative Business Modeling.* Mason, OH: South-Western, 2002.

Michell, V., and Fitzgerald, G. "The IT Outsourcing Marketplace: Vendors and Their Selection." *Journal of Information Technology* 12, no. 3 (1997): 223–237.

Milgate, M. *Alliances, Outsourcing, and the Lean Organization.* Westport, CT: Quorum Books, 2001.

Render, B.; Stair, R. Jr.; Hanna, M.; and Stair, R. *Quantitative Analysis for Management.* 8th ed. Upper Saddle River, NJ: Prentice Hall, 2002.

Savage, S. L. *Decision Making with Insight.* Belmont, CA: Brooks/Cole-Thomson Learning, 2003.

Schniederjans, M. J.; Hamaker, J. L.; and Schniederjans, A. M. *Information Technology Investment Decision Making Methodology.* Singapore: World Scientific, 2004.

8

Methodologies for Allocating Business Activities Between Outsourcers and Insourcers

Learning Objectives   After completing this chapter you should be able to:

- Describe how game theory can be used in determining optimal proportion allocations of business activities between outsourcers and insourcers.
- Formulate game theory models for international O-I decision problems.
- Understand the value of the information provided by game theory for international O-I decision problems.
- Describe how linear programming can be used in determining optimal proportion allocations of business activities between outsourcers and insourcers.
- Formulate linear programming models for international O-I decision problems.
- Understand the value of the information provided by linear programming for international O-I decision problems.

Introduction

In Chapters 1 through 4, we introduced the international O-I process (see Figure 8.1) of identifying non-core business activities and considering them as candidates for outsourcing. The number or the proportion of these activities to be outsourced must be decided in a way that optimizes results for the client firm.

Chapter 1 introduced different types of outsourcing arrangements. In *business process outsourcing* (BPO), an entire business function (e.g., all accounting activities, information systems activities, production activities, etc.) can be completely removed from the client firm and handled

by the outsource provider. In most other types of outsourcing some of the business activities in a given functional area are outsourced, while the rest are insourced. Consider the manufacture of a tangible product, like a muffler for an automobile. Prefabrication, metal cutting, welding, and assembly are all required to produce the finished muffler. Or consider an intangible service product, like developing a new customer service product. There are R&D tasks, customer survey work, marketing analysis, and engineering tasks required to completely finish the development and delivery of a new service product. All or some of these varied activities, which make up a finished product, can be identified as non-core activities and can become

150

Figure 8.1   **Application of This Chapter's Methodologies in International O-I Planning**

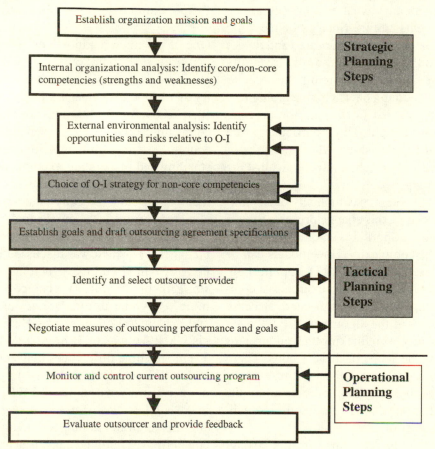

candidates for outsourcing. Having identified them as outsourcing candidates does not in itself mean they will or can be outsourced in a way which optimizes the allocation decision.

The situation where some, but not all, activities are outsourced leads to a question client firms face in the international O-I decision: what proportion of business activities should be outsourced and what proportion should be insourced? This is a common problem that many first-time client firms tend to experiment with by only outsourcing a small portion of activities to see how, in the long run, this strategy will work. In terms of the international

O-I planning process this decision can be made at the strategic or tactical levels (note Figure 8.1). In both cases it helps managers to identify goals, which need to be achieved, and the outsourcing and insourcing requirements necessary to achieve those goals.

To arrive at the ideal O-I proportion involves consideration of many differing variables and multiple criteria. Some proportions can be in terms of actual business activities, while others may be in terms of departmental budgets, product lines, or service categories. Most literature on this subject is conceptual in nature (Cullen and Willcocks 2003,

51–66). Suggestions or guidelines are given as to how a firm can identify what may or may not be appropriate for outsourcing. Such guidelines tend only to consider what can be allocated and do not always include the possible economic trade-offs that may exist favoring insourcing. In order to optimize an outsourcing decision, insourcing factors should be included in the decision process, but not as an afterthought. This is particularly true in international O-I decisions, where the risks of outsourcing must be weighed directly against the risks of insourcing.

Because of the potential complexity of an international O-I decision, this chapter presents the use of decision-making algorithms uniquely capable of dealing with the complexity. How models can be identified for use in a particular O-I application, as well as formulating them for input into a computer software application, is presented. Because of the complexity of the algorithms used, the actual procedural process of making these algorithms work is beyond the scope of this textbook. These computational aspects are left to software applications. But for those seeking more detail on the computational aspects of the algorithms, we will reference a number of useful sources.

The methodologies examined in this chapter are all capable of providing proportioned answers to international O-I decisions. They include game theory and linear programming. These methodologies originate from the field of *operations research* and are considered general purpose methodologies applicable to model a broad range of business, engineering, and economic decision-making situations. In addition, all of the methodologies presented in this chapter are considered *optimization methods,* since solutions cannot be improved upon. Such methodology is rare in international O-I decision making and provides opportunities for application and future use in this important decision-making area of concern.

Game Theory Methodology for O-I Proportional Allocation Decisions

One of the main justifications for outsourcing is that firms that do not outsource will be at a competitive disadvantage to others in the same industry that adopt this strategy ("Discover Weights the Risk" 2004; Smith 2004). In other words, industry competition drives strategic planners to use the outsourcing strategy for competitive reasons. Understanding and responding to competitive moves or behavior is essential for any successful firm. One methodology that is ideally suited to aid in strategy choice decisions is "game theory."

Game theory (GT) is an extension of *decision theory* (DT) (which was discussed in Chapter 7), both of which address problems with multiple *strategies* or *alternatives*, a choice of which results in *payoffs* under differing *states of nature* (Dixit and Skeath 2004; Hargreaves-Heap and Varoufakis 2004; Miller 2003; Montet and Serra 2004). There are some differences between DT and GT. Unlike DT problems that exist in certainty, risk, or uncertainty environments, a GT problem exists in a *"conflict" decision environment*. In *conflict situations,* strategic choices involve moves and countermoves until the game is at an end and final payoff is derived. Since the outsourcing decision is usually based on competitor behavior, GT is ideally suited to model such behavior.

Also unlike DT, which allows only *pure strategy* decisions (i.e., only one alternative is selected), GT allows for *mixed strategy* decisions, where proportions of more than one strategy or alternative can be selected (e.g., 80 percent of Alternative 1 and 20 percent of Alternative 2). GT can solve both pure strategy and mixed strategy games, which makes it ideal for determining the allocation proportion decision between outsourcers and insourcers.

Lastly, while DT does not guarantee an optimal solution, GT does. In GT problems a compromise is the optimal solution possible if both players are playing a perfect game to win. This is reasonable for the O-I decision, since all firms in any industry play to win profits, market share, etc. GT solution methodologies give the exact strategy or proportions of strategies to achieve an optimal, compromised solution.

Game Theory Model Elements

While game theory problems can have more than two players, we will limit this discussion to a two-person, zero-sum game. In a *two-person, zero-sum game* there are two players; what one player gains, the other loses. For any firm conducting business in an industry of competitors, one can safely assume that a firm opposes all of its competitors, hence giving rise to a two-sided or two-person, zero-sum game. For example, consider market share in a single industry. What one firm gains in market share is taken away from other firms in the industry as a whole. The two persons in GT models are usually referred to as Player A and Player B, as in this explanation of the GT model.

The general statement of a two-person, zero-sum game model is presented in Table 8.1. In Table 8.1 the GT model can have as many m Player A strategies and n Player B strategies. It is common in O-I problems that strategies will vary, so it is unlikely both players will have the same number of strategies (i.e., m does not have to equal n). Player A's strategies (for A_i, where $i=1, 2, \ldots, m$ strategies) are always positioned as rows in the model formulation, and Player B's strategies (for b_j, where $j=1, 2, \ldots, n$ strategies) are always positioned as columns. The intersection of the rows and columns define the *payoffs* (i.e., P_{ij}; where $i=1, 2, \ldots, m; j=1, 2, \ldots, n$) for any combined two player strategy selection. This table can be called a *game theory payoff table* and represents the model formulation of the GT problem. Similar

Table 8.1

Generalized Statement of the GT Model

Player A's strategies	Player B's strategies			
	B_1	B_2	...	B_n
A_1	P_{11}	P_{12}	...	P_{1n}
A_2	P_{21}	P_{22}	...	P_{2n}
:	:	:	:	:
A_m	P_{m1}	P_{m2}	...	P_{mn}

to a DT problem, the payoffs can be positive, zero, negative, financial or non-financial, such as ratings, scores, or percentages.

The interpretation of the GT payoff table is different from that of DT payoff tables. The payoffs are always expressed in terms of what Player A "gains" and what Player B "loses." To explain this difference look at the O-I strategy selection decision presented in the GT payoff table in Table 8.2. Assume there are two players in this game: a firm and its competitor. The firm could be facing an individual firm, a group of firms, or the entire industry, so long as what the firm gains, the others lose. Both players have a choice of two strategies: to outsource or insource production. Assume also that the payoff values in Table 8.2 represent millions of dollars in profit. If the firm (i.e., Player A) selects the Outsource Strategy 1 and the competitor (i.e., Player B) also selects the Outsource Strategy 1, the payoff is a gain of $40 million to Player A and a loss of $40 million to Player B. Likewise, if Player A selects the Outsource Strategy 1 and Player B selects the Insource Strategy 2, the payoff is an $80 million loss to Player A and a gain of $80 million to Player B. So a negative value in the payoff table is actually a gain for Player B. If Player A selects the Insource Strategy 2 and Player B selects the Outsource Strategy 1, the payoff is a $20 million gain to Player A and a $20 million loss

Table 8.2

GT Formulation of the O-I Proportion Decision Model

Firm's alternative strategies (Player A)	Competitor alternative strategies (Player B)	
	Outsource (Strategy 1)	Insource (Strategy 2)
Outsource (Strategy 1)	40	−80
Insource (Strategy 2)	20	50

to Player B. If both players select their Insource Strategy 2, Player A gains $50 million and Player B loses $50 million.

GT methodology seeks to achieve two objectives: (1) maximize the payoffs to Player A and (2) minimize the losses to Player B, thus achieving an optimal compromise between the two cross-purposed objectives. GT methodology provides both players with an individual strategy to select or a proportional combination of strategies to achieve an optimal compromise solution. The optimal solution is called the *value of the game* for both players. When a GT player selects a single or individual strategy, it is called a *pure strategy* solution, just like those obtained in DT problems. If proportions of several strategies are selected it is called a *mixed strategy* solution. Note, the sum of the proportions for either player must add up to one. Just as the pure strategy represents 100 percent of a players' choice, so must the sum of the mixed strategies add up to 100 percent.

As previously mentioned, one of the underlining assumptions that holds true in a GT problem is both players always make choices in their own best economic interest. That is, Player A always makes choices that will maximize payoffs and Player B makes choices to minimize losses. A GT solution forces both players to achieve an optimal, compromised solution. Specifically, once the optimal solution is arrived at and followed by one player, it does not matter what the other player chooses to do, since both players receive respective, optimal compromised payoffs. (This payoff property will be demonstrated with an example later in this section.)

Game Theory Model Formulation Procedure

The GT model formulation procedure consists of the following steps:

1. Determine Player A's strategies.
2. Determine Player B's strategies.
3. Construct GT payoff table (row and column headings).
4. Enter payoff values to complete GT payoff table.

To illustrate the formulation procedure with an O-I proportion allocation decision problem, suppose a client firm wishes to allocate its marketing budget to either its own marketing department (i.e., Insource) or two other marketing sources (i.e., Outsourcer A or Outsourcer B). A main competitor of the client firm outsources marketing to four competitive outsourcing organizations (i.e., Outsourcers W, X, Y, and Z). The client firm wants to take market share away from its competitor and feels a combined, proportional O-I strategy will help achieve this goal.

A marketing consulting firm has estimated if the client firm allocates all of the budget to its marketing department, and the competitor selects Outsourcer W, the net gain in market share to the client firm will be 10 percent. If the competitor selects Outsourcer X, the gain to the client firm will be 20 percent; if Outsourcer Y is selected, the gain

Table 8.3

GT Model of the O-I Strategy Selection Problem

Client firm's alternative strategies (Player A)	Competitor's alternative strategies (Player B)			
	Outsourcer W (Strategy 1)	Outsourcer X (Strategy 2)	Outsourcer Y (Strategy 3)	Outsourcer Z (Strategy 4)
Insource (Strategy 1)	10	20	5	−12
Outsourcer A (Strategy 2)	2	9	11	−15
Outsourcer B (Strategy 3)	−4	−6	21	25

to the client firm will be 5 percent; if Outsourcer Z is selected, the client firm will lose 12 percent.

If the client firm allocates all of its budget to Outsourcer A, and the competitor selects Outsourcer W, the net gain in market share to the client firm will be 2 percent. If the competitor selects Outsourcer X, the gain to the client firm will be 9 percent; if Outsourcer Y is selected, the gain to the client firm will be 11 percent; if Outsourcer Z is selected, the client firm will lose 15 percent.

If the client firm allocates all of its budget to Outsourcer B, and the competitor selects Outsourcer W, the loss in market share to the client firm will be 4 percent. If the competitor selects Outsourcer X, the loss to the client firm will be 6 percent; if Outsourcer Y is selected, the gain to the client firm will be 21 percent; and if Outsourcer Z is selected, the client firm will gain 25 percent. What is the formulation of this GT model?

Using the four-step procedure above, first determine Player A's or the client firm's strategies. The client firm has three strategies: Insource, Outsourcer A, and Outsourcer B. Next determine Player B's or the competitor's strategies. The competitor has four strategies: Outsourcer's W, X, Y, and Z. Then construct the GT payoff table as presented in Table 8.3. Finally, enter the payoffs as defined

in the problem above, completing the formulation of the GT model in Table 8.3.

Computer-Based Solutions for Game Theory Problems

There are several analytical procedures based on matrix algebra that can be used to derive GT pure strategy or mixed strategy proportions. The computational procedures are quite tedious and will not be presented here. For those interested in a basic review of some of these computational procedures, see Ecker and Kupferschmid (2004) or Hillier et al. (2005). For a more extensive discussion of the mathematics see Kelly (2002), Montet et al. (2003), and Rasmusen (2000). The Weiss (2000) software application is one of many that are commercially available for solving GT problems. To demonstrate the software, use AB:QM (Lee 1996) to generate a solution. First generate the solution for the GT O-I proportion decision model previously presented in Table 8.2. The AB:QM computer printout with the solution proportions for this model is presented in Figure 8.2.

As seen in Figure 8.2, the printout is divided into ***Input Data*** and ***Program Output*** sections. The Input Data section restates

Figure 8.2   **Computer Solution for GT O-I Proportion Decision Model**

Program: Game Theory
Problem Title : O-I Proportion Decision
***** Input Data *****

A \ B	Strategy 1	Strategy 2
Strategy 1	40	–80
Strategy 2	20	50

***** Program Output *****

Mixed Strategy

For Player A:
Probability of Strategy 1   0.200
Probability of Strategy 2   0.800

For Player B:
Probability of Strategy 1   0.867
Probability of Strategy 2   0.133

Value for this game is   24.00

***** End of Output *****

the input data for the GT problem. The Program Output section states the solution proportions (referred on the printout as a "Probability") of each strategy for selection. What does the Probability of Strategy 1 proportion of 0.200 and the Probability of Strategy 2 proportion of 0.800 mean? In this problem the client firm wants to decide how to allocate production activities between outsourcing (i.e., Strategy 1) and insourcing (i.e., Strategy 2). The proportions in the computer printout represent the solution to the proportion the production activities allocated between the outsourcer and insourcer. Specifically, Player A should allocate 20 percent of production to an Outsource Strategy 1 and 80 percent to the Insource Strategy 2. If the client firm adopts this optimal O-I proportional

strategy, it will receive a payoff of $24 million in profit (given in the printout where it states "Value for this game is"). It also means that Player B loses $24 million. So if the client firm allocates 20 percent of production activities to outsourcing and 80 percent to insourcing, they will realize $24 million regardless of what strategies the competitor chooses. That is, the optimal proportions from the GT solution guarantee the client firm $24 million despite competitor actions. To illustrate this payoff it can be seen in the solution that Player B should select 0.867 or 86.7 percent of Strategy 1 (i.e., outsourcing) and 0.133 or 13.3 percent of Strategy 2 (i.e., insourcing). Suppose Player B does not follow the proportional recommendations and chooses to simply Outsource everything (i.e., no insourcing at all)? If that course of action is taken by Player B, the value of the game to Player A is a function of the payoffs in the Outsource column of Table 8.2. The value of the game can be computed simply as:

$$\text{Value of the game} = 40\,x_1 + 20\,x_2 \qquad (1)$$

where x_1 is the optimal proportion for Outsourcing Strategy 1 and x_2 is the optimal proportion for Insourcing Strategy 2 for Player A. Plugging these optimal values in equation (1) above, the expected value of the game for Player A is as follows:

$$\text{Value of the game} = 40\,(0.2) + 20\,(0.8) = 24 \quad (2)$$

Now suppose Player B selects only Insourcing Strategy 1 instead of the Outsourcing Strategy 2. Will it make any difference? No! Plugging in the optimal proportions to that situation will again arrive at the same payoff for Player A:

$$\text{Value of the game} = -80\,x_1 + 50\,x_2 =$$
$$-80\,(0.2) + 50\,(.80) = 24 \quad (3)$$

It makes no difference what Player B chooses to do (i.e., any proportions of either strategy); it will not alter the optimal value of the game for Player A or the loss for Player B.

Look at the solution for the other GT problem formulated. The AB:QM computer printout solution for the GT O-I strategy selection model from Table 8.3 is presented in Figure 8.3. In this model the decision is one of selecting optimal O-I proportional strategies for purposes of allocating a client firm's marketing budget to achieve an increase market share. As the solution in Table 8.3 shows, Player A (i.e., the client firm) should select 0.569 or 56.9 percent of Strategy 1 (i.e., Insource strategy), 0 percent of Strategy 2 (i.e., Outsourcer A), and 0.431 or 43.1 percent of Strategy 3 (i.e., Outsourcer B). The value of the game turns out to be 3.96 percent of market share gain for Player A, which means that Player B (i.e., a competitor) will lose 3.96 percent of the market share in this two-person, zero-sum game.

Note the occurrence of a proportion of 0 percent for several of the strategies. This 0 percent denotes a *"dominated" strategy*. A *dominated* strategy should never be selected because some other single strategy is a preferable choice. Since one of the underlying assumptions of GT is that players will always act rationally in their own best interest, a strategy that should never be selected will end up with 0 proportion in an optimal GT solution.

Linear Programming for O-I Proportional Allocation Decisions

There are few O-I decisions that are not in some way limited or constrained. Client firm's have budget limitations, trust issues, computer security issues, compliance with labor agreements, etc. Adding the international context to the O-I decision creates additional limitations, like international governmental constraints, exporting issues, and regulations. All of these limitations act as constraints on any O-I

Figure 8.3 Computer Solution for GT O-I Strategy Selection Model

Program: Game Theory
Problem Title : O-I Strategy Selection Model
***** Input Data *****

A \ B	Strategy 1	Strategy 2	Strategy 3	Strategy 4
Strategy 1	10	20	5	−12
Strategy 2	2	9	11	−15
Strategy 3	−4	−6	21	2

***** Program Output *****

Mixed Strategy

For Player A:
Probability of Strategy 1   0.569
Probability of Strategy 2   0.000
Probability of Strategy 3   0.431

For Player B:
Probability of Strategy 1   0.725
Probability of Strategy 2   0.000
Probability of Strategy 3   0.000
Probability of Strategy 4   0.275

Value for this game is   3.96

***** End of Output *****

proportion decision. Trying to figure out allocation proportions between insourcing and outsourcing, while considering many possible constraints a client firm may face, offers an almost impossibly complex problem. Fortunately, there is an equally powerful modeling decision aid that can deal with the almost infinite number of constraints and still manage to arrive at an optimal allocation proportion for international O-I proportion decisions. This decision aid is called linear programming.

Linear programming (LP) is a deterministic, multivariable, constrained, single-objective optimization methodology (Hillier et al. 2005). So an LP model has known constant parameters (i.e., deterministic values), has more than one unknown or decision variable, has mathematical expressions that constrain the values of the decision variables, and seeks a single-objective optimal solution. LP is one of the most diverse methodologies in the field of operations research, permitting application to just about every possible problem situation that fits the model's assumptions. (Assumptions of the LP model will be discussed later in this section.) LP has been suggested in the outsourcing literature as a useful decision-making tool (Coman and Boaz 2000).

LP Model Elements

A generalized LP model can be stated as:

$$\text{Maximize (or Minimize): } Z = \sum_{j=1}^{n} c_j x_j \qquad (4)$$

$$\text{subject to: } \sum_{j=1}^{n} a_{ij} x_j \geq, =, \leq b_i, \text{ for } i=1, \ldots, m \quad (5)$$

$$\text{and: } x_j \geq 0, \text{ for } j=1, \ldots, n \qquad (6)$$

where x_j is the $j = 1, 2, \ldots, n$ non-negative *decision variable* or unknown; c_j is the $j = 1, 2, \ldots, n$ *contribution coefficient* that represents the marginal contribution to Z for each unit of the respective decision variable; m is the number of *constraints*; and a_{ij} where $i = 1, 2, \ldots, n$ and $j=1, 2, \ldots, m$ is *technological coefficient* that represents per-unit usage by x_j of the *right-hand-side coefficient* of b_i. The a_{ij}, b_i, and c_j are parameters in this model.

All LP model formulations consist of three elements: an *objective function* (i.e., equation (4) above), *constraints* (i.e., equation (5) above), and the *non-negativity* or *given requirements* (i.e.,

equation (6) above). The objective function is generally expressed as one of the following:

$$\text{Maximize: } Z = c_1 x_1 + c_2 x_2 + \ldots + c_n x_n, \text{ or} \quad (7)$$

$$\text{Minimize: } Z = c_1 x_1 + c_2 x_2 + \ldots + c_n x_n \qquad (8)$$

where Z is an unknown that is not a variable but one that will be solved when we the values of the x_j decision variables are determined. The objective function is always an equality with the same form and style as the two above. If the problem has a single objective of maximizing, say profit, then use "Maximize" Z as in equation (7) above. If the objective is to minimize, say costs, then use the "Minimize" Z function as in equation (8) above. The singularity of the objective function is why LP is referred to as a single objective methodology.

The objective function is "subject to" or limited by the constraints in an LP model. The constraints can be generally expressed in terms of $\geq$, $=$, or $\leq$ expressions as follows:

$$a_{11} x_1 + a_{12} x_2 + \ldots + a_{1n} x_n \leq b_1 \qquad (9)$$

$$a_{21} x_1 + a_{22} x_2 + \ldots + a_{2n} x_n \geq b_2 \qquad (10)$$

$$a_{m1} x_1 + a_{m2} x_2 + \ldots + a_{mn} x_n = b_m \qquad (11)$$

where b_i is a right-hand-side value usually representing the availability of some economic resource, such as a budget in dollars or hours of labor available. The a_{ij} technology coefficients represent the per unit usage of the related decision variable (e.g., number of hours per one unit of its related decision variable).

Consider an example. A client firm has a maximum of only 100,000 hours of labor with which to achieve production goals. Suppose we let x_1 be the number of hours of labor allocated to an outsourcer, and let x_2 be the number of hours of labor for insourcing. The total available resources (i.e., 100,000 hours of labor) is the right-hand-side b_i, so an LP constraint for this situation would be (note there is an implied "1" for the a_{ij} in front of both decision variables in equation (12)):

$$x_1 + x_2 \leq 100,000 \text{ [Labor hours]} \qquad (12)$$

Now suppose dollar values are brought into the model to reflect differing costs of labor hours. With LP, there is no problem in using completely different criteria (e.g., dollars versus hours) in the same model as a different constraint. Assume the cost per hour for the outsourcer is $45, and the cost per hour for the insourcer is $40, with a total available budget for hourly costs of $4 million. This constraint would be:

$$45\, x_1 + 40\, x_2 \leq 4,000,000 \text{ [Dollars]} \qquad (13)$$

Constraints come in only three expressions: $\leq, \geq$, or $=$. Some models only have one type of expression for all constraints, other models use all three types. When should a particular type constraint should be used? It depends on the related right-hand-side b value. If b is a total maximum value, then use a less-than or equal-to expression. If b is a total minimum value, then use a greater-than or equal-to expression. If b is an exact value, then use an equality expression.

The left-hand-side of the constraint represents resources used with the decision variable values to stay within a particular constrained value. The right-hand-side represents a targeted amount of the resource used. When the model solves for the optimal decision variable values, it will have to conform to the limitations posed by these constraints. This is why the set of constraints in the model begins with the two words "subject to."

How many constraints are enough in modeling a problem? The answer depends on the problem. As many constraints can be placed in the model

as there are data for support. Fortunately, LP is a robust model that can eliminate or make redundant constraints not needed in the solution effort. On the other hand, too many incorrectly formulated constraints may unrealistically bind the solution and cause a misformulation.

The decision variables in LP models must be real numbers (i.e., zero or some positive value). As a formal part of the correct way to formulate an LP model, one must add an additional statement:

$$\text{and} \qquad x_1, x_2, \ldots, x_n \geq 0 \qquad (14)$$

These constraints on the decision variables communicate the type of LP model being formulated and are treated uniquely from the model's regular constraints. As presented above, this states the model requires decision variables to be zero or any positive value, including fractional values. But what if the decision variable values need to be whole units? That requires the solution to generate only integer values. This is done by revising the non-negativity requirements to also include the integer given requirement:

$$\text{and} \qquad x_1, x_2, \ldots, x_n \geq 0 \text{ and all integer} \qquad (15)$$

What this non-negativity and given requirement states is the need for an *integer LP* solution procedure solving the LP model that will force decision variables to be integer values. An even more specialized version of integer LP is called *zero-one LP*, which has its own non-negativity and given requirements statement:

$$\text{and} \qquad x_1, x_2, \ldots, x_n = 0 \text{ or } 1 \qquad (16)$$

These non-negativity and given requirements dictate a solution procedure that generates only a zero or a one for each of the decision variables. The zero-one LP model is particularly useful in selection problems, such as outsourcer provider selection problems (the type covered in Chapter 7).

Linear Programming Model Formulation Procedure

The procedure for formulating any kind of LP model includes the following steps:

1. *Determine the type of problem*: An LP problem has to be either a maximization or minimization. If the problem's main objective is about profit or sales, it will be a maximization problem. If the problem is about cost, it will be a minimization problem. The same values used to determine the type of problem are also used as contribution coefficients or c_j in the objective function.

2. *Define the decision variables*: In Step 1 the type of problem is determined by finding profit or cost contribution coefficients. How many profit or cost contribution coefficients determines the number of decision variables, since these are attached to the decision variables in the objective function. Two things to remember in defining the decision variables are: be precise in what the decision variables are determining; state any "time horizon" the problem implies.

3. *Formulate the objective function*: Since the contribution coefficients have already been identified in Step 1, and the decision variables in Step 2, all that is left is to combine these into the form of an objective function as presented in either equations (7) or (8).

4. *Formulate the constraints*: Here are two strategies that may help. Using a *right-hand-side strategy,* identify lists of available or targeted resource objectives that need to be achieved by the model. These are the right-hand-side *b* parameters. Create a column vector (i.e., a column of numbers) that will represent the *b* values in the model. Then go back and find technology coefficients to finish the

left-hand side of the constraint. Alternatively, use a *left-hand-side strategy*, where resource utilization rates (i.e., technology coefficients) are identified in tables or reports. Take the technology coefficients and align them by row or column to form the left-hand side of the constraints. Then go back and find the right-hand-side values that match up with the technology coefficients.

5. *State the non-negativity and given requirements*: Simply use the statement of non-negativity and given requirements in equations (14), (15) or (16).

To illustrate this formulation procedure with an example, let us suppose a client firm must decide the proportion of information system "help desk" service calls to allocate between existing insource labor and two outsourcers (i.e., Outsourcer Providers A and B) for one year. The primary selection criterion is to minimize variable cost per phone call. The estimated variable cost per help desk service call when insource labor is used is $120. From the *Request for Information* (RFI) responses the variable cost bid from Outsource Provider A is $80, and the bid from Outsource Provider B is $75. All of the service calls must be covered by either insourcing labor or the two outsource providers, regardless of how the final proportion of service calls are assigned. The client firm has a total, maximum fixed cost budget of $4 million for the one-year period. The estimated fixed costs for insourcing are $1.2 million, $2 million for Outsource Provider A, and $2.5 million for Outsource Provider B. One additional constraint on the final proportion decision is a labor agreement the client firm must observe. It was agreed that the current insource labor force would at minimum handle at least 10 percent of all the service calls, even if outsourcers are employed by the client firm. Given that information, what is the LP model formulation for this O-I proportion decision help desk problem?

Utilizing the five-step procedure for formulating an LP O-I proportion decision help desk problem model, note the following:

1. *Determine the type of problem*: This problem's main objective is minimizing the variable cost per service call from the three potential providers (an insourcer and two outsourcers). Thus, it is clearly a minimization problem. The three cost values of 120, 80, and 75 are the contribution coefficients, or c_j, in the objective function.

2. *Define the decision variables*: In Step 1, we identified three cost contribution coefficients. Thus we will also have three decision variables, since these contribution coefficients are attached to the decision variables in the objective function. Note also that the problem specifies a time horizon of one year. Using this information, we can define the decision variables for this problem as follows:

x_1 = proportion of help desk service calls to be covered during the year by insource labor

x_2 = proportion of help desk service calls to be covered during the year by Outsource Provider A

x_3 = proportion of help desk service calls to be covered during the year by Outsource Provider B

3. *Formulate the objective function*: Having identified the contribution coefficients in Step 1 as 120, 80, and 75, and the decision variables in Step 2 as x_1, x_2, and x_3, we will now use them in an objective function:

$$\text{Minimize: } Z = 120x_1 + 80\,x_2 + 75\,x_3 \qquad (17)$$

4. *Formulate the constraints*: The constraints in this problem can be modeled in any order; we will model them in the order given in the word problem above. The specification that all service calls "must be covered by either the insourcing labor or the two outsource providers" means that the sum of the percentages of the calls handled in-house and allocated to the two outsource providers must add up to 100.

This can be represented as the following equality LP constraint:

$$x_1 + x_2 + x_3 = 1 \qquad (18)$$

The next constraint involves the fact that the client firm has a total maximum fixed-cost budget for help desk calls of $4 million for the one-year period. This is a right-hand-side b value for the next constraint. The estimated fixed costs of $1.2 million for insourcing, $2 million for Outsource Provider A, and $2.5 million for Outsource Provider B give us the technology coefficients, a_{ij}, related to the $4 million right-hand-side value. Knowing this permits us to formulate the second constraint (note that the $4 million right-hand-side value is a maximum value, so the constraint is a less-than-or—equal-to):

$$1.2\text{ x}1 + 2.0\text{ x}2 + 2.5\text{ x}3 \le 4 \qquad (19)$$

The last constraint concerns the labor agreement, "It was agreed that the current insource labor force would at minimum handle at least 10 percent of all the service calls, even if outsourcers are employed by the client firm," which means the proportion of insourcing is greater than or equal to 10 percent. This can be stated as an LP constraint in this model as:

$$x_1 \ge 0.10 \qquad (20)$$

5. *State the Non-Negativity and Given Requirements:* Simply use a similar statement of non-negativity given in equation (14) as:

$$\text{and } x_1, x_2, x_3 \ge 0 \qquad (21)$$

The complete LP model formulation for the O-I proportion decision help desk problem is given in (22) below:

Minimize $Z = 120\,x_1 + 80\,x_2 + 75\,x_3$

[Variable cost per service call]

subject to:

$x_1 + x_2 + x_3 = 1$ [Sum of percentages]

$1.2\,x_1 + 2.0\,x_2 + 2.5\,x_3 \leq 4$ [Fixed costs in dollars]

$x_1 \geq 0.10$ [Minimum labor contract requirement]

and $x_1, x_2, x_3 \geq 0$ (22)

Now look at another proportion allocation problem, but this time formulate it using integer LP and allocating hours rather than percentages. Suppose a client firm provides phone service trouble shooting for a major computer software developer's customers (i.e., phone service help desk for software problems). The firm offers phone service 10 hours a day, 7 days a week, 52 weeks a year, or for 3,640 hour per year. The client firm must decide how to allocate these hours of service coverage. The firm has in the past outsourced all phone service work coverage to three different outsourcers (i.e., Outsource Providers A, B, and C). Now the firm believes it may be better to *backsource* (i.e., defined in Chapter 1 as reversing outsourcing and bringing the work back inside the firm) in an effort to maximize profits. The client firm estimates by insourcing it can make $57 in profit on each customer phone call. The firm also estimates it can make $45 on each call handled by Outsource Provider A, $55 on each call handled by Outsource Provider B, and $60 on each call handled by Outsource Provider C. In order to maintain service agreements with outsourcing firms, the client firm has agreed to allocate a minimum of 1,500 hours to the three outsourcers. Recent government regulations that reward firms for insourcing jobs, which make the $57 per call profit possible, require a minimum of 1,200 hours of labor to be insourced. Stated in the reply to the

RFI, Outsource Provider C has a service capacity limitation that prevents them from being allocated more than 750 total hours. Finally, the client firm has a total budget of $138,000 to pay for required business services. The estimated costs per hour for the insourced hours and three outsourcers are $36, $43, $39 and $37, respectively. Assuming whole hours have to be assigned, what is the integer LP formulation for this phone service problem?

Utilizing the five-step procedure for formulating an LP model, one should:

1. *Determine the type of problem*: This problem's primary criterion a for arriving at a solution is maximizing profit per phone call for the four potential providers (i.e., an insourcer and three outsourcers). As such, it is clearly a maximization problem. The four profit values of 57, 45, 55, and 60 are the contribution coefficients or c_j in the objective function.

2. *Define the decision variables*: Step 1 identified four profit contribution coefficients, which also determine the number of decision variables, since these contribution coefficients are attached to the decision variables in the objective function. Note also a one-year time horizon is stated in the problem. The resulting decision variables for this problem are:

x_1 = number of hours of phone service to be covered during the year by insource labor

x_2 = number of hours of phone service to be covered during the year by Outsource Provider A

x_3 = number of hours of phone service to be covered during the year by Outsource Provider B

x_4 = number of hours of phone service to be covered during the year by Outsource Provider C

3. *Formulate the objective function*: Having identified the contribution coefficients in Step 1 (i.e., 57, 45, 55, and 60), and the decision variables in Step 2 (i.e., x_1, x_2, x_3, and x_4), all that is left is to combine these into the form of an objective function:

Maximize: $Z = 57 x_1 + 45 x_2 + 55 x_3 + 60 x_4$ (23)

4. *Formulate the constraints*: For the first constraint, "The client firm must decide how to allocate these hours of service coverage," it is known that the sum of the allocation of hours to all four of the service providers must total 3,640. This can be structured as an equality LP constraint as:

$$x_1 + x_2 + x_3 + x_4 = 3,640 \qquad (24)$$

In the sentence, "In order to maintain agreements for service, the client firm agrees to allocate a minimum of 1,500 hours to the three outsourcers," a total, minimum amount of hours is given, which must be allocated to the three outsourcers. This constraint is:

$$x_2 + x_3 + x_4 \geq 1,500 \qquad (25)$$

In the sentence, "Recent government regulations that helped reward firms for insourcing jobs (which make the $57 per call profit possible) require a minimum of 1,200 hours of labor to be insourced," a minimum number of hours must be allocated exclusively to insource labor. This constraint can be structured as:

$$x_1 \geq 1,200 \qquad (26)$$

In the sentence, "Stated in the reply to the RFI, Outsource Provider C has a service capacity limitation, which prevents them from being allocated more than 750 total hours," no more than 750 hours can be allocated to Outsource Provider C. This constraint is structured as:

$$x_4 \leq 750 \qquad (27)$$

In the sentences, "Finally, the client firm has a total budget of $138,000 to pay for the required

business services. The estimated costs per hour for the insourced hours and three outsourcers are $36, $43, $39 and $37, respectively," the budget constraint is structured as:

$$36 x_1 + 43 x_2 + 39 x_3 + 37 x_4 \leq 138,000 \qquad (28)$$

5. *State the Non-Negativity and Given Requirements*: Since we are seeking an answer that allocates whole hours, simply use a statement of non-negativity and given requirements similar to that given in equation (15):

and $x_1, x_2, x_3, x_4 \geq 0$ and all integer   (29)

The complete integer LP model formulation for the O-I proportion decision problem is given in (30) below:

Maximize: $Z = 57x_1 + 45x_2 + 55x_3 + 60x_4$
[Total profit]

subject to:

$x_1 + x_2 + x_3 + x_4 = 3,640$
[Total phone service hours per year]

$x_2 + x_3 + x_4 \geq 1,500$
[Minimum hours to outsourcers]

$x_1 \geq 1,200$
[Minimum hours to insourcer]

$x_4 \leq 750$
[Maximum hours for Outsourcer C]

$36 x_1 + 43 x_2 + 39 x_3 + 37 x_4 \leq 138,000$
[Total budget for the year]

and $x_1, x_2, x_3, x_4 \geq 0$ and all integer   (30)

For one final LP model formulation, revisit some of the various decision-making criteria discussed in prior chapters in the context of an international O-I selection decision, then bring them together into one model. To formulate this model use zero-one LP decision variables. Suppose a multi-national client firm

Table 8.4

Risk Factors for International O-I Zero-One LP Provider Selection Problem

Risk factors in international O-I	Possible IP or OP countries							
	IP 1	IP 2	IP 3	OP1	OP2	OP3	OP4	OP5
Economic: Labor	7	6	8	3	7	6	5	6
Economic: Capital	3	7	5	6	8	3	7	6
Economic: Infrastructure	8	8	5	6	6	7	3	8
Total Economic Risk Rating (Target = 48)	18	21	18	15	21	16	15	20
Culture: Language	2	9	2	3	7	6	5	9
Culture: Social norms	3	2	5	2	5	3	7	6
Culture: Gender roles	2	5	10	6	9	2	3	5
Total Culture Risk Rating (Target = 45)	7	16	17	11	21	11	15	20
Demographics: Migration	3	9	10	4	10	3	3	4
Demographics: Population	7	4	3	10	3	7	10	10
Demographics: Urbanization	4	7	10	9	4	10	9	3
Total Demographic Risk Rating (Target = 52)	14	20	23	23	17	20	22	17
Politics: Ideology	9	6	4	7	5	9	8	5
Politics: Instability	8	6	9	4	8	3	5	3
Politics: Legalities	7	8	5	9	9	9	3	6
Total risk Politics Risk Rating (Target = 54)	24	20	18	20	22	21	16	14

must select one insource provider (IP) facility from three (i.e., labeled IP1, IP2, IP3) located in differing countries and two outsource provider (OP) facilities from five (i.e., labeled OP1, OP2, OP3, OP4, OP5) located in differing countries to handle production of a new product. The yearly cost of the eight facilities are $1.21 million, $1.05 million, $1.25 million, $1.08 million, $1.23 million, $1.15 million, $1.1 million, and $1.17 million, respectively. Because all eight facilities are in different countries, consultants are hired to analyze various international risk factors directly related to the facility operations, which are required to complete the client firm's agreement from selected providers. Based on a rating system, where 1 is High Risk, 5 or 6 is Average Risk, and 10 is Low Risk, the consultants developed survey questions (see examples in Chapter 5, Table 5.8) that could be grouped into

total categories of risk, including economic, culture, demographic, and politics as presented in Table 8.4. Each of these are added to arrive at a total risk rating for the four risk categories. Since the client firm plans on selecting all three facilities together, total risk target ratings for a set of three facilities chosen simultaneously are stated in Table 8.4 (e.g., Total economic risk rating target = 48) as a minimum target for the set of three facilities to be selected.

In addition to international risk, the client firm wants to maximize return on investment (ROI—see Chapter 6). Based on estimated investment costs and profit projections, eight facilities can achieve an ROI of 15 percent, 17 percent, 19 percent, 12 percent, 20 percent, 22 percent, 18 percent, and 21 percent, respectively. Since three facilities are being selected at one time, the client firm sets a minimum total ROI of 55 percent for the three facilities (i.e., the sum of the ROIs for the facilities must total 55 percent or more).

Another operations criterion is customer satisfaction benchmarks (see Chapter 7) from previous production experiences in customer service. To measure customer service, a *benchmark team* is established by the client firm, which uses executive polling (see Chapter 5) to rate on a 100-point rating scale (where 100 points is a perfect score) how they perceive the customer service performance of the eight service providers using a variety of customer service criteria (see Chapter 7, Table 7.6). Their resulting estimates are 93, 99, 87, 95, 98, 94, 98, and 94, respectively. The outsourcing team sets a minimum, collective target rating for the three facilities at 285. What is the zero-one LP model formulation for this problem?

Utilizing the five step procedure for formulating an LP model one should:

1. *Determine the type of problem*: This problem is specifically focused on minimizing total agreement costs in the selection of the potential providers (i.e., an insourcer and two outsourcers) from the set of eight. As such, it is clearly a minimization problem. The cost values, "... $1.21 million, $1.05 million, $1.25 million, $1.08 million, $1.23 million, $1.15 million, $1.1 million, and $1.17 million, respectively," are the contribution coefficients or c_j in the objective function.

2. *Define the decision variables*: Step 1 states there are eight cost contribution coefficients, which also determines the number of decision variables. Using zero-one decision variables, when the value of a variable equals one, it means that facility is chosen. When the value of the decision variable is zero, it means that provider is not chosen. Note the one-year time horizon stated in the problem. The resulting decision variables for this problem are:

x_1 = if 1, select IP1 facility for one year; if zero, do not select IP1

x_2 = if 1, select IP2 facility for one year; if zero, do not select IP2

x_3 = if 1, select IP3 facility for one year; if zero, do not select IP3

x_4 = if 1, select OP1 facility for one year; if zero, do not select OP1

x_5 = if 1, select OP2 facility for one year; if zero, do not select OP2

x_6 = if 1, select OP3 facility for one year; if zero, do not select OP3

x_7 = if 1, select OP4 facility for one year; if zero, do not select OP4

x_8 = if 1, select OP5 facility for one year; if zero, do not select OP5

3. *Formulate the objective function*: Having identified the contribution coefficients in Step 1 (i.e., 1.21, 1.05, 1.25, 1.08, 1.23, 1.15, 1.1, and 1.17), and the decision variables in Step 2 (i.e., x_1, x_2, x_3, x_4, x_5, x_6, x_7, and x_8), all that is left is to combine these into the form of an objective function:

$$\text{Minimize } Z = 1.21x_1 + 1.05x_2 + 1.25x_3 + 1.08x_5 + 1.23x_5 + 1.15x_6 + 1.1x_7 + 1.17x_8 \qquad (31)$$

4. *Formulate the constraints*: With zero-one decision variables the value of three decision variables, representing x_1 for IP1, x_2 for IP2, and x_3 for IP3 must add up to one (for the selection of one of the three). This is structured as an equality LP constraint as follows:

$$x_1 + x_2 + x_3 = 1 \qquad (32)$$

Likewise, considering, "... and two outsource facilities from five (i.e., labeled OP1, OP2, OP3, OP4, OP5) located in differing countries to handle the production of a new product they are planning," the remaining variables are set to equal two in the following constraint:

$$x_4 + x_5 + x_6 + x_7 + x_8 = 2 \qquad (33)$$

For the next set of four constraints representing the inclusion of the economic, demographic, culture, and politics risk factors, use the "left-hand-side strategy" mentioned in the LP model formulation procedure. In Table 8.4 the total risk factor rows for the four criteria are the left-hand-side values of the four constraints. Why? Because they represent the per provider contribution toward achieving the right-hand-side targeted goal. The remaining minimum target right-hand-side values representing the b_i values in the constraints are also listed in Table 8.4. These constraints are structured as:

$$18x_1 + 21x_2 + 18x_3 + 15x_4 + 21x_5 + 16x_6 + $$
$$15x_7 + 20x_8 \geq 48 \text{ [Economic risk rating]} \qquad (34)$$

$$7x_1 + 16x_2 + 17x_3 + 11x_4 + 21x_5 + 11x_6 + $$
$$15x_7 + 20x_8 \geq 45 \text{ [Culture risk rating]} \qquad (35)$$

$$14x_1 + 20x_2 + 23x_3 + 23x_4 + 17x_5 + 20x_6 + $$
$$22x_7 + 17x_8 \geq 52 \text{ [Demographic risk rating]} \qquad (36)$$

$$24x_1 + 20x_2 + 18x_3 + 20x_4 + 22x_5 + 21x_6 + $$
$$16x_7 + 14x_8 \geq 54 \text{ [Politics risk rating]} \qquad (37)$$

Continuing, the problem states, "In addition to international risk, the client firm wants to maximize their return on investment (ROI). Based on estimated investment cost and profit projections the eight facilities can achieve an ROI of 15 percent, 17 percent, 19 percent, 12 percent, 20 percent, 22 percent, 18 percent, and 21 percent, respectively. Since three facilities are being selected at one time, the client firm sets a minimum total ROI of 55 percent target for the three facilities (i.e., the sum of the ROIs for the facilities must total 55 percent or more)," structure this constraint as:

$$15x_1 + 17x_2 + 19x_3 + 12x_4 + 20x_5 + $$
$$22x_6 + 18x_7 + 21x_8 \geq 55 \text{ [Maximize ROI]} \qquad (38)$$

Lastly, the problem concludes, "Another operations criterion is customer satisfaction benchmarks . . . established by the client firm which uses executive polling (see Chapter 5) to rate on a 100-point rating scale (where 100 points is a perfect score) . . . Their resulting estimates are 93, 99, 87, 95, 98, 94, 98, and 94, respectively. The outsourcing team sets a minimum collective target rating for the three facilities at 285," structure this customer satisfaction constraint as:

$$93x_1 + 99x_2 + 87x_3 + 95x_4 + 98x_5 + $$
$$94x_6 + 98x_7 + 94x_8 \geq 285$$
$$\text{[Maximize customer satisfaction]} \qquad (39)$$

5. *State the Non-Negativity and Given Requirements:* Since the answer either selects (i.e., $x_j = 1$) or does not select ($x_j = 0$) a provider, use a statement of non-negativity and given requirements as:

$$\text{and} \qquad x_1, x_2, x_3, x_4, x_5, x_6, x_7, x_8 = 0 \text{ or } 1 \qquad (40)$$

The complete zero-one LP model for the O-I facility provider decision is given in (41) on page 167.

One point that should be noted in the various LP models above is that many additional constraints representing selection criteria can be added to these models in any order. Moreover, the criteria between constraints does not need to be converted into the same units of measure (i.e., constraints can be in dollars, rating points, ROI, etc.). This feature of modeling flexibility demonstrates one advantage of these models over less flexible methodologies presented in other chapters.

Minimize $Z = 1.21 x_1 + 1.05 x_2 + 1.25 x_3 + 1.08 x_4 + 1.23 x_5 + 1.15 x_6 + 1.1 x_7 + 1.17 x_8$

[Minimize costs]

subject to:

$x_1 + x_2 + x_3 = 1$ [Select one insource provider from three]

$x_4 + x_5 + x_6 + x_7 + x_8 = 2$ [Select two outsource providers from five]

$18x_1 + 21x_2 + 18x_3 + 15x_4 + 21x_5 + 16x_6 + 15x_7 + 20x_8$	≥ 48	[Seek to minimize total economic risk rating, Chapter 5, Table 5.9]
$7x_1 + 16x_2 + 17x_3 + 11x_4 + 21x_5 + 11x_6 + 15x_7 + 20x_8$	≥ 45	[Seek to minimize total culture risk rating, Chapter 5, Table 5.11]
$14x_1 + 20x_2 + 23x_3 + 23x_4 + 17x_5 + 20x_6 + 22x_7 + 17x_8$	≥ 52	[Seek to minimize total demographic risk rating, Chapter 5, Table 5.12]
$24x_1 + 20x_2 + 18x_3 + 20x_4 + 22x_5 + 21x_6 + 16x_7 + 14x_8$	≥ 54	[Seek to minimize total politics risk rating, Chapter 5, Table 5.10]
$15x_1 + 17x_2 + 19x_3 + 12x_4 + 20x_5 + 22x_6 + 18x_7 + 21x_8$	≥ 55	[Seek to maximize ROI, Chapter 6]
$93x_1 + 99x_2 + 87x_3 + 95x_4 + 98x_5 + 94x_6 + 98x_7 + 94x_8$	≥ 285	[Seek to maximize customer satisfaction, Chapter 7]

and $\qquad\qquad x_1, x_2, x_3, x_4, x_5, x_6, x_7, x_8 \qquad = 0$ or $1 \qquad\qquad (41)$

Computer-Based Solutions for Linear Programming Problems

Once the LP models are formulated, they are used to generate solutions for the problems they represent. The LP methodologies utilize an algorithmic *iteration process* (i.e., a set of steps used in a repeating process that changes the parameters in the model to achieve an optimization solution). Because of the enormous computational effort necessary to generate answers, various software packages are used for solution purposes. LP software packages such as *Premium Solver Platform* (solver.com) are capable of solving LP problems with 200,000 decision variables and an almost unlimited number of constraints. Complete surveys of dozens of LP software packages can be routinely found in the *OR/MS Today* publication or online at the Web site: www.lionhrtpub.com/orms/surveys/LP/LP-survey.html. Additional software information and general information on LP can be accessed on many

Web sites including http://www-fp.mcs.anl.gov/otc/guide/optweb/continuous/constrained/linearprog/. For purposes of illustration, the AB:QM, Version 4.0 software (Lee 1996) is used. This software application has similar output found in most personal computer-based systems.

Begin looking at AB:QM solutions by first solving the LP O-I Proportion Decision Help Desk Problem originally formulated in equation (22). The resulting solution using the AB:QM system is presented in Figure 8.4. The computer printout starts with a "Input Data" restatement of the model formulation, followed by the "Program Output," where the solution is obtained. The three constraints in the "Input Data" are labeled by row as C1, C2, and C3. The optimal solution for the decision variables are found in the columns of the lower sub-table labeled "Variable" and "Value," such that $x_1 = 0.100$, $x_2 = 0.000$, and $x_3 = 0.900$. This means in the O-I proportion decision help desk problem the client firm should allocate 0.10 or 10

Figure 8.4 **Computer Solution for LP O-I Proportion Decision Help Desk Problem**

Program: Linear Programming
Problem Title : LP Help Desk Problem
***** Input Data *****
Min. $Z = 120X1 + 80X2 + 75X3$
Subject to
C1 $1X1 + 1X2 + 1X3 = 1$
C2 $1.2X1 + 2X2 + 2.5X3 <= 4$
C3 $1X1 >= 0.1$
***** Program Output *****
$Z = 79.500$

Variable	Value
X1	0.100
X2	0.000
X3	0.900

Constraint	Slack/Surplus
C2	1.630
C3	0.000

***** End of Output *****

percent of the proportion of help desk service calls to be covered during the year to insource labor (i.e., x_1), 0 percent of the calls to be covered during the year to Outsource Provider A (i.e., x_2), and 0.90 or 90 percent of the calls to be covered during the year to Outsource Provider B (i.e., x_3). If the client firm follows this optimal proportion, it will realize a minimized cost per service call of only $79.50 (i.e., $Z = 79.50$).

The LP solution also identifies any ideal resources or deviation from the constraint's right-hand-side values in the sub-table labeled "Constraint" and "Slack/Surplus" below the solution sub-table. In an equality constraint (i.e., C1), there can be no variation from the right-hand-side value possible, so this constraint is not listed. For constraints that are expressed with < or >, there can be possible variation from the right-hand-side values. With a <

constraint it is possible to have *slack resources*, or a deviation represented by the sum of the products of the optimal decision variables and the respective technology coefficients, which are less than that for the right-hand-side value. When this happens, the right-hand value has not been fully achieved (i.e., deviation from targeted goal), or there are slack resources not used from the particular b_i value. Likewise, when there is a > constraint, it is possible to have *surplus resources* or the sum of the products of the optimal decision variables and the respective technology coefficients are greater than that for the right-hand-side value. When this happens, the right-hand value is exceeded or surplus resources have been used beyond those stated for a particular b_i value.

In the solution in Figure 8.4, constraint C2, representing a desire not to exceed the $4 million budget, has slack (i.e., slack because it is a < constraint) of $1.63 million. The informational value of knowing ahead of time there will be some slack budget may be useful in planning allocations to other firm projects. Since there is zero surplus in C3 (i.e., surplus because it was a > constraint) the desired minimum allocation of 10 percent is fully achieved for the insource labor hours. In summary, LP provides an optimal solution defining proportions that should be used to determine the O-I decision and identify excess budget resources, which can be reallocated to other projects.

Looking at the Integer LP O-I Proportion Decision Phone Service Problem previously presented in equation (30), and again using the integer LP AB:QM (Lee 1996), the resulting solution for the O-I proportion decision phone service problem is presented in Figure 8.5. The "Input Data" restates the model formulation, followed by the "Program Output" where the solution is obtained. The optimal solution for the all integer decision variables is $x_1 = 2,140$, $x_2 = 0$, $x_3 = 750$, and $x_4 = 750$. In the O-I proportion decision, the phone service problem

Figure 8.5 Computer Solution for Integer LP O-I Proportion Decision Phone Service Problem

Program: All Integer Programming
Problem Title : Integer LP Phone Service Problem
***** Input Data *****
Max. $Z = 57X1 + 45X2 + 55X3 + 60X4$
Subject to
C1 $1X1 + 1X2 + 1X3 + 1X4 = 3640$
C2 $1X2 + 1X3 + 1X4 >= 1500$
C3 $1X1 >= 1200$
C4 $1X4 <= 750$
C5 $36X1 + 43X2 + 39X3 + 37X4 <= 138000$
***** Program Output *****
$Z = 208230$

Variable	Value
X1	2140
X2	0
X3	750
X4	750

Constraint	Slack/Surplus
C2	0
C3	940
C4	0
C5	3960

***** End of Output *****

means the client firm should allocate 2,140 hours of phone service to be covered during the year by insource labor (i.e., x_1), 0 hours to be covered during the year by Outsource Provider A (i.e., x_2), 750 hours to be covered during the year by Outsource Provider B (i.e., x_3), and 750 hours to be covered during the year by Outsource Provider C (i.e., x_4). If the client firm follows this optimal allocation of hours, it should realize a total, maximized profit for phone service of $208,230 (i.e., $Z = 208230$).

In the solution in Figure 8.5, we can also identify the slack and surplus in the solution. Constraint C2, representing the desire to allocate at least 1,500

hours to the three outsourcers (A, B, and C or x_2, x_3, or x_4), has no surplus, meaning exactly 1,500 hours are allocated in the optimal solution. In constraint C3, representing the desire to allocate at least 1,200 hours to meet the insource labor requirement, is more than satisfied, since there is a surplus of 940 hours beyond the 1,200 target (i.e., $2,140 - 1,200 = 940$). The zero slack in constraint C4, representing the capacity limitation for Outsource Provider C, a maximum of 750 hours, is exactly equaled. Finally, the slack of $3,960 in the C5 constraint is the difference between the allowable total cost budget to pay for phone services (i.e., $138,000) and what is needed in the optimal solution (i.e., $36 \times (2,140) + 43(0) + 39(750) + 37(750) = \$134,040$). In summary, there is an optimal solution defining allocation of service hours and identifying excess budget resources that can be reallocated to other client firm projects.

Lastly, consider the Zero-one LP O-I Provider Selection Problem previously presented in equation (41). Using the zero-one LP AB:QM software (Lee 1996), the resulting solution for the international zero-one LP O-I provider selection problem is presented in Figure 8.6. The model formulation is restated in the "Input Data" section, and optimal solution is given in the "Program Output" section. The optimal solution for the all integer decision variables are $x_1 = 0$, $x_2 = 1$, $x_3 = 0$, $x_4 = 0$, $x_5 = 0$, $x_6 = 1$, $x_7 = 0$, and $x_8 = 1$. In the zero-one LP O-I provider selection problem this means the client firm should select the insource provider IP2 (i.e., $x_2 = 1$) and the outsource providers OP3 (i.e., $x_6 = 1$) and OP5 (i.e., $x_8 = 1$) to handle the production of the new product they are planning. If the client firm follows that optimal selection, it will minimize total costs to $3.370 million (i.e., $Z = 3.370$). This solution does not determine the "proportion of production" that should be allocated to each provider, but simply makes the initial provider selection. Then use one of the previous models to solve for

Figure 8.6   **Computer Solution for Zero-one LP O-I Provider Selection Problem**

Program: Zero One Programming
Problem Title : Zero-One LP Provider Selection Problem
***** Input Data *****
Min. Z = 1.21X1 + 1.05X2 + 1.25X3 + 1.08X4 + 1.23X5 + 1.15X6 + 1.1X7+ 1.17X8
Subject to
C1   1X1 + 1X2 + 1X3 >= 1
C2   1X4 + 1X5 + 1X6 + 1X7 + 1X8 >= 2
C3   18X1 + 21X2 + 12X3 + 15X4 + 21X5 + 16X6 + 15X7 + 20X8>= 48
C4   7X1 + 16X2 + 17X3 + 11X4 + 21X5 + 11X6 + 15X7 + 20X8>= 45
C5   14X1 + 20X2 + 23X3 + 23X4 + 17X5 + 20X6 + 22X7 + 17X8>= 52
C6   24X1 + 20X2 + 18X3 + 20X4 + 22X5 + 21X6 + 16X7 + 14X8>= 54
C7   15X1 + 17X2 + 19X3 + 12X4 + 20X5 + 22X6 + 18X7 + 21X8>= 55
C8   93X1 + 99X2 + 87X3 + 95X4 + 98X5 + 94X6 + 98X7 + 94X8>= 285
***** Program Output *****
Z =   3.370

Variable	Value
X1	0
X2	1
X3	0
X4	0
X5	0
X6	1
X7	0
X8	1

***** End of Output *****

an optimal proportion for each of the providers. Also, this particular software program does not provide the slack and surplus values as part of the printout, but those can be quickly determined by simply substituting the optimal solution into each constraint and solving for the slack/surplus. (That is left as an exercise for students.)

Extending the LP Solution with Duality and Sensitivity Analysis

When solving an LP problem, we seek to determine the primary or *primal solution* between the decision variable values and their use (represented by a_{ij}) of available resources (represented by b_i). One of the unique informational features of LP modeling is its ability to have its solution extended by two additional analyses: duality and sensitivity analysis. *Duality* refers to a *dual solution*, which provides useful economic trade-off information that can be used to explore *ex post* changes in model parameters. The procedural methods for duality can be found in any basic operations research textbook and will not be discussed here. For additional information on the theory and procedural aspects of LP duality, see Ecker and Kupferschmid (2004) and Hillier et al. (2005).

To illustrate the usefulness of the dual solution, return to the LP printout for the O-I proportion decision help desk problem model originally presented in

Figure 8.4 but restated with dual and sensitivity analysis values in Figure 8.7. As can be seen in Figure 8.7, there are added tables and columns of solution values. All of these values extend from the same algorithmic iterative process used to arrive at a solution from the LP model. They are a by-product of the LP solution process and are usually included in all available LP software applications. There are two sets of dual solution values: one related to the decision variables, found in the "Reduced Cost" column of the AB:QM printout, which are "dual decision variables" labeled as y_j, and one for the right-hand-side value, found in the "Shadow Price" column, which are "shadow prices" and labeled as s_i.

The *dual decision variables* y_j can be defined as the relative economic loss in Z for each unit of the related primal decision variable x_j. Simply stated, they represent what one stands to lose when going against the optimal solution. This loss is expressed in units of Z (i.e., usually dollars). As can be seen in Figure 8.7, for each primal solution decision variable, x_j, there is a dual decision variable y_j. The dual decision variable values in this problem are: $y_1 = 0$, $y_2 = 5$, and $y_3 = 0$. There is no relative economic loss in using the O-I solution proportions for x_1 and x_3, as stated in the optimal solution. This must always be the case, since the optimal primal values of $x_1 = 0.100$ and $x_3 = 0.900$ indicate it is necessary to allocate units to these variables in order to be optimal. The variable $y_2 = 5$ means for each whole unit of x_2 (i.e., if all 100 percent of the proportion is shifted away from current allocations) $5 per call handled is added. So, if it is decided ex post to force the LP model solution (perhaps with a new constraint) to shift toward increasing x_2 to 1, $5 per call (i.e., the relative economic loss in reallocation) would be added to the total cost of a phone call. This is the relative economic loss of shifting from the optimal solution to one that includes an allocation to x_2. Since the objective of this LP model is to minimize costs, do not choose

Figure 8.7 Computer Solution with Duality and Sensitivity Analysis for LP O-I Proportion Decision Help Desk Problem Model

Program: Linear Programming
Problem Title : LP Help Desk Problem
***** Input Data *****
Min. Z = 120X1 + 80X2 + 75X3
Subject to
C1   1X1 + 1X2 + 1X3 = 1
C2   1.2X1 + 2X2 + 2.5X3 <= 4
C3   1X1 >= 0.1
***** Program Output *****
Z =   79.500

Variable	Value	Dual Variable	Reduced Cost
X1	0.100	Y1	0.000
X2	0.000	Y2	5.000
X3	0.900	Y3	0.000

Constraint	Slack/Surplus	Dual Variable	Shadow Price
C2	1.630	S2	0.000
C3	0.000	S3	45.000

Right Hand Side Ranges

Constraints	Lower Limit	Current Values	Upper Limit	Allowable Increase	Allowable Decrease
C2	2.370	4.000	No limit	No limit	1.630
C3	0.000	0.100	1.000	0.900	0.100

***** End of Output *****

to go against the existing optimal solution. In some situations, perhaps because outsource providers fail to meet agreements or an outsource provider runs out of production capacity, there may be a need to know what the additional costs of bringing in a more costly outsource provider will be. The dual decision variables provide an economic valuation that can be used as an estimate of costs of changing outsourcers. Where would this information be of value in outsourcing? These added costs might be used as a penalty estimate that can be allocated to the outsource provider for breaking a contract.

The *shadow price* or s_i variables can be defined as the marginal contribution to Z (usually in terms of dollars) for one unit of the related constraint's b_i. For *binding constraints* (i.e., a constraint that has zero slack or zero surplus and represents an actual limitation in the final solution), adding to the right-hand-side value adds to Z. For binding constraints decreasing the right-hand-side value decreases Z. As can be seen in Figure 8.7, for each primal right-hand-side b_i, there is a dual shadow price variable, s_i. The dual shadow price values in this problem are $s_2 = 0.000$ and $s_3 = 45.000$. There is no shadow price for the right-hand-side values from equality constraints (note there is no s_1 dual variable in the sub-table in Figure 8.7). The variable $s_2 = 0$ means there is no marginal contribution that can be made to Z if the right-hand-side value for the C2 constraint is increased. To explain this result, one can see that the b_2 value is $4 million dollars, which is the budget constraint limiting the total amount of payment for provider services. Since there is a slack of $1.63 million, it makes economic sense that increasing a budget not fully used will not change Z, but only add to the budgetary slack. The variable $s_3 = 45$ shadow price means for each whole unit of the proportion (i.e., a whole unit is 100 percent, since the current right-hand side is in decimal values) either decrease Z by $45 through reduction of one unit from the right-hand-side value, or increase Z by $45 through an increase of the right-hand-side value by one. Of course, it is impossible to add or subtract one from the 0.1 proportion without violating the problem (i.e., you cannot have a -90 percent or 110 percent proportion in a problem where there is only 100 percent to allocate in the first place). To avoid the duality problem, an additional analysis is required to set boundaries for realistic changes in parameters. This analysis is called "sensitivity analysis."

Sensitivity analysis is a methodology applied in LP problems to generate threshold values where change in parameters alter an existing solution. This provides an indication of how much change in a parameter can be allowed before it invalidates an existing dual or primal solution. There are different forms of LP sensitivity analysis focusing on different parameters in the model. These types of LP sensitivity analyses include the a_{ij}, b_i, and c_j parameters. The procedural methods of LP sensitivity analysis can again be found in any basic operations research textbook, but fortunately are usually provided as add-on tables in most LP software applications. This discussion of sensitivity analysis will be limited to just changes in the b_i parameter.

The AB:QM software system provides b_i sensitivity analysis information in the sub-table labeled "Right-Hand-Side Ranges" (see Figure 8.7). The b_i sensitivity analysis provides possible ranges where the shadow price remains true and the obvious out-of-bound problem proportions mentioned in the previous paragraph are avoided. Looking at the b_i ranges in the AB:QM printout sub-table labeled "Right-Hand-Side Ranges," notice the designated upper and lower limits in this sensitivity analysis table. These are the boundaries or threshold boundaries under which a change in a right-hand-side b_i value impacts the existing primal solution and invalidates the shadow price valuations. Beyond the threshold boundaries the solution breaks down and the dual values become inaccurate. The informational value of these ranges must be put in the context of the problem. In Figure 8.7 there is no right-hand-side range for constraint C1 because it is an equality preventing any change from the right-hand-side value.

The sensitivity analysis for b_2 ranges from a lower limit of 2.370 with no upper limit. The current value of $4 million can be reduced to $2.37 million (i.e., an allowable decrease of $1.630 million) without changing the existing Z. This is true since the change takes place within the sensitivity analysis range, and the current value for the dual decision variable remains true at a value of 0. So a decrease of $1.630 (or any lesser amount) times 0 is still 0, or there is no change in Z. If a change lower than $1.630 is made, the solution alters and Z will change. The outcome of this change is not known without re-running the model. (This is left as a problem for students to confirm.)

The sensitivity analysis for b_3 ranges from a lower limit of 0.100 and an upper limit of 1.000 (note Figure 8.7). The current value of 0.10 represents the contractual labor requirement of allocating at least 10 percent of the proportion of the service calls to insource labor. The upper limit could be increased up to 100 percent (i.e., 1.000 in Figure 8.7), and the lower limit could be reduced down to 0 percent (i.e., 0.000 in Figure 8.7). Staying within this sensitivity analysis range means that the shadow price from the duality solution of $45 per unit will remain true. For example, if this requirement is ex post reduced from 0.1 down to 0 percent (i.e., in effect eliminating the insourcing requirement), the cost per call could further be reduced from the current optimal level of $79.50 by another $4.50 (i.e., 0.1 x $45). Alternatively, to increase the proportion to give insourcing labor 30 percent, instead of 10 percent, it would increase costs by $9.00 (i.e., 0.2 x $45). If the proportion allocated to insource labor is increased to 100 percent, it would increase the costs $40.50 (i.e., 0.9 x $45), up to $120 per call. This makes sense because the current cost per call by insource labor is $120. Where this has value is in planning through clear identification of labor costs, necessary to make insourcing cost effective. In other words, the dual solution combined with the sensitivity analysis boundary information can be used to estimate the economic value of trading-off insourcing for outsourcing. Another application is in negotiating labor contracts where exact cost information can be used to make negotiations more objective.

One last point about the example problems presented here should be mentioned. While an astute student may be able to see where the duality and sensitivity analyses values originate in these simple, illustrative examples, which is the intent of using simple examples, most real world, international O-I problem models make it impractical and virtually impossible to see all interactions of variables with constraints accurately, so as to determine the dual solution or threshold boundaries. Only LP and methodologies derived from it provide the duality and sensitivity analyses capable of handling and providing answers to O-I proportional problems with an optimal solution.

While the informational value of duality valuations and sensitivity analyses are useful in planning ex post parameter changes, they are limited to one parameter change at a time. That is, no simultaneous changes of parameters are permitted if the valuations are to remain true. Each time one single b_i is changed, it is necessary to re-run the model without making other parameter changes if the original duality and sensitivity analyses information is to be useful. This should not be viewed as a major limitation, since a model can be run repeatedly and quickly using a computer. There are, though, other LP limitations, which must be considered in using this modeling methodology.

Linear Programming Model Assumptions/Limitations

The LP model presented in this chapter implicitly requires the following assumptions to be met in order to accurately arrive at an optimal solution and provide the duality and sensitivity analysis information (Schniederjans 1995, 3):

- *Proportionality*: Each unit of each decision variable x_j contributes c_j units to the objective function, and utilizes a_{ij} units of the b_i values in the constraints.
- *Additivity*: The contribution to the objective function and the technological coefficients in

Table 8.5

Methodologies Useful in Selecting O-I Provider Proportions

Name of methodology	Usefulness and application to outsourcing decision
Non-linear programming	Useful for dealing with LP problems when non-linear decision variables are present in the problem (Hillier et al. 2005). Useful in situations where a profit or cost objective function may have a geometric relationship, or where the technology coefficient usage is non-linear. This methodology might be employed by a client firm with low product quality that could improve its reputation by association with an outsource provider that is a quality product industry leader.
Fuzzy linear programming	Useful when LP model parameters are not known with certainty (Kickert 1979). In this model weights can be applied allowing for upper- and lower-level targeted resource goals. This methodology might be used when cost or profit estimates of an O-I arrangement range widely and cannot be brought to a specific, deterministic value necessary for an LP model.
Goal programming	Useful in situations where there are multiple goals to be considered (Schniederjans 1995). Whereas LP models either maximize profit or minimize costs, goal programming permits every constraint in an LP model to be considered as a goal to be achieved. Goal programming also permits ranking and weighting of goals. This methodology might be used by client firms that have strong preferences for fully utilizing specific resources (e.g., minimizing labor hours while maximizing profit). Goal programming permits constraints to be ranked higher or lower, permitting them a higher priority of consideration in a final optimal solution over less important or lower-ranked constraints.
Dynamic programming	Useful in dealing with a sequence of interrelated decisions, where the objective is to optimize the overall outcome of the entire sequence of decisions over time (Hillier et al. 2005). Since the basic international O-I decison process requires a sequence of decisions, from strategic to tactical to operational, this methodology is ideal for the O-I sequential decision process.
Data envelopment analysis	Useful in constrained problems where the efficiency of trade-offs in terms of inputs and outputs required in an outsourcing agreement can be used to compare differing outsource proposals (Cooper et al. 2000). This method can be used to determine the weighting that can select outsource providers (based on efficiency) as well as mathematical weighting that can be used in other decision models (e.g., decision theory models). It is very useful in modeling the O-I proportion decision problem.

the constraints are independent of the values of the decision variables (i.e., there is no synergistic impact for any combination of decision variables that may end up on a solution, or two plus two has to equal four).

- *Divisibility*: Decision variables are permitted to be fractional values.
- *Certainty*: All parameters, a_{ij}, b_i, and c_j must be known with certainty.
- *Linearity*: The objective function and all constraints are linear.

The Divisibility requirement above is relaxed in the case of integer LP and zero-one LP, since these models have integer given requirements. In addition to these assumptions, the accuracy of all LP model solutions are completely dependent on the accuracy of the a_{ij}, b_i, and c_j parameters.

Some of these limitations can be further relaxed by the use of other operations research methodologies listed in Table 8.5. These methods are based in part on the LP formulation and algorithmic solution procedures.

Summary

The decision to undertake an outsourcing strategy requires consideration of what is to be outsourced and what will remain insourced. This chapter presented methodologies useful in determining an optimal proportion, which seeks to allocate business activities between outsourcers and insourcers. Two methodologies are game theory and linear programming. Game theory was shown to be useful as a logical extension of decision theory methods in conflict situations often encountered in international O-I decision making. Linear programming was demonstrated to be a highly flexible methodology capable of considering multiple variables and multiple criteria in rendering an optimal proportion allocation between outsourcing and insourcing business activities.

While this is the last chapter of this textbook, there is an Epilogue that follows. It represents both a collective summation of what this textbook is about and a probable look into the future of the outsourcing industry if businesses choose a wrong course of action in outsourcing activities.

Review Terms

Additivity
Alternatives
Backsource
Benchmark team
Binding constraints
Business process outsourcing (BPO)
Certainty
Conflict situations
Constraints
Contribution coefficients
Data envelopment analysis
Decision theory (DT)
Decision variables
Divisibility
Dominated strategy
Dual decision variables
Dual solution
Duality
Dynamic programming
Ex post
Fuzzy linear programming
Game theory (GT)
Game theory payoff table
Goal programming
Integer LP

Iteration process
Left-hand-side strategy
Linear programming (LP)
Linearity
Mixed strategy
Non-linear programming
Operations research
Optimization methods
Payoffs
Primal solution
Proportionality
Pure strategy
Request for Information (RFI)
Right-hand-side coefficient
Right-hand-side strategy
Sensitivity analysis
Shadow price
Slack resources
States of nature
Strategies
Surplus resources
Technological coefficients
Two-person, zero-sum game
Value of the game
Zero-one LP

Discussion Questions

1. What is an international O-I proportional decision?
2. How is the two-person, zero-sum game theory problem related to O-I decision making?
3. Does it make sense that in any type of O-I decision-making situation, payoff values modeled using game theory can be both negative and positive? Explain.
4. Why does game theory solution proportions provide a strategy that ensures the same value of the game to both players?
5. Why are linear programming solutions optimal?
6. Why is there a need for differing types of decision variables (i.e., real values, integer values, zero-one values) in LP models?
7. How is it possible to incorporate risk factors or risk criteria into a linear programming model?
8. Why use LP duality and sensitivity analysis when solving an O-I problem?

Concept Questions

1. What types of answers do game theory models provide a decision maker?
2. What are the modeling differences between decision theory and game theory?
3. What is the formulation procedure for a game theory model?
4. What is the value of the game in a game theory problem?
5. How many constraints or decision variables can be modeled in an LP problem?
6. What is the formulation procedure for a linear programming model?

7. What is the definition of a dual decision variable?
8. What is the informational value of a right-hand-side sensitivity analysis range?

Methodology Problems

1. Assume there are two players in this game: a firm and a competitor. The firm will be Player A and the competitor will be Player B. Both players have a choice of two strategies: to outsource accounting business processes or to insource them. If the firm selects the outsource strategy, and the competitor also selects the outsource strategy, the payoff is a gain of $20 million to Player A. If Player A selects the outsource strategy and Player B selects the insource strategy, the payoff is a $40 million loss to Player A. If Player A selects the insource strategy and Player B selects the outsource strategy, the payoff is $15 million gain to Player A. If both players select the insource strategy, Player A gains $40 million. What is the GT model formulation of this problem?

2. Assume a client firm wants to allocate its production budget to either its own production department or two other production sources (i.e., Outsourcer A or Outsourcer B). The client firm's main competitor outsources the production to three alternative outsourcing organizations (i.e., Outsourcers X, Y, and Z). The client firm wants to maximize its profit. The client firm has estimated that if it insources all of its budget, and the competitor selects Outsourcer X, the net profit to the client firm will be $12 million. If the competitor selects Outsourcer Y, the gain to the client firm will be 15 million, and if Outsourcer Z is selected, the gain to the client firm will be $9 million. If the client firm allocates all of its budget to Outsourcer A, and the competitor selects Outsourcer X, the net profit to the client firm will be $4 million. If the competitor

selects Outsourcer Y, the gain to the client firm will be $1 million, and if Outsourcer Z is selected, the client firm will lose $5 million. If the client firm allocates all of its budget to Outsourcer B, and the competitor selects Outsourcer X, the net profit to the client firm will be $1 million. If the competitor selects Outsourcer Y, the loss to the client firm will be $7 million, and if Outsourcer Z is selected, the client firm will lose $11 million. What is the GT model formulation of this problem?

3. Assume a client firm wants to allocate its information systems budget to one of four outsourcers (i.e., Outsourcers A, B, C, and D). The competition outsources its information systems to five alternative outsourcing organizations (i.e., Outsourcers V, W. X, Y, and Z). The client firm wants to maximize market share and has estimated in the table below the possible market share results, given the various selection combinations. What is the GT model formulation of this problem?

Firm/Comp.	V	W	X	Y	Z
A	5	8	9	11	12
B	−8	−9	−3	2	1
C	−1	1	2	4	4
D	13	15	17	20	19

4. Suppose you have modeled a profit maximizing GT problem for a client firm, where the payoffs are in millions of dollars, and the firm is allocating a budget to a possible combination of three outsourcers (i.e., Strategy 1, Strategy 2, and Strategy 3) to achieve them. The AB:QM solution for this model is given below in the printout. What are the optimal strategy proportions that the client firm should use to allocate its budget? What is the resulting value of the game to the client firm?

***** Input Data *****

A \ B	Strategy 1	Strategy 2	Strategy 3
Strategy 1	34	23	54
Strategy 2	12	34	21
Strategy 3	22	26	27

A \ B Strategy 1

***** Program Output *****

Mixed Strategy

For Player A:

Probability of Strategy 1	0.667
Probability of Strategy 2	0.333
Probability of Strategy 3	0.000

For Player B:

Probability of Strategy 1	0.333
Probability of Strategy 2	0.667
Probability of Strategy 3	0.000
Value for this game is	26.67

***** End of Output *****

5. Suppose you have modeled a market share maximizing GT problem for a client firm, where the payoffs are in percentages of increased market share to the client firm, given the client firm allocates its budget to a possible combination of four outsourcers (i.e., Strategy 1, Strategy 2, Strategy 3, and Strategy 4) to achieve them. The AB:QM solution for this model is given below in the print-

out. What are the optimal strategy proportions that the client firm should use to allocate its budget? What is the resulting value of the game to the client firm? Does this problem have any dominated alternatives? Explain.

***** Input Data *****

A \ B	Strategy 1	Strategy 2	Strategy 3
Strategy 1	12	22	14
Strategy 2	15	18	11
Strategy 3	10	9	20
Strategy 4	13	12	25

***** Program Output *****

Mixed Strategy

For Player A:

Probabilty of Strategy 1	0.000
Probabilty of Strategy 2	0.750
Probabilty of Strategy 3	0.000
Probabilty of Strategy 4	0.250

For Player B:

Probabilty of Strategy 1	0.875
Probabilty of Strategy 2	0.000
Probabilty of Strategy 3	0.125

Value for this game is 14.50
***** End of Output *****

6. Suppose a client firm has to decide the hour allocation of information system work between existing insource labor and one outsourcer provider for a period of one year. Their primary selection criteria is to minimize variable costs per hour of service. The estimated variable costs per hour of service by insource labor is $200. The outsource provider costs per hour is estimated at $185. All 4,000 hours of the service must be covered by either the insourcing labor or the outsource provider, regardless of how the final proportion is assigned. It is expected that the outsource provider will receive at least 25 percent of the hours allocated, and the insource labor must receive at least 20 percent. The insource labor cannot handle more than 80 percent of the total hours, because of labor limitations. What is the integer LP model formulation for this O-I hour allocation problem?

7. A client firm must allocate production between its own internal department and two outsourcers (i.e., Outsourcers A and B). The primary objective is to maximize profit. The total profit possible for the three sources of production are $3 million, $2.7 million, and $4 million, respectively. There are constraints that limit production. The internal department can at maximum handle 40 percent of the total production. Each outsourcer is limited at maximum to handling 50 percent of the total production. There is an internal department labor agreement requiring at least 15 percent of the production to be handled by the internal department. What is the LP model formulation for this O-I proportional allocation problem?

8. A client firm must select one provider from three: one internal department and two outsourcers (i.e., Outsourcers A and B) to provide services during a one year planning horizon. The primary objective is to maximize profit. The total profit possible during the next year for the three providers are $21 million, $25 million, and $27 million, respectively. The client firm has set a

quality service target rating of at least 90 percent customer satisfaction. The three providers currently have a 91, 93, and an 87 percent rating, respectively. The client firm also has set a delivery service target rating of at least 85 percent on-time delivery rating. The three providers currently have an 87, 84, and a 95 percent rating, respectively. The client firm also has set a risk target rating of no more than 15 percent rating. The three providers currently have a 10, 8, and 5 percent risk rating, respectively. What is the zero-one LP model formulation for this O-I provider selection problem?

9. Below is an AB:QM computer printout of an LP model. The constraints are labeled for the types of resources they represent. In this model the decision variables are defined as: x_1 = number of hours of service to be covered by insource labor; x_2 = number of hours of service to be covered by Outsource Provider A; and x_3 = number of hours of service to be covered by Outsource Provider B. What is the optimal allocation hours in this problem? What slack or surplus hours exist? What is the maximized profit for the year?

***** Input Data *****

Max. Z = 175X1 + 185X2 + 170X3

     [Profit per hour]

Subject to

C1   1X1 + 1X2 + 1X3 = 10000

         [Total hours that must
         be covered by all three
         providers]

C2   1X1 >= 1000

         [Minimum hours that insource
         labor must cover]

C3   1X2 + 1X3 <= 7500

         [Maximum hours that both
         outsourcers can provide]

***** Program Output *****

Z =1825000.000

Variable	Value	Dual Variable	Reduced Cost
X1	2500.000	Y1	0.000
X2	7500.000	Y2	0.000
X3	0.000	Y3	15.000

Constraint Slack/Surplus Dual Variable Shadow Price

Constraint	Slack/Surplus	Dual Variable	Shadow Price
C2	1500.000	S2	0.000
C3	0.000	S3	10.000

Right-Hand-Side Ranges

Constraints	Lower Limit	Current Values	Upper Limit	Allowable Increase	Allowable Decrease
C1	8500	10000	No limit	No limit	1500.000
C2	No limit	1000	2500	1500	No limit
C3	0	7500	9000	1500	7500

***** End of Output *****

10. (Use the LP problem printout solution from Problem 9 to answer these questions.) What are the dual decision variable values? What do they mean in this problem? What are the shadow price values of the resources in this problem? What do they mean? What is the b_2 sensitivity analysis range? What do the range values mean in this problem?

11. Below is an AB:QM computer printout of an LP model. The constraints are labeled for the types of resources they represent. In this model the decision variables are defined as: f: x_1 = number of hours of service to be covered by Outsource Provider A; x_2 = number of hours of service to be covered by Outsource Provider B; x_3 = number of hours of service to be covered

by Outsource Provider C; and x_4 = number of hours of service to be covered by Outsource Provider D. What is the optimal allocation hours in this problem? What slack or surplus hours do we have? What is the minimized cost for the year?

***** Input Data *****

Min. Z = 19X1 + 18X2 + 15X3 + 21X4
　　　　[Cost per hour]

Subject to

C1　　　1X1 + 1X2 + 1X3 + 1X4 = 100000
　　　　[Total hours to be outsourced]
C2　　　1X2 + 1X3 <= 50000
　　　　[Maximum hours for Outsourcers B and C]
C3　　　1X1 + 1X2 + 1X4 >= 80000
　　　　[Minimum hours for Outsourcers A, B and D]
C4　　　1X1 + 1X4 >= 35000
　　　　[Minimum hours for Outsourcers A and D]

***** Program Output *****
Z =1790000.000

Variable	Value	Dual Variable	Reduced Cost
X1	50000	Y1	0
X2	30000	Y2	0
X3	20000	Y3	0
X4	0	Y4	2

Constraint	Slack/ Surplus	Dual Variable	Shadow Price
C2	0	S2	1
C3	0	S3	–3
C4	15000	S4	0

Right-Hand-Side Ranges

Constraints	Lower Limit	Current Values	Upper Limit	Allowable Increase	Allowable Decrease
C1	85000	100000	130000	30000	15000
C2	20000	50000	65000	15000	30000
C3	50000	80000	100000	20000	30000
C4	No limit	35000	50000	15000	No limit

***** End of Output *****

12. (Use the LP problem printout solution from Problem 11 to answer these questions.) What are the dual decision variable values? What do they mean in this problem? What are the shadow prices values of the resources in this problem? What do they mean? What is the four b_j sensitivity analysis ranges? What do these range values mean in this problem?

References

Coman, A., and Boaz, R. "Production Outsourcing: A Linear Programming Model for the Theory-of-Constraints." *International Journal of Production Research* 38, no. 7 (2000): 1631–1639.

Cooper, W. W.; Seiford, L. M.; and Tone, K. *Data Envelopment Analysis*. Boston: Kluwer Academic Publishers, 2000.

Cullen, S., and Willcocks, L. *Intelligent IT Outsourcing*. London: Butterworth-Heinemann, 2003.

"Discover Weights the Risk." *Outsourcing Intelligence Bulletin: FSO Magazine* 11, no. 1 (Sept. 19–26, 2004), editor@fsoutsourcing.com.

Dixit, A. K., and Skeath, S. *Games of Strategy*. 2nd ed. New York: W. W. Norton, 2004.

Ecker, J. G., and Kupferschmid, M. *Introduction to Operations Research*. Malabar, FL: Kreiger Publishing, 2004.

Hargreaves-Heap, S. P., and Varoufakis, Y. *Game Theory: A Critical Introduction*. London: Routledge, 2004.

Hillier, F. S.; Lieberman, G. J.; and Lieberman, G. *Introduction to Operations Research*. New York: McGraw-Hill, 2005.

Kelly, A. *Decision Making Using Game Theory.* Cambridge: Cambridge University Press, 2002.

Kickert, W. J. *Fuzzy Theories on Decision Making.* The Hague: Martinus Nijhoff, 1979.

Lee, S. M. *AB:QM Software.* Boston: Allyn and Bacon, 1996.

Miller, J. D. G*ame Theory at Work: How to Use Game Theory to Outthink and Outmaneuver Your Competition.* New York: McGraw-Hill, 2003.

Montet, C.; Dexter, C.; and Serra, D. *Game Theory and Economics.* New York: Palgrave/MacMillan, 2003.

Montet, C., and Serra, D. *Game Theory and Economics.* Houndmills, England: Palgrave/Macmillan, 2004.

Rasmusen, E. *Games and Information: An Introduction to Game Theory.* 3rd ed. Malden, MA: Blackwell Publishers, 2000.

Schniederjans, M. J. *Goal Programming: Methodology and Applications.* Boston: Kluwer Academic Publishers, 1995.

Smith, I. "Outsourcing Would Benefit U.S. Economy in the Long Run." *Outsourcing Intelligence Bulletin: FSO Magazine* 9, no. 2 (June 27–July 4, 2004), editor@fs outsourcing.com.

Weiss, H. J. *DS for Windows.* 2nd ed. Upper Saddle River, NJ: Prentice Hall, 2000.

Epilogue: There Are Wrong Ways and Rights Ways to Outsource-Insource in an International Context

Learning Objectives   After completing this chapter you should be able to:

- Identify and avoid possible wrong ways of performing outsourcing-insourcing.
- Understand possible consequences of performing outsourcing-insourcing the wrong way.
- Identify and seek possible right ways of performing outsourcing-insourcing.
- Understand possible consequences of performing outsourcing-insourcing the right way.
- Understand possible future changes that may impact the outsourcing industry.

Introduction

Sadly, there are many books and articles whose titles are similar to that of Schartz and Gibb's (1999) book *When Good Companies Do Bad Things* decrying the wrong way to conduct business. The notion of "bad or good," "wrong or right" implies values based on what societies define as codes of ethical conduct. There are as many codes of ethical conduct as there are societies.

Downing et al. (2003) has empirically shown there is value in outsourcing if it is done "right." It is interesting to note recent suggestions on industry best practices in outsourcing warn as much of how not to use it, as how it can be used (Reifer 2004).

While this textbook has tried to reveal right ways of undertaking an O-I project, it is important to stress how outsourcing has been wrongly employed in the past, so that those practices can be avoided in the future. To emphasize this point, the trends for the industry of outsourcing should be extrapolated in order to explore possible future negative consequence scenarios. Not wanting to end negatively, a review and summary of some of the right ways of conducting outsourcing are presented as well as suggestions of where O-I should be heading in the future. It is hoped this speculation on the O-I industry may provide guidelines to aid the reader in maximizing outcomes of future outsourcing projects and better preparing for possible risk situations.

The Wrong Way to O-I

While the listing of possible wrong ways of conducting an O-I project could be endless, discussion will be limited here to those that have appeared in the literature and which particularly need to be avoided.

- Avoid outsourcing non-core business activities that could become core business activities in the future.
- Avoid outsourcing critical information and relying on trust.
- Avoid outsourcing just to make the accounting books look good.
- Avoid outsourcing just to handle or deal with labor problems.
- Avoid outsourcing just to mitigate risks.
- Avoid outsourcing business activities that are easily copied by outsourcing firms.
- Avoid international outsourcing risks in foreign countries where you will be at a disadvantage for reasons of politics, culture, economics, or demographics.

Now, this chapter will consider each of these and examine the related available literature to better define what is at risk.

Avoid Outsourcing Critical or Non-Core Business Activities That Could Become Core Business Activities in the Future

As Adler (2003) points out in a listing of risks client firms run, there is a potential they might outsource what could become (or could have become) a core activity in the future. While multi-criteria scoring methodologies have been introduced in this textbook, permitting a more objective way of identifying non-core business activities, the final selection process of non-core activities is basically subjective and lacks any precise, organized decision framework.

Here is an example of an extreme outsourcing situation. Capgemini Energy is an outsourcing firm specializing in outsourcing to energy industry clients. TXU Corporation is an energy producing/delivering firm. According to Wijnen (2004) these firms entered into a joint venture where Capgemini provides outsourcing services to TXU. Yet, Capgemini owns 97 percent of the joint venture, and TXU Corporation only owns 3 percent. While TXU believes its core competencies are best utilized in this type of arrangement, the ownership percentage does not appear to allow for potential growth to find or develop new core competencies in this joint venture in the future.

The current literature supporting *business process outsourcing* (BPO) is substantial, indicating it is presently the leading economic growth segment in the outsourcing industry ("Bangladesh to Provide Outsourcing . . ." 2004; "Dubai Has Business Process . . ." 2004). The BPO sector in India has been growing at almost 60 to 70 per cent per annum ("India Is the Leading Outsourcing . . ." 2004). Indeed, some organizations consider it foolish to waste time experimenting with smaller outsourcing projects of only select business activities. Client firms should instead jump into a BPO relationship to avoid coordination activities necessary when only a partial segment of a business function (e.g., outsourcing only accounts payable from all of the accounting activities) is outsourced and must be coordinated in differing locations ("Outsourcing Expectations Surpass . . ." 2004). While research generally supports the idea of outsourcing specific non-core competency business activities, and even multiple outsourcing activities from a single functional area (see Rabinovich et al. 1999), we believe future research on BPO will most likely reveal that this poses real risks of disrupting business organizations, potentially revealing proprietary secrets, and preventing future core competencies from being developed. It has been observed, recently, that some firms are having second thoughts about BPOs. The META Group, Inc. (i.e., a research group) has reported, while 70 percent of the businesses in a recent survey will renew outsourcing agreements, many will reduce both the scope and the duration of the original agreement ("Eighty Percent Financial Firms to Outsource . . ." 2004). How can any client firm maintain secrets if all accounting or information systems' business activities are outsourced? How can any client firm hope to maintain markets if all of its marketing business activities are outsourced to providers who also outsource to their competitors? How can any client firm quickly adapt to its home market customer product needs if they have outsourced all operations to a foreign outsource provider, particularly when a change in the market reveals a new potential for a core competency that could be developed?

One additional point in the development of core competencies is the impact that outsourcing has on retarding the growth of new technologies in client firms. Many firms have tried to avoid increasing costs of information technology by using an outsourcing strategy, where the provider is responsible for purchasing and maintaining technologies. Unfortunately, many firms, particularly in the banking industry, have rushed offshore to outsource without investigating the practice and technology abilities of providers ("Challenges to Consider" 2004). As a result, many banks find a hands-off management of information technology means spending much more money for low quality work. Trying to rebuild an information technology group without hands-on experience is considerably more costly and time consuming than had the banks simply retooled existing technologies.

Another way of looking at this problem is in forgone opportunities, or risk of opportunity loss. For example, there have been a number of large outsourcing deals cancelled over the last few years. J.P.

Morgan Chase organization, for example, announced cancellation of a more than $5 billion outsourcing contract with IBM ("J.P. Morgan Takes . . ." 2004). This change involves taking back over 4,000 information technology employees. Just think of the loss of loyalty those 4,000 employees may have toward their old employer! J.P. Morgan CIO believes managing its own IT infrastructure is the best policy for long-term growth and success of the company and its shareholders. This change in policy was brought about by J. P. Morgan's acquisition of Bank One, a financial institution. How can firms know ahead of time what future mergers or acquisitions might lead to in the development of longer-term, new, strategic core competencies? Put another way, what opportunities have client firms forgone by a BPO, where much of the human and capital resources are outsourced?

Avoid Outsourcing Critical Information and Relying on Trust

Referred to by Adler (2003) as *spillover risk*, outsourcing firms are exposed to the possibility that confidential or critical information might leak to competitors or be used by the outsourcing firm to eventually take over the client firm's business. To help avoid this risk situation some accounting organizations, like the *American Institute of Certified Public Accountants* (AICPA), have drafted new standards for members ("U.S. Accounting Firms . . ." 2004). The AICPA standard now requires outsource providers to inform client firms if they have outsourced client work to third parties that might be competitors of the client firm. The standards also require under the new rules that third-party service providers maintain confidentiality of the client's information.

Industry insiders have remarked the international context of outsourcing adds risks, which presently, client firms have ignored or failed to consider in their outsourcing strategy ("Challenges to Consider" 2004, O'Bryan 2004). Customers are not oblivious and can react with negative consequences to the client firm as noted by Wolosky (2004) when U.S. customers found out their U.S. tax returns were processed in India. Diddi (2004) outlines how countries, like Russia and China, are currently major players in the worldwide outsourcing industry. Considering how recently these same nations considered themselves the enemy of western nations and their agents (i.e., western business organizations), does it make sense for a client firm to open itself (i.e., revealing the most intimate, business operations secrets, the client firm markets, and resulting in the eventual dependency on an outsource provider for specific business activities) to the risks of dealing with governments or competitive businesses in foreign countries, which might gain advantages by sharing confidences existing between a client and outsource provider? It is only prudent to weigh risks and consider them in any outsource provider decision making in an effort to avoid potential losses in the future.

Trust is a difficult condition to define in the international context, since the differences in culture, politics, economics, and demographics create differences in how people view "right and wrong." A business person doing something perfectly "right" in one country may be viewed as doing something "wrong" in another. These differences can lead inevitably to groundless distrust of a foreign outsource provider. To avoid this it is best to initially base everything, which can be defined and delineated, in a contractual arrangement. A legal, binding document or contract is the best way to begin a relationship in an international context. As presented in the case studies in Chapter 3, even a document can be misinterpreted and result in distrust, but it is an accepted means of interaction and exchange respected the world over. As such, a contract acts as a bridge upon which trust can be built and over time earned through mutually beneficial cooperative efforts.

Avoid Outsourcing Just to Make the Accounting Books Look Good

If stockholders do not like what they see on the accounting books of a company, they tend to sell shares of stock, which causes the company's stock price to drop. This is bad for CEO's and boards of directors. So they tend to make decisions, like going with an outsourcing strategy, which will have immediate results on the bottom line. This puts pressure on firms to keep the books always looking attractive, sometimes despite the reality or true condition of the firm. Outsourcing agreements can be used to make a company's accounting books look better than they actually are, at least in the short-term. Called *uplifting the balance sheet* by Chorafas (2003, 39–44), it is little more than a set of creative accounting practices to improve a company's books. There are many of these creative accounting methods, but for the sake of an example, assume a company requires in an agreement with an outsource provider that the provider accepts a large portion of the existing, fully depreciated client firm's technology for partial payment of the provider's services. On the client firm's books the assets are fully depreciated, so there is little impact on reduction of assets. On the other hand, the increased income for the provider's services will appear at little expense to the client, while the revenues from the products/ services sold increase the return on investments of the remaining technologies of the client firm. Therefore, the client firm's income goes up, return on investment increases, there is little impact on short-term expenses, and it appears productivity from the remaining technology is increasing (when in fact these may not be true).

It is because of these uplifting tactics and concerns about possible prosecution that there have been calls from the accounting profession for a transparency in outsourcing of accounting practices from members of the accounting industry (Wolosky 2004). Of more direct concern is the fact that governments are starting to establish accounting rules that will not only prevent firms from unfairly taking advantage of the outsourcing strategy for unethical conduct, but forcibly take some of the present ethical profits out of the industry. A single ruling by the *Financial Accounting Standards Boards of the United States* against the EDS Corporation completely wiped out their operating profits on an outsourcing arrangement ("Accounting Rule Wipes . . ." 2003).

The fact is U.S. companies do not have to cheat at outsourcing to make money. The U.S. government currently extends substantial benefits to firms that outsource in an international context. For example, current corporate tax rules require U.S. companies to pay a standard rate of 35 percent on profits, but only if the money is in the U.S. ("U.S. Companies Benefit . . ." 2004). For profits from overseas operations, dollars that are kept abroad are taxed at zero percent ("U.S. Companies Eager . . ." 2004).

Avoid Outsourcing Just to Handle or Deal with Labor Problems

Managers should seek to avoid *downsizing* (i.e., reducing head counts of employees) their organizations by utilizing an outsourcing strategy. They also should not try to deal with union labor cost problems by outsourcing them. The research findings of Benson and Littler (2002) demonstrate the labor cost savings and productivity outsourcing is supposed to afford may ultimately be lost in declining work effort and lower product or service quality caused by insecurity among employees over the possible or perceived loss of jobs through outsourcing.

Avoid Outsourcing Just to Mitigate Risks

The point of mitigating risks by outsourcing, as explained in Chapter 2, is a fallacy. While it must be recognized there are many types of risk in outsourcing, and some can be reduced through an outsourcing project, it must also be recognized firms add risk to operations by using the outsourcing strategy. As Natovich (2003) has shown, many organizations consider outsourcing projects as an attractive, risk-mitigating approach. Yet it does not eliminate risk at all. The outsource provider may agree to complete a project for a fixed cost and according to a defined time schedule. Although the provider accepts some liability for traditional project risks, those, along with other forms of risk, are also shared by the client firm. A provider's failure is in fact the client firm's failure; provider risks are the client firm's risks. In addition, some risks are unique to the situation of allowing a provider to do work for a client. These include (Domberger 1998, 119–126):

- *Confidentiality risks:* Unique client firm information on markets or competitors that the client firm is targeting can be shared or even sold to a competitor.
- *Controlling risks:* If a client firm has completely outsourced production activities (i.e., a BPO), and the outsource provider does not want to enhance the product or quality as much as the client firm desires, what can the client firm do in the short term? Very little! This lack of control is also true of accounting practices, marketing planning, financial analysis, or the information systems services when BPOs are undertaken. Of course, it appears that a client firm might switch over to a new outsource provider, but at what cost to the firm and its customers?

- *Environmental risks:* In an international context outsourcing to countries that have limited or no laws on environmental pollution may sound attractive to U.S. manufacturers that pollute in excess. Nonetheless, anti-pollution "watch-dog" groups track U.S. polluters worldwide and report misgivings everywhere. These firms cannot hide bad behavior. Moreover, the U.S. firm is still liable in world courts for environmental losses. Since the outsource provider is in control of such activities, the client firm might find itself facing a dangerously costly environmental risk over which they have little control.

- *Intellectual property risks:* The client firm may have proprietary processes and technology that an outsource provider must use in completion of services for the client. Access and use of these intellectual properties constitutes a risk, since they might be shared with competitors once an outsourcing agreement with the original client has expired. Of course, an outsourcing agreement can be written to provide protection from these risks, but in reality few firms have the financial clout to extol grievances in international courts.

The best advice in trying to mitigate risks is to write the strongest outsourcing agreement possible ("Negotiating the Contract." 2004) including, but not limited to, the following points:

- Define the scope of the contract explicitly so the client can assume the provider will at least perform all of the services of the outsourced function, which the client performed prior to outsourcing.

- The agreement should include service levels and performance milestones for provider compliance, and impose stringent penalties for failure.

- The agreement should obligate the provider to remain current with evolving practices and technology.

- Pricing protection mechanisms should be formally included in the agreement such as benchmarking and market-based pricing.

- Include the client firm's right to re-bid the services to a third party or to perform the services internally if desired.

- The provider's key personnel will effectively serve as adjuncts to the client's management. In addition, the client firm should have a right to approve all individuals filling these key positions.

- Ownership of the client's intellectual property should continue to be owned by the client firm.

- It is important to establish measures wherever possible to define the client's right to terminate an agreement for just cause. This must include the right to obtain from the vendor most of the resources used by the provider to perform services, the license rights to software and materials, the right to acquire dedicated equipment, the right to assume contracts, and the right to make offers to provider personnel dedicated to providing services to the client.

- The contract should include an extraordinary events provision that obligates the provider, upon the client's request, to re-configure the service arrangement and to pass on to the client any cost reductions the provider can achieve.

Avoid Outsourcing Business Activities That Are Easily Copied by Outsourcing Firms

In an outsourcing arrangement, the client firm can unwittingly become a superfluous middle agent, unnecessary to the outsource provider's eventual takeover of the client firm's market. Many U.S. firms view their core competencies as access to the U.S. market and customer service capabilities. Many of these firms outsource back-office business activities to countries like India and China. India and China are encouraging fluency in the English language to support the growing outsourcing industry ("English Language Skills . . ." 2004). India, for example, is increasing employment of their highly educated, English-speaking workers by one million per year ("Boston Consulting Group . . ." 2004). How much longer will it be before firms, based in India or China, want to initiate competitive businesses in the U.S., so they can outsource back to their home countries in order to take advantage of the wage structures which will give them a competitive advantage over U.S.-based firms?

One suggestion by Adler (2003) that can help avoid this problem is to create an interdependence of processes between client and provider. Basically, by tying various business activities required of the outsource provider to other activities insourced by the client firm, the client will be in a better position to control and monitor outsource provider contributions. This way it would be more convenient to monitor the input and output of the provider, while not making it easy for the provider to duplicate activities to become a successful competitor. This tactic of control is another reason why the BPO strategy of outsourcing an entire functional area is not wise. Clearly, it is not as easy to create an independent and competitive business if only part of the business activities of a functional area are outsourced.

Avoid International Outsourcing Risks in Foreign Countries Where You Will Be at a Disadvantage for Reasons of Politics, Culture, Economics, or Demographics

It is wrong to ignore the international risks that are part of every outsourcing arrangement. When asked

in an interview with a partner in a leading outsourcing firm if understanding culture and political/legal issues is really important in an international context, the partner replied, "Understanding the cultural and legal environment of the offshore vendor is essential . . ." ("Negotiating a Contract . . ." 2004). The interviewee went on to say it is particularly important to understand the governing laws that exist in a provider's country, because they will undoubtedly impact human resource decisions, intellectual property rights, and data privacy issues. (For a good review of the legal issues in outsourcing see Burnett (1998).) Others, such as Meisler (2004) and Elmuti and Kahawala (2000) point out that failure to consider political, cultural, economic and other international risk factors can and often do lead to outsourcing project failure.

The *Information Security Forum* (ISF), a global not-for-profit organization with over 260 corporate and public sector members, highlights the unique risks to information presented by outsourcing critical and non-critical business functions ("Outsourcing Has Some Risky Issues . . ." 2004). The ISF and other outsourcing organizations publish reports on types of outsourcing risks firms are currently facing, as well as providing information on how they can be overcome, minimized, or controlled.

Possible Consequences of Wrong Way O-I

Discussion will be limited to three possible areas of consequence: how the outsourcing industry is at risk, the possible evolution of industries as a response to outsourcing, and the possible loss of the outsourcing industry.

Outsourcing Industry at Risk

Review of outsourcing literature undertaken in preparing this textbook reveals outsourcing as a business practice or strategy is not under control of any government or institutional body at this time. While some laws and guidelines have been created, the process of outsourcing in an international context has no governing body or reporting system established, other than individual countries' legal systems. Only the trust and legal agreements that bind outsource providers and client firms hold this form of business strategy accountable. While this freedom has allowed outsourcing to rapidly grow ("Large Outsourcing Deals on the Rise . . ." 2004), it has also positioned world economics in a riskier situation. Considering nations, particularly India, Russia, and China, which have made major economic resource allocations to train and develop millions of workers for the outsourcing industry, the possibility of a sudden decline in demand for outsourcing poses an increased risk of major economic difficulties, not just for those three nations, but all nations, since most have citizens involved in the outsourcing industry. Unlike many business mergers, an outsourcing agreement can in many cases be terminated much more quickly than an alliance or a partnership. Indeed, most outsourcing agreements are designed with a fairly short-term period in mind.

Countless articles state outsourcing is here to stay and its growth makes it seem to be a winning strategy, which is true in most cases. What could possibly come along to stop it? As stated above, trust and legal agreements are what keep outsourcing going. Suppose something would happen to cause distrust in outsourcing? Look at the possible interactive chain-effect scenario in Figure E.1, where distrust is caused by outsource providers in one country that impact the world. What is viewed as secret information in one country may be expected to be reported nationally in another. There are disclosure laws in the U.S. that require many business activities be reported in such a way that the public has full access to the information. In other countries such information is considered proprietary. While Figure E.1 proposes a dire final outcome worldwide,

it is a real possibility according to IMF economists ("Anti-Outsourcing Would Effect . . ." 2004).

The relatively short-term nature of many outsourcing agreements, the fact that client firms are often in differing countries from the provider and therefore, less concerned about possible negative consequences of discontinuing an agreement, makes all such agreements vulnerable to rapid termination. Trusting an outsource provider can quickly turn into distrust because of differences of culture, which are invariably part of doing business internationally. The speed with which trust can be turned into distrust and outsourcing agreements terminated places the outsourcing employees, the outsourcing industry, and even the government's investments in the industry at considerable risk. There is some support for this in the literature. It has been observed that negative comments about outsourcing aired in the U.S. 2004 presidential election caused a marked shift of outsourcing activities in just a matter of months from Indian firms to U.S. firms ("Outsourcing Backlash to Benefit U.S. . . ." 2004). With as much as 70 percent of India's BPOs originating from the U.S., a sudden halt in this relationship would result in billions of dollars of loss to Indian firms and hundreds of thousands of jobs lost in a relatively short period of time ("Indian BPO Industry . . ." 2004).

Another risk to the outsourcing industry is in the shift from offshore outsourcing to just offshoring. A former managing director of Compaq India put it this way, "Anything that can be outsourced can be offshored" (Meisler 2004). The offshore outsourcing industry is starting to feel the impact of firms that believe it is politically unwise to hire a foreign outsourcer when they can simply start up an offshore firm ("Knowledge Storm Releases . . ." 2004; "U.S. Firms Set Up . . ." 2004; "U.S. Companies to Shift Jobs . . ." 2004). Many firms feel that it is better to take advantage of the cost reduction possibilities in foreign countries by establishing their own busi-

Figure E.1   **A Negative Interactive Chain-effect Resulting from Distrust**

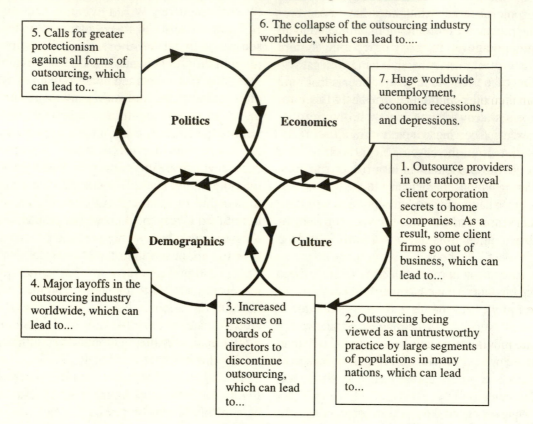

nesses in those countries than to be seen hiring a third-party outsourcing firm. The offshoring international business strategy has its own advantages and disadvantages (Caslione and Thomas 2002), but is perceived as a major threat to growth of the outsourcing industry.

Evolution of Industries

Any business strategy, like outsourcing, can be used in differing ways to have a significant impact on ways all business is conducted. Outsourcing can be viewed as a strategy by the outsource provider to acquire the client firm and its markets. This acquisition process can take a variety of forms. For example, it was previously mentioned how an initial relationship between an outsource provider with a client may result in the outsource provider taking over the markets of the client firm (see Chapter 2, Samsung's take-over of microwave products from GE). Another, more evolutionary change is now being forecast by outsource researchers. This is the natural evolution of outsourcing firms to become the best at what they do, better than any client firm. Zhao and Calantone (2003) have observed the trend of outsourcing firms specializing in research and development (R&D) to attract the very best human resource talent available, worldwide. Like a magnet, outsourcing firms are draining the best and most talented people in specialized areas to manage operations. In many cases they acquire this talent from client firms that BPO their human resources to the outsourcing firm. The outsourcing firm can then pick-and-choose the best to keep for their longer-term goals and to work with other firms as they receive other outsourcing contracts. The point is that outsourcing firms are expected to become the arbiters of industry best practices, controlling which client firm will have services and be a winner, and which client firms will have to select lesser outsourcing services (or relegating them to a loser status by comparison). It has been observed that talent in U.S. firms is drying up because outsourcing firms, even those located in the U.S., are being attracted to outsourcing permanently ("Outsourcing Backlash to Benefit U.S. . . ." 2004). It has also been observed that firms are moving from using outsourcing for small selective applications to larger BPO applications to acquire industry best practices ("IT Outsourcing Likely to Grow . . ." 2004). Additionally, Adler (2003) has observed the trend in human resource outsourcing firms to evolve into full-service BPOs from smaller selective outsourcing firms.

Loss of Outsourcing Industry

Many believe that outsourcing fails half of the time (Hall 2003). At what point might boards of directors and managers find outsourcing is not a viable strategy? Many factors can lead to major curtailment or elimination of the outsourcing industry as known today. Some firms are *backsourcing* or bringing their work back to their home countries because of poor labor or inadequate service by outsource providers (Metz 2004). Other economic factors can also contribute to a decline. For example, the demand on competent human resources in India has contributed to a labor shortage there ("Indian Outsourcing Industry . . ." 2004). This is viewed as a potentially serious issue in that country's desire to provide global labor market needs of quality employees. Not only can a shortage of quality employees slow outsourcing industry growth, it can lead to lesser quality being utilized with long-term negative consequences. Firms are starting to recognize that in some instances, the best and most cost-effective work can be done inside their own organization (Hall 2003). Also, if a government believes outsourcing is costing more than benefiting a country, it could put an end to these agreements. For example, governments control a nation's telecommunications, and telecommunications are a driving force behind the outsourcing of service jobs. It would be easy to discontinue types of telecommunications that hinder or could bring an end to select outsourcing jobs. So, it is possible to eliminate the outsourcing industry within a country if a country chooses to do so. Furthermore, the act of one country could cause others to follow suit, bringing a major reduction in worldwide outsourcing.

The Right Way to O-I

The following suggestions on the right way of conducting an O-I project are offered as a culmination to the content of the prior chapters and are based on the observations of the authors. They include:

- *Seek to use O-I as an organizational transformational process*
  - learn new ideas (to tune-up the firm)
  - train personnel
  - implement new technologies and processes
  - learn to avoid transformation risks

- *Seek to use O-I as a means to further international and global business*
  - learn about international markets (e.g., labor markets)
  - learn to identify and avoid international risks
- *Seek to use O-I to augment existing business activity resources*
  - handle production shortfalls (as temporary help)
  - handle very costly special projects (e.g., consulting projects, like facility location analysis, legal issues, etc.)

Seek to Use O-I as an Organizational Transformational Process, to Learn New Ideas, Train Personnel, and Implement New Technologies/ Processes

Sometimes referred to as *business transformation outsourcing* (BTO), organizations can take advantage of the higher level of new business process ideas, skills, and technology available through specialized outsourcing firms in order to vastly upgrade the organization ("Transforming Outsourcing . . ." 2003; Lacity et al. 1992). That is, improve the processes, skills, and technology of the firm, not substitute them for an outsourcing firm partner. Unlike traditional outsourcing, where infrastructure and personnel are handed over to the provider at a fixed price, BTO focuses on helping the client create a new infrastructure, process, technological level of performance, or business model. BTO outsourcers are often tied to meeting business performance metrics, rather than service-level agreements. In essence, BTO deals are an evolution of the standard outsourcing contract. Previously, the traditional outsource provider was responsible for maintaining a business activity at a fixed price. Now the BTO provider is expected to

change or improve the process, to return the operations to the client firm at the end of the contract, so that the client becomes self-sufficient in running the new infrastructure.

Examples of the BTO approach to outsourcing are appearing in the literature. Dun & Bradstreet (D&B), for example, recently signed an outsourcing contract with IBM to handle data acquisition and delivery services, customer service, and financial processes ("IBM Signs $180M Outsourcing . . ." 2004). Working with IBM, D&B expects to improve IBM's quality process, bolster its customer service and reduce costs. To achieve these goals, D&B will utilize IBM's ability to leverage delivery scale, global process expertise, and advanced technologies.

Another example of a BTO mentioned in Chapter 2, involved a production facility needing to upgrade their *information technology* (IT) monitoring equipment to protect against critical heating (Sawyer 2003). The use of a state-of-the-art outsourcing firm, which specialized in IT, was ideal for these needs. It resulted in substantial savings for the client firm and development of a computer monitoring system that would continuously serve the needs of the client to a better degree than what the client itself could have afforded.

There is also a need to avoid transformational risks undertaken during outsourcing in an international context. *Human resources* (HR) is an important area of risk avoidance since this usually represents the primary reason for outsourcing. Alder (2003) has found that human resource firms are advised not to trust all of their HR needs to one outsourcing firm. They should instead spread them over several outsource providers. Research reported by Alder (2003) has shown that the average number of outsourcers employed to cover HR needs by a client firm is 4.5. Natovich (2003) supports this idea as it relates to technology usage and the avoidance of outsource project failure. This research shows that a client firm cannot mitigate risks by simply assigning them to an outsource provider. Instead, Natovich (2003) and Klepper (1995) suggest the best course of action is to share risk with the outsource provider to foster the idea that the client and provider are partners. Indeed, it has been observed by Natovich (2003) that the best way to create a failed outsourcing project is to simply place the entire risk burden on the provider via the outsourcing agreement. Research findings reported in Kern and Willcocks (2001, 48) have shown that an ideal partnership in outsourcing should include:

- Non-reliance on the outsourcing agreement as a basis for the relationship
- Mutual desire to work things out and give and take
- Fair profit for the provider
- Ability to work together on a personal relationship level
- Good cultural fit between the client firm and the provider firm
- Fair treatment by the provider for transferred client firm personnel
- Perception the provider understands a client's needs and problems

Handling the various risks in global or international outsourcing has been viewed as a critical factor leading to outsourcing success (Crowley 1999). Elmuti and Kathawala (2000) found the most serious risk is the fear of job loss by everyone in the client firms. Just the thought of international outsourcing of jobs is shown to create disharmony in firms and a hostile atmosphere. It should come as no surprise that once an outsourcing strategy is adopted in one area of the firm, other employees in other areas begin to believe their jobs may be outsourced next. Elmuti and Kathawala's (2000) research suggests the best

way to deal with this risk and minimize fear is through communication and honesty about the future of job opportunities.

Another way a firm can avoid many transformational risks is illustrated by Discover Bank, the issuer of Discover Card ("Discover Weighs the Risk" 2004). They experimented with various call service outsource providers in India over a period of years and found which banking processes worked well in offshore operations, yielding the greatest savings. From this, they determined the best policy is to not outsource inbound customer service calls. Instead, the firm insourced these to U.S. call centers.

Seek to Use O-I as a Means to Further International and Global Business

By taking advantage of the finance, marketing, and operations knowledge, market access, and supply-chain connections, international outsource providers can educate a client firm as to the best ways for entering and capturing foreign markets. This education could be specifically defined within an outsourcing agreement and/or delivered through the experience client firm managers' share during the life of an outsourcing agreement.

Seek to Use Outsourcing to Augment Existing Business Activities

Rather than replacing personnel or transferring them to outsourcers, which develops fear complexes, a less threatening and more productive approach is to use outsourcing to augment existing process, human, and technology resources. In this regard outsourcing can be used to fill resource shortfalls during peak demand periods. Peak management research suggests there will be times when demand exceeds capacity, resulting in lost profits and customers (Ronen et al. 2001). Why not use outsourcing to deal with these periods of excessive demand. Doing so minimizes investments for infrequently used peak resources. This is a common strategy used by utility companies that want to avoid purchasing power equipment only used at peak power demand times during the year.

A logical extension of the peak management idea is to use outsourcing to deal with the infrequently performed tasks many business organizations face. Fortunately most organizations do not face a facility location analysis project or major legal matter overseas, requiring specialized skills that are very expensive and infrequently used. They represent stand-alone, unique projects and are ideal applications for specialized outsourcing services. These infrequently performed activities will never become a core competency. So using an outsource provider, the client firm benefits from the advantages of outsourcing while avoiding most of the disadvantages associated with the strategy (see Chapter 2).

When necessary, it only makes sense to outsource projects to the very best talent a firm can find to handle them. Since outsourcing firms are expected to continue to develop and acquire the best talented people over time, they will be the rational solution for organizations that cannot afford to hire and maintain permanent staff to handle infrequent problems.

Possible Consequences of Right Way O-I

When outsourcing is used in the right way its life cycle, which all business models have, may be long, similar to subcontracting, where outsourcing's origins can be found. What will extend the life cycle of the outsourcing industry is its benefit for all people in every country. This is why the consideration of the international context is so important to long-term success. Unless all parties or stakeholders in an outsourcing arrangement believe they are benefiting, there will be pressure to reduce or eliminate it as a business practice. Alternatively, as suggested in the interactive chain-effect in Figure E.2, continuous growth can be the future of the outsourcing industry, if it chooses the right path by seeking to benefit all participants.

What Needs to Be Done?

There are two important activities that should be undertaken immediately: First, institute sensible government regulation of the outsourcing industry by all countries. Second, develop ethical practices in outsourcing that can be used as guides and benchmarks for acceptable outsourcing behavior.

Government Regulation

The first and most important function of any country's government is to protect its people. By establishing clear government regulations on outsourcing within each country, outsourcers will be less likely to knowingly or unknowingly violate political, cultural, economic, or demographic mores within a particular country. Simply put, a clear set of legal guidelines will help outsourcing arrangements to comply with the many international risk areas currently impacting outsourcing arrangements negatively.

The fact is most governments are far behind in development of outsourcing, and may not even be aware when they utilize the industry. As noted in the literature ("Several U.S. States Unaware . . ." 2004) some U.S. state governments are actually unaware they are outsourcing IT offshore because of the generalities of the outsourcing agreements. This research study reveals most

Figure E.2   **Creating a Growth Interactive Chain-effect Resulting from Positive Experience**

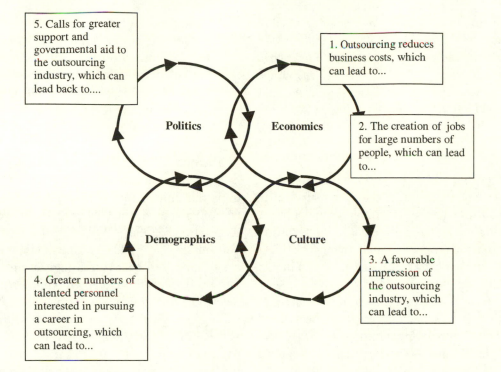

state taxpayers and lawmakers are ill-equipped to respond to growth in outsourcing trends because they have little or no power to regulate work performed offshore or the providers with whom they deal.

Effective legislation is needed, not politically motivated acts, which costs citizens more than helps them (Hoxter 2004). For example, politicians in at least 36 U.S. states have drafted over 100 legislative bills seeking to restrict and even punish companies that outsource offshore ("U.S. Federal Anti-Outsourcing . . ." 2004). Currently, some U.S. state governments, such as Arizona, arbitrarily restrict all international outsourcing of jobs to U.S. labor ("Arizona Governor Stops . . ." 2004). A California bill would limit bidding on state contracts to companies with employees operating within the state

or national borders. In New York, lawmakers are considering curtailing offshoring companies access to the state's popular Empire Zone program, which attracts companies to New York by offering tax cuts and public money to offset building and construction costs ("Several U.S. States . . ." 2004). Members of the U.S. Senate have introduced the *Keep American Jobs at Home Act* to eliminate tax deductions for businesses that ship U.S. jobs to foreign countries and to provide wage insurance and training assistance for service sector workers whose jobs have been outsourced to foreign firms. It also offers legal protection for companies refusing to outsource their workforce to maximize profits ("U.S. Senator Introduces . . ." 2004).

Such regional and national laws against the practice of outsourcing in all countries are expected to fail ("U.S. Legislation Bills . . ." 2004). For-rester Research predicts protectionist measures fail as inventive companies use stealth tactics to avoid barriers ("Europe to Offshore . . ." 2004). U.S. Federal Reserve chairman Alan Greenspan believes that using the U.S. tax code to encourage American companies to bring jobs shifted overseas back to the United States will not work ("U.S. Tax Code . . ." 2004). Other reasons for possible failure include:

- Offshoring jobs to countries with lower costs is widely regarded as critical to survival in industries where outsourcing is a major trend. Hiring outsourcers abroad affords flexibility to adjust personnel strength to meet business requirements at a lower cost and with higher levels of expertise.
- There are powerful agencies, such as the *U.S. Chamber of Commerce*, which represent over 3 million companies that have declared their resolve to fight all legislative moves against outsourcing ("U.S. Chamber of Commerce . . ." 2004).
- There is now some question about the consti-tutionality of any federal legislation that bans outsourcing in an international context ("U.S. Federal Anti-Outsourcing . . ." 2004). Such anti-outsourcing laws may violate U.S. inter-national trade obligations, the *North America Free Trade Agreement* (NAFTA), and *World Trade Organization* (WTO) regulations.
- Ending outsourcing in one country could lose jobs for that country. For example, India outsources jobs to the U.S. and they might retaliate if the U.S. ceases outsourcing to their country ("India Companies Outsourcing to U.S." 2004). Asian firms are also outsourc-ing an increasing number of jobs to the U.S. ("Asian Companies Outsource . . ." 2004). In-deed, some U.S. states, like California have gained 700,000 "in-sourced" jobs created by

subsidiaries of foreign companies ("No Use Opposing Offshoring . . ." 2004).
- Ending outsourcing may be counterproduc-tive to all international trade. While there may be some short-term job losses resulting from offshore outsourcing to India and China, consider the long-term benefits of these na-tions developing into prime markets for U.S. exports (Kolawa 2004).

The outsourcing industry is currently besieged by incoherent and confusing government regula-tions that hinder the effectiveness of the indus-try rather than aid it ("Managing the Weight of Regulation." 2004; "Why Regulating Offshore Outsourcing . . ." 2004). Many outsourcing firms are so confused over recent legislation that their latest action has been to hire more lawyers to help determine if they should continue an outsourcing strategy or give it up (Regulatory Compliance Pause U.S. . . ." 2004). Indeed, research on mo-tivations for offshore outsourcing shows nine out ten firms use this outsourcing to avoid compliance with ever increasing regulation by governments ("Global Competition Forcing . . ." 2004).

Yet there is a surprising willingness of business firms to accept special conditions and additional taxes on outsourcing activities ("U.S. Companies Eager . . ." 2004). In a survey of executives 40 per-cent reveal they are willing to make concessions in order to continue moving jobs out of the U.S. They would pay higher taxes (i.e., an offshoring out-sourcing tax) to compensate for jobs sent offshore; they would be willing to help pay for improvements in the quality of American education and worker retraining to help the U.S. maintain its competitive edge in technology. Nearly 58 percent of all the business respondents believe companies that out-source should pay higher taxes to fund retraining of workers who have lost jobs to offshoring. This survey's results are backed up by actual deeds. For example, *Lloyds TSC,* a financial institution in the United Kingdom, has signed an agreement to work with the finance union, *Unifi,* to protect interests of U.K. staff when jobs are offshored ("Lloyds TSC Signs Offshoring . . ." 2004). Specifically, they have agreed to make training and re-tooling workers, whose jobs have been outsourced, a central part of their offshoring process. Both Lloyds and the unions are working together to offer staff comprehensive training. In addition, Lloyds offers jobs to anyone wishing to continue working for them and will pay up to £2000 to re-train staff members preferring to leave the firm.

Industry Ethics Program

It will take time for legislation to be developed and instituted in every country that seeks to protect its citizens from potential harm that outsourcing can cause. This first step is to establish a set of ethical standards of behavior for outsourcing firms to follow, which will lead to universal or worldwide outsourcing legislative acts. Why establish an outsourcing industry ethics program? One reason is because ethical conduct is a successful strategy for building trust. If a firm or a country can see that outsourcers have a history of behaving ethically, they will be more likely to accept the risks of outsourcing ventures and support the industry. But trust must be earned and with it can come better legislation that is mutually beneficial to all participants. Without trust, outsourcing can fail (Natovich 2003).

A process to develop these ethical standards and eventual legislative acts may follow these steps:

1. Governments should encourage professional organizations and societies to develop self-help guidelines for firms undertaking an international outsourcing strategy. These guides can help direct firms in the right way to conduct outsourcing, and

help them avoid counterproductive behavior of the past. The importance of these guidelines directed as "self-interest" is critical for universal adoption. All companies, by their very nature, are focused on self-interest. Such professional guidelines are now being developed by select practitioner organizations. For example, the *Joint Forum* has developed its principles in conjunction with the *International Organization of Securities Commissions* (IOSCO) for the securities industry ("Joint Forum Helps . . ." 2004). The Joint Forum's principles are high-level and cross-sectoral, designed to provide a minimum benchmark against which all financial institutions can gauge their approach to outsourcing. These principles are designed to assist regulated entities in determining minimum steps that should be taken when considering outsourcing activities, and include establishing a coherent policy with specific risk management programs.

2. Governments should develop a set of basic, international, ethical practices for outsourcing firms and the outsourcing industry. Extending from the self-help guidelines, these principles of ethics can be based upon those most common in ethics literature, but focused specifically on outsourcing practices. Businesses need specific advice and very clear statements concerning what is ethical and what is not. Research has shown international business, if left to its own control, is likely to be conducted in an unethical manner (Carter 2000). By reviewing the many codes of conduct available in the literature, one can see there are several tenets that have fairly universal acceptance. These common tenets are presented in Table E.1 (De George 1993; Engholm and Rowland 1996, 140–153; Rodrigues 1996, 476–485; Schniederjans 1998, 152–154).

3. Governments should draft legislation based on the ethics guidelines. The outsourcing firms that have been guided by their associations practices (from Step 1 above) and then sought to follow governmental conduct codes (from Step 2 above),

Table E.1

Ethical Principles and Related Outsourcing Linkages

Ethics principle	Outsourcing linkage
Seek to do no harm to indigenous cultures	Don't use outsourcing in a way that violates religious holidays (e.g., making Jews work during the Sabbath).
Seek to do no harm to the ecological systems of the world	Don't use outsourcing to move polluting business practices from one country to another.
Seek to uphold basic human rights	Don't use outsourcing to take advantage of cheap child labor that leads to child abuse.
Seek to uphold universal labor standards	Don't use outsourcing as a strategy to decrease union membership and weaken unions.
Seek to pursue long-term involvement in foreign countries	Don't use outsourcing as a short-term arrangement to reduce costs; view it as a long-term partnership.
Seek to share knowledge and technology with foreign countries	Don't think an outsourcing agreement will prevent sharing of technology, but use the inevitable sharing to build a good relationship with foreign outsourcing firms.

should have no problem accepting or working within the boundaries of legislation.

Concluding Point on the Future of Outsourcing

Companies can give many different reasons why they outsource, but the reality is that outsourcing's most attractive feature is it helps firms cut costs. In a survey conducted by the *Boston Consulting Group* the economics of outsourcing appear to show it will have continued importance as a cost reduction strategy long into the future ("Boston Consulting Group . . ." 2004). They found factory workers in low-cost countries work much more cheaply than their U.S. and European counterparts. For example, a comparable hourly wage in the U.S. of $15 and Europe of $30 is well above the $1 per hour in China, yet China quickly achieves quality levels equivalent to or even higher than plants in the West. Most interesting is the long-term prospects for the gap in wages. Most economists assume lower-wage countries will experience in-

creases while higher wage countries will see wage levels fall, making the comparative advantage of cost reduction by outsourcing less attractive in the future. This may not be the case. The survey reports that wages are increasing at an annual rate of 8 percent in China, compared to the United States and Germany with increase in annual rates of 2.5 percent and 2 percent, respectively ("Boston Consulting Group . . ." 2004). Projecting growth in hourly wage rates through the year 2009, the average hourly wages will be approximately $1.30 in China, $25.30 in the United States, and $34.50 in Germany. So, in dollar terms, the wage gap will expand rather than shrink, resulting in a probable increase of the outsourcing industry in the foreseeable future.

Just as there is a growing need for outsourcing, so too there is a need for planning outsourcing to make it beneficial for all participants and their societies. In other words, outsourcing should be done the "right way," to favor all.

Review Terms

American Institute of Certified Public
Accountants (AICPA)

Backsourcing

Business process outsourcing (BPO)

Business transformation outsourcing (BTO)

Confidentiality risks

Controlling risks

Downsizing

Environmental risks

Human resource (HR)

Information Security Forum (ISF)

Information technology (IT)

Intellectual property risks

International Organization of Securities
Commissions (IOSCO)

North America Free Trade Agreement (NAFTA)

Spillover risk

Uplifting the balance sheet

World Trade Organization (WTO)

Discussion Questions

1. If there are no laws defining an outsourcing relationship, how can anyone call what a firm does "wrong"?
2. Why might governments be reluctant to institute outsourcing legislation?
3. What are reasons why a government should institute outsourcing legislation?
4. How can ethics be beneficial for the outsourcing industry?

Concept Questions

1. What are five things a firm should avoid doing in an outsourcing project?
2. What are three things a firm should seek to accomplish in conducting an outsourcing project?
3. What risks exist in international outsourcing?
4. What are some of the possible consequences of doing outsourcing badly?

References

"Accounting Rule Wipes Billions from Outsourcers' Profits." *Global Computing Services* (Oct. 17, 2003): 2–3.

Adler, P. S. "Making the HR Outsourcing Decision." *MIT Sloan Management Review* 45 (Fall 2003): 53–60.

"Anti-Outsourcing Would Effect Economic Growth, Says IMF." *Outsourcing Intelligence Bulletin: FSO Magazine* 4, no. 4 (April 25–May 2, 2004), editor@fsoutsourcing.com.

"Arizona Governor Stops State's Outsourcing." *Outsourcing Intelligence Bulletin: FSO Magazine* 4, no. 7 (April 18–25, 2004), editor@fsoutsourcing.com.

"Asian Companies Outsource Services to U.S. Conglomerates." *Outsourcing Intelligence Bulletin: FSO Magazine* 4, no. 7 (May 23–30, 2004), editor@fsoutsourcing.com.

"Bangladesh to Provide Outsourcing Services to U.S. Financial Firms." *Outsourcing Intelligence Bulletin: FSO Magazine* 4, no. 7 (August 8–15, 2004), editor@fsoutsourcing.com.

Benson, J., and Littler, C. "Outsourcing the Workforce Reductions: An Empirical Study of Australian Organizations." *Asia Pacific Business Review* 8, no. 3 (2002):16–31.

"Boston Consulting Group Urges American Firms to Outsource More Jobs to India." *Outsourcing Intelligence Bulletin: FSO Magazine* 4, no. 7 (July 11–18, 2004), editor@fsoutsourcing.com.

Burnett, R. *Outsourcing IT: The Legal Aspects.* Aldershot, England: Gower Publishing, 1998.

Carter, C. R. "Precursors of Unethical Behavior in Global

Supplier Management." *The Journal of Supply Chain Management* 36, no. 1 (2000): 45–56.

Caslione, J. A., and Thomas, A. R. *Global Manifest Destiny.* Chicago: Dearborn Trade Publishing, 2002.

"Challenges to Consider." *Outsourcing Intelligence Bulletin: FSO Magazine* 4, no. 7 (September 19–26, 2004), editor@fsoutsourcing.com.

Chorafas, D. N. *Outsourcing, Insourcing and IT for Enterprise Management.* Houndmills, Great Britain: Palgrave/MacMillan, 2003.

Crowley, D. "Taming the Ferocious Outsourcing Beast." *PC Week* (February 15, 1999): 85.

De George, R. *Competing with Integrity in International Business.* New York: Oxford University Press, 1993.

Diddi, R. "The Rebuttal: FSU and East Europe Prepare for a Rebuttal to Indian Outsourcing and BPO Capability." *Outsourcing Intelligence Bulletin: FSO Magazine* 4, no. 5 (May 2–9, 2004), editor@fsoutsourcing.com.

"Discover Weighs the Risk." *Outsourcing Intelligence Bulletin: FSO Magazine* 4, no. 7 (September 19–26, 2004), editor@fsoutsourcing.com.

Domberger, S. *The Contracting Organization: A Strategic Guide to Outsourcing.* Oxford: Oxford University Press, 1998.

Downing, C. E.; Field, J. M.; and Ritzman, L. P. "The Value of Outsourcing: A Field Study." *Information Systems Management* 20, no. 4 (2003): 86–91.

"Dubai Has Business Process Outsourcing (BPO) Growth Potential." *Outsourcing Intelligence Bulletin: FSO Magazine* 4, no. 7 (May 9–16, 2004), editor@fsoutsourcing.com.

"Eighty Percent of Financial Firms to Outsource Operations by 2005, Says Report." *Outsourcing Intelligence Bulletin: FSO Magazine* 4, no. 7 (May 23–30, 2004), editor@fsoutsourcing.com.

Elmuti, D., and Kathawala, Y. "The Effects of Global Outsourcing Strategies on Participants' Attitudes and Organizational Effectiveness." *International Journal of Manpower* 21, nos.1/2 (2000): 112–129.

Engholm, C., and Rowland, D. *International Excellence.* New York: Kodansha International, 1996.

"English Language Skills Become China's National Priority Due to Outsourcing." *Outsourcing Intelligence Bulletin: FSO Magazine* 4, no. 7 (July 11–18, 2004), editor@fsoutsourcing.com.

"Europe to Offshore 1.2 Million Jobs to India by 2015, Says Forrester Research." *Outsourcing Intelligence Bulletin: FSO Magazine* 11, no. 1 (August 22–29, 2004), editor@fsoutsourcing.com.

"Global Competition Forcing Companies in UK to Outsource." *Outsourcing Intelligence Bulletin: FSO*

Magazine 4, no. 7 (November 7–14, 2004), editor@fsoutsourcing.com.

Hall, M. "Outsourcing Deals Fail Half the Time." *Computerworld* 37, no. 44 (2003): 10.

Hoxter, C. J. "Outsourcing: The Latest Target of Protectionist Forces." *Caribbean Business* 32, no. 6 (2004):10+.

"IBM Signs $180M Outsourcing Deal with Dun and Bradstreet." *ComputerWorld,* http://www.computerworld.com/managementtopics/outsourcing/story/0,10801,96824,00.html, November 5, 2004.

"India Is the Leading Outsourcing Destination Among Competitors." *Outsourcing Intelligence Bulletin: FSO Magazine* 4, no. 7 (May 30–June 6, 2004), editor@fsoutsourcing.com.

"Indian BPO Industry to Touch $3.6bn in 2004 Despite Outcry on Outsourcing in the U.S." *Outsourcing Intelligence Bulletin: FSO Magazine* 4, no. 7 (July 25–August 1, 2004), editor@fsoutsourcing.com.

"Indian Companies Outsourcing to U.S." *Outsourcing Intelligence Bulletin: FSO Magazine* 4, no. 7 (May 9–16, 2004), editor@fsoutsourcing.com.

"Indian Outsourcing Industry Struggling with Employee Shortage." *Outsourcing Intelligence Bulletin: FSO Magazine* 14, no. 1 (November 5–12, 2004), editor@fsoutsourcing.com.

"IT Outsourcing Likely to Grow, Says Gartner." *Outsourcing Intelligence Bulletin: FSO Magazine* 4, no. 7 (May 23–30, 2004), editor@fsoutsourcing.com.

"J.P. Morgan Takes on Workers as IBM Outsourcing Deal Ends: Four Thousand Employees Providing Tech Services to Return to Wall St. Firm." *Outsourcing Intelligence Bulletin: FSO Magazine* 4, no. 7 (September 19–26, 2004), editor@fsoutsourcing.com.

"Joint Forum Helps Enable Financial Sector with Outsourcing Guidance." *Outsourcing Intelligence Bulletin: FSO Magazine* 4, no. 7 (August 8–15, 2004), editor@fsoutsourcing.com.

Kern, T., and Willcocks, L. P. *The Relationship Advantage: Information Technologies, Sourcing, and Management.* Oxford: Oxford University Press, 2001.

Klepper, R. "The Management of Partnering Development in IS Outsourcing." *Journal of Information Technology* 10, no. 4 (1995): 249–258.

"KnowledgeStorm Releases 'Corporate IT Spending and Offshore Services' Report." *Outsourcing Intelligence Bulletin: FSO Magazine* 4, no. 7 (May 9–16, 2004), editor@fsoutsourcing.com.

Kolawa, A. "Why Regulating Offshore Outsourcing Will Hurt the U.S. Economy." *Outsourcing Intelligence*

Bulletin: FSO Magazine 11, no. 1 (September 12–19, 2004), editor@fsoutsourcing.com.

Lacity, M. C., and Hirschheim, R. "Determinants of Information Technology Outsourcing: A Cross-Sectional Analysis." *Journal of Management Information Systems* 9, no. 1 (1992): 334–358.

"Large IT Outsourcing Deals on the Rise, Says TPI Study." *Outsourcing Intelligence Bulletin: FSO Magazine* 4, no. 7 (October 24–31, 2004), editor@fsoutsourcing.com.

"Lloyds TSC Signs Offshoring Agreement with Unifi." *Outsourcing Intelligence Bulletin: FSO Magazine* 4, no. 7 (May 9–16, 2004), editor@fsoutsourcing.com.

"Managing the Weight of Regulation." *Outsourcing Intelligence Bulletin: FSO Magazine* 4, no. 7 (October 1, 2004),www.fsoutsourcing.com/AspxForms/FSOChannels/FSO.

Meisler, A. "Think Globally, Act Rationally." *Workforce Management* 83, no. 1 (2004): 40–45.

Metz, C. "Tech Support Coming Home?" *PC Magazine* 23, no. 3 (February 17, 2004): 20.

Natovich, J. " Vendor Related Risks in IT Development: A Chronology of an Outsourced Project Failure." *Technology Analysis and Strategic Management* 15, no. 4 (2003): 409–420.

"Negotiating the Contract: Best Practices in Mitigating the Risks of Changing Business Needs, Evolving Technology, Rising Costs and More." *Outsourcing Intelligence Bulletin: FSO Magazine* 4, no. 7 (June 13–20, 2004), editor@fsoutsourcing.com.

"No Use Opposing Offshoring, Says Silicon Valley Network Study." *Outsourcing Intelligence Bulletin: FSO Magazine* 4, no. 7 (July 25–August 1, 2004), editor@fsoutsourcing.com.

O'Bryan, S. "Economic Impact of Outsourcing Risks: The U.S. Is Overlooking Critical Infrastructure Risk Again." *Outsourcing Intelligence Bulletin: FSO Magazine* 4, no. 7 (May 23–30, 2004), editor@fsoutsourcing.com.

"Outsourcing Backlash to Benefit U.S. IT Sector, Says CCI President." *Outsourcing Intelligence Bulletin: FSO Magazine* 4, no. 7 (August 8–15, 2004), editor@fsoutsourcing.com.

"Outsourcing Expectations Surpass Just Cost Savings As CFOs Demand More." BOBSGUIDE, November 5, 2004, http://www.bobsguide.com/guide/news/7137.html.

"Outsourcing Has Some Risky Issues, Says International Security Forum." *Outsourcing Intelligence Bulletin: FSO Magazine* 4, no. 7 (June 27–July 4, 2004), editor@fsoutsourcing.com.

Rabinovich, E.; Windle, R.; Dresner, M.; and Corsi, T.

"Outsourcing of Integrated Logistics Functions." *International Journal of Physical Distribution and Logistics Management* 29, no. 6 (1999): 353–375.

"Regulatory Compliance Pause U.S. Companies to Outsource Services Abroad." *Outsourcing Intelligence Bulletin: FSO Magazine* 4, no. 7 (May 30–June 6, 2004), editor@fsoutsourcing.com.

Reifer, D. J. "Seven Hot Outsourcing Practices." *IEEE Software* 21, no. 1 (January/February 2004): 14–16.

Rodrigues, C. *International Management.* Minneapolis/St. Paul: West Publishing, 1996.

Ronen, B.; Coman, A.; and Schragenheim, E. "Peak Management." *International Journal of Production Research* 39, no. 14 (2001): 3183–3194.

Sawyer, J. W. "The Optimization Triangle Proves an Rx for Success." *Energy User News* 28, no. 11 (2003): 24–26.

Schniederjans, M. J. *Operations Management in a Global Context.* Westport, CT: Quorum Books, 1998.

Schwartz, P., and Gibb, B. *When Good Companies Do Bad Things.* New York: Wiley, 1999.

"Several U.S. States to Curb Outsourcing of Jobs Overseas." *Outsourcing Intelligence Bulletin: FSO Magazine* 4, no. 7 (July 11–18, 2004), editor@fsoutsourcing.com.

"Several U.S. States Unaware of Offshore Outsourcing, Says Study." *Outsourcing Intelligence Bulletin: FSO Magazine* 4, no. 7 (July 25–August 1, 2004), editor@fsoutsourcing.com.

"Transformational Outsourcing—It's All in the Contract." *Global Computing Services* (July 25, 2003): 4.

"U.S. Accounting Firms to Inform Clients Before They Outsource Work to Third Parties." *Outsourcing Intelligence Bulletin: FSO Magazine* 4, no. 7 (November 7–14, 2004), editor@fsoutsourcing.com.

"U.S. Companies Benefit Tax-Breaks from Outsourcing Jobs Overseas." *Outsourcing Intelligence Bulletin: FSO Magazine* 4, no. 2 (April 4–11, 2004), editor@fsoutsourcing.com.

"U.S. Chamber of Commerce Against Outsourcing Curbs." *Outsourcing Intelligence Bulletin: FSO Magazine* 4, no. 7 (April 18–25, 2004), editor@fsoutsourcing.com.

"U.S. Companies Eager to Move Jobs Offshore." *Outsourcing Intelligence Bulletin: FSO Magazine* 4, no. 7 (May 9–16, 2004), editor@fsoutsourcing.com.

"U.S. Companies to Shift Jobs by Offshoring Rather Than Outsourcing." *Outsourcing Intelligence Bulletin: FSO Magazine* 4, no. 5 (May 2–9, 2004), editor@fsoutsourcing.com.

"U.S. Federal Anti-Outsourcing Laws Violate Anti-

Protectionist Trade Rules." *Outsourcing Intelligence Bulletin: FSO Magazine* 4, no. 7 (April 18–25, 2004), editor@fsoutsourcing.com.

"U.S. Firms Set Up Offshoring Units in India." *Outsourcing Intelligence Bulletin: FSO Magazine* 4, no. 7 (May 9–16, 2004), editor@fsoutsourcing.com.

"U.S. Legislation Bills on Anti-Outsourcing Bound to Fail." *Outsourcing Intelligence Bulletin: FSO Magazine* 15, no. 1 (December 5–12, 2004), editor@fsoutsourcing.com.

"U.S. Senator Introduces Anti-Outsourcing Bill." *Outsourcing Intelligence Bulletin: FSO Magazine* 4, no. 7 (June 27–July 4, 2004), editor@fsoutsourcing.com.

"U.S. Tax Code Might Not Stop Job Outsourcing, Says Greenspan." *Outsourcing Intelligence Bulletin: FSO Magazine* 4, no. 4 (April 25–May 2, 2004), editor@fsoutsourcing.com.

"Why Regulating Offshore Outsourcing Will Hurt the U.S. Economy." *Outsourcing Intelligence Bulletin: FSO Magazine* 11, no. 1 (September 12–19, 2004), editor@fsoutsourcing.com.

Wijnen, R. "Turning on the Lights: Capgemini Energy and TXU Aim to Jumpstart Utility Outsourcing." *Outsourcing Intelligence Bulletin: FSO Magazine* 4, no. 7 (September 19–26, 2004), editor@fsoutsourcing.com.

Wolosky, H. W. "Transparent Outsourcing." *Practical Accountant* 37, no. 3 (2004): 4.

Zhao, Y., and Calantone R. J. "The Trend Toward Outsourcing in New Product Development: Case Studies in Six Firms." *International Journal of Innovation Management* 7, no. 1 (2003): 51–66.

INDEX

Marc J. Schniederjans is the C. Wheaton Battey Distinguished Professor of Business in the College of Business Administration at the University of Nebraska-Lincoln. He teaches classes in operations management, decision sciences, and management information systems. He also teaches in the College's partnership MBA program at Offutt Air Force Base. Dr. Schniederjans has won several distinguished teaching awards and has authored or co-authored 14 books in the field of management. He has published more than 90 journal articles. Professor Schniederjans is serving on various journal editorial review or advisory boards, and has served as a journal editor. He has been an active member of the Decision Sciences Institute for over twenty years and has served as a consultant and trainer to a wide variety of business and government agencies. Ashlyn M. Schniederjans is at Johns Hopkins University. Dara G. Schniederjans is at the University of Minnesota-Twin Cities.